CHERYL ALFREY WALDECK

Occasions

SEASONAL MENUS & ENTERTAINING SECRETS

The JOY of FOOD

CHERYL ALFREY WALDECK

Occasions

SEASONAL MENUS & ENTERTAINING SECRETS

Published & printed in the United States of America

First Edition

ISBN 978-0-692-80201-4

For information about special discounts for bulk purchases
please contact the author:

Cheryl A. Waldeck at cherwaldeck@cox.net

Art direction by Carl Brune

Cover photo by Ace Cuervo

for Todd

He rises to the occasion.

CONTENTS

Entertaining Secrets & Social Graces

Spring

Summer

Autumn

Winter

Baking Technique
354

Glossary
367
INGREDIENTS, TECHNIQUES & TERMS

Index
391
RECIPES & TECHNIQUES BY CATEGORY

Acknowledgements
395

Entertaining Secrets & Social Graces

Classic Entertaining
The Guest List • Menus: Feasting with the Five Senses • Invitations • Accepting an Invitation
The Thank You Note

Entertaining Options
A Formal Seated Dinner • Buffet Service • Outdoor Entertaining • Entertaining Children

Larger Occasions
Entertaining Groups of Ten or More • Successful Co-Hosting

Wines
Choosing a Wine • Opening Wine • How to Pour Wine • Serving Wines • Calculating Amount
Glossary of Wines & Liqueurs

The Table
Setting a Formal Table • Folding Napkins • Caring for Linens

Getting Organized
Utilizing Time Lines • Good Cooking Habits • Stocking the Pantry & Freezer • Kitchen Essentials
How Long Will It Keep?

The Cocktail Glass

Utilizing Flowers
Basic Arranging • The Meaning of Flowers • Symbolic Herbs & Flowers • Edible Flowers & Herbs
Chilling with Style • Tussie Mussies

Greeting & Managing Guests
Greeting, Seating & Managing • Introductions

At Ease at the Table
At Ease at the Table • When Accidents Happen

Hosting Overnight Guests
Weekend Entertaining • The Gracious Guest • The Guest Room

Hostess Gifts & Party Favors
Hostess Gifts • Party Favors for Guests • Gifts for the New Baby & Sweet Sixteen
Traditional Wedding Anniversary Gifts

Entertaining Secrets & Social Graces

My view of entertaining is to simply slow down and take the time to creatively present something special – and that is what this book is all about.

It does not matter if you live in a one bedroom apartment or a colossal estate, the spirit of entertaining is the same.

It is about enabling a warm and comfortable atmosphere, providing sustenance to others, and preserving and thus relishing life's special moments. You will find that the entertaining secrets and social graces outlined here are not about stuffy rules, but are about a creative process that demonstrates style and finesse, along with a caring way of being that makes entertaining a relaxed experience. In an age where we all rush, multi-task, and spend so much time in front of a screen, I like to organize occasions that encourage us to talk and cherish one another. When successful, guests begin to reflect upon and describe memories and special times, and engage in thoughtful conversations that too become long remembered – and isn't that what life is all about?

Everything the home entertainer needs, from creating a formal seated dinner to crafting a casual patio buffet, is outlined in this section. For when thoughtful hospitality is coupled with good foods and an imaginative approach, a simple meal is transformed into a treasured, and long-remembered, *Occasion.*

Classic Entertaining

The Guest List • Menus: Feasting with the Five Senses
The Invitation • Accepting an Invitation • The Thank You Note

The first thing to consider when entertaining is who to include and what to serve. Having a mix of people that can easily engage in conversation with one another will make your occasion both interesting and fun for everyone. When crafting "the right mix" consider interest, age and gender. When working through a menu, consider the five senses.

The Guest List

Invite Folks with Similar Interest

To easily ensure party conversation starts off on a positive note include friends with things in common. Even if people are meeting for the first time, when they have things in common they will feel comfortable initiating an exchange. As you introduce guests upon their arrival, try to make a point of also mentioning things they both enjoy.

Guests of the Same Age Always Work Well

When crafting "the right mix," consider friends both younger and older as well. A young face or seasoned acquaintance can make enchanting additions to any party.

All Male and All Female Parties are Easy

When you begin mixing it can get tricky. If you'd like to invite single guests, it's nice to either include other single guests, or encourage single friends to bring a date. That way no one will feel like the odd man out while mixing with couples.

Menus: Feasting with the Five Senses

Bring All of Your Senses into Menu Planning

Be attentive to color, aroma, texture and even the sounds different foods make as you eat them. Think of each of the five senses as you craft menus and consider how sight, smell, taste, feel and sound will be perceived.

Be Visual

The visual presentation of a dish has an uncanny way of also enhancing the pleasure derived from it. Even a platter for make-your-own sandwiches can be a visually sensuous experience by the simple act of using slices from three different colors of tomatoes in red, yellow and orange. Add sliced Bermuda onion to the platter, with its deep purple color, and your display will become mouth-watering.

Keep in mind that how a dish looks will also affect perception of its flavor. For example, a deep red glaze will be associated with intense berry flavor and bright greens with garden fresh foods.

Explore the Four Basic Tastes When Crafting Menus

Consider sweetness, saltiness, sourness and bitterness – then find a balance. Consider temperature, and incorporate at least one hot and one cold dish into your menu for variety. Further activate the senses with texture – from puréed and creamy to crunchy and crisp, a combination will stimulate the appetite.

Try to avoid meals that are all one shade of color or all a similar texture. And finally, be sure to incorporate aromatic ingredients like herbs and spices to enhance your dishes and their flavors.

Give Thought to What is Available and in Season

Fruits and vegetables consumed in the height of their growing season are cost effective and will always taste better.

A listing of fruits and vegetables fresh in each season of the year can be found with the four seasonal sections of menus that follow.

Think About the Weather

The subliminal cravings associated with outdoor temperature can be powerful. If it's cold outside consider a hot soup or heartier entrée, because warm and substantial foods are what our bodies crave when we are chilled.

Likewise, when the weather is warm or hot, serve cold drinks and dine outside with light dishes like fresh corn and something grilled.

Consider the Importance & Significance of the Occasion

Any meal can be elevated to something special, but a true occasion like a birthday or holiday calls for thinking ahead and planning something equally special on the menu. When the occasion is a significant one, consider things like an extra special or showy dessert, an exceptional cut of meat, a really good wine and/or an elegant table setting.

Choose the Entrée or Dessert First

When crafting your own menus, it's a good idea to pick either the dessert or entrée first and then build the meal around the style of these dishes. For example, if you want to make a rich and decadent chocolate cake for dessert, then serve a lighter entrée like grilled chicken or fish. People simply can't eat large and heavy meals anymore, nor do they want to. But one splurge is usually welcome.

Likewise, if you want to prepare an entrée that requires last-minute time in the kitchen, avoid choosing a dessert that also requires last-minute preparation. Serve the more elaborate entrée, but pair it with an easy dessert that can be made the day ahead – or vice versa.

Use Your Imagination

Remember that we eat for sustenance but also for pleasure, and experiment with presentation. Your guests are sure to enjoy novelty in the composition and presentation of dishes. Think ahead to the serving of each dish and consider how a garnish of fresh herbs, fruits and flowers might stimulate the senses.

It is fun to also choose unusual serving pieces, creatively mix plates and glassware, and let your personality shine in both the food presentation and table setting. These things not only create a welcoming and fun atmosphere, but let your guests know you cared enough to make this effort.

With each of the twenty-four menus in Occasions I have included a visual gallery of table setting concepts designed for the season and celebration. Use these examples as your starting point and create your own imaginative tables when entertaining at home.

A few other tips to consider:

Make Enough

It's better to have too much than not enough – you can always make a "party favor" of extra desserts.

Keep It Simple

It is easier on the host/hostess and also helps guests not regret overeating if you streamline your menus. Always serve a protein, starch and vegetable or fruit for balance, with appetizers and desserts as options in accordance with your guest list and occasion.

Stay Within Your Means

Set a budget and stick to it. When you make entertaining doable you are more apt to enjoy hosting again.

Avoid Experimenting

Serve recipes you are comfortable making when entertaining at home, and avoid substitutions so that you can be assured the meal will be a success.

Respect the Pre-Work

Do as much in advance as you possibly can so you will have time with your guests and enjoy the occasion as much as they will. When you invite friends and family to dinner you don't want to be stressing in the kitchen or be too tired to have fun. Getting tasks out of way beforehand will allow you to relax during the party and have time to talk and enjoy what you have worked hard to create.

With each menu in Occasions, an organized time line is included to help stagger tasks and develop an understanding of the work that can be completed pre-party.

The Invitation

Invitations set the tone for a party and capture the degree of formality/casualness of the gathering. When hosting a large themed party, shower or special occasion, create an inviting paper invitation that is mailed. It is fun to match the type face with graphics and paper to convey just the kind of mood you want to create. For example, the Kentucky Derby party invitation below is playful and sporty because that is the kind of event being planned. For a formal event, the invitation wording, paper choice and font type should also be formal.

WHAT TO INCLUDE IN AN INVITATION

WHO

Trainers Jane & Wade Brown

WHAT

Invite you to join them for

A Kentucky Derby Party

WHEN

The first Saturday in May

Post Time: 3:00 pm

WHERE

Track Address:

1234 Horse Park Avenue in Lexington

PROGRAM

Southern Buffet & Running of the Roses

DRESS CODE

Jockey Silks and Hats for the Ladies

RESPONDE S'IL VOUS PLAIT — R.S.V.P.

Please reply by April 28th to 122-222-3345

Continue Invitation & Party Theme by Decorating the Venue
Greet guests with a Derby banner tied to an outside lamp post.

Have fun creating a festive atmosphere by labeling rooms in your home as:

Paddock (the closet), Watering Hole (the bar), Infield (the kitchen), Club House (the dining room), etc. *A tried and true Kentucky menu for a Derby party can be found in the Spring section of this publication.*

Accepting an Invitation–R.S.V.P.

When you are the guest, be sure to respond as quickly as possible when invited to a party, dinner in a friend's home, or for a weekend at the lake. Your reply will enable the host/hostess to get an accurate count for meals and other necessities and will be greatly appreciated.

Invitations should not be treated lightly. Entertaining guests in your home takes time and effort, not to mention expense. And guests should never cancel at the last minute without a believable excuse, such as illness.

Regrets

If you cannot attend but would like to, let your host know: *I am so tickled to be invited. May I ask for a rain check?*

If you are invited and your (new) significant other is not: Subtly let your host know you are now a couple by saying, *I'd love to come another time with the lady I'm seeing a lot of these days, Libby Matt. I know you don't have room for both of us this time, but I'd really like for you to meet her.*

This way you let your host know something he/she did not, and they can choose to make room or call you at another time – and all is well.

BEFORE LEAVING THE PARTY

Always remember to seek out your host and/or hostess to thank them for including you in the affair, and let them know what a nice time you had.

The Thank You Note

Merci, Gracias, Danke, Grazie

No matter what language you speak, a sincere and hand written thank you note is one of the most generous ways you can show your appreciation for a gift or kindness.

HERE'S A SIMPLE FORMULA TO FOLLOW:

DATE YOUR NOTE

Tuesday -or- December 28, 2016

SALUTATION TO THE PERSON/PEOPLE YOU ARE THANKING

Dearest Aunt Amy, Uncle Nicky and family,

STATE WHO IS DOING THE THANKING (IF MORE THAN ONE PERSON)

John Reed and I…

STATEMENT OF THANKS FOR THE GIFT

…Reed and I would like to express our sincere appreciation for your most generous Christmas gifts.

NAME THE GIFT — BE SPECIFIC

The serving platter and bowl in our wedding china pattern have long been coveted and will be put to much good use.

MENTION SOMETHING NOTEWORTHY ABOUT HOW YOU PLAN TO ENJOY, OR USE THE GIFT. OR, HOW YOU APPRECIATE THE EFFORT/CONSIDERATION.

In fact, we are looking forward to using both pieces at a dinner party in our new home in February.

REMARK ABOUT WARM HOSPITALITY AND/OR THOUGHTFULNESS OF THE GIVER

Thanks too for hosting the family for Christmas this year. It is always such fun to see Betty Jo and little Sammy and be in your warm and wonderful home!

THANK THEM AGAIN — ALWAYS IN AN UPBEAT AND PLEASANT KEY

Thanks again for being so generous to the two of us as we build our own home together. Happy New Year to you and your family.

SIGN YOUR NAME

Most sincerely,

Karen

Write neatly and leave good margins. Avoid an overuse of exclamation marks, watch for misspelled words, and be sure to include your return address on the outside of the envelope.

Entertaining Options

A Formal Seated Dinner • Buffet Service • Outdoor Entertaining

A Formal Seated Dinner

Invitations

Invitations to a formal seated dinner should be issued at least two weeks in advance, and the wise host/hostess sends out a reminder a day or two prior to the event to confirm all guests. For when you are planning something formal it is always nice to avoid last minute surprises.

The invitations can be issued in person, by phone or mail and the reminder can be as easy as a text, if you don't have the chance to talk in person.

Arrivals

As the host/hostess, be sure to greet each guest as they arrive and get them settled.

As a guest, make every effort to arrive at the stated time, *especially for a luncheon when both the host and other guests have afternoon plans and things cannot be delayed.* Likewise, avoid arriving too early, for your host(s) may not yet be ready!

If you arrive late, and the event has already started, simply slip in quietly and go briefly to your host/hostess to make your apologies and then sit down.

Setting the Stage - Creating a Warm Environment

When hosting, playing music and lighting lamps in each room as a nice way to "set the stage" for guests. The host/hostess will also want to make sure everyone has a drink or glass of water, and then be sure to sit down themselves to enjoy family and friends and the afternoon or evening they have worked to create.

Seating Guests

When the meal is ready, the host or hostess should announce something like, *Let's go in to dinner now,* and then lead guests to the dining area and designate where everyone is to sit.

The host and hostess are typically seated at the ends (or heads) of the table, and the woman guest of honor (if you have one) is seated at the host's right. The honored male guest is at the hostess' right. Guests of honor can be old friends, visitors from another state or country, or those celebrating a birthday or anniversary.

It is nice to also mix the men and women in your party. Even newly married couples enjoy being seated next to someone unfamiliar and being given the chance to discuss a-typical subjects.

As the meal progresses the host and hostess should be mindful of the table conversation. If one person seems quiet, encourage them to join in by asking a friendly question or by complimenting something they've done recently. This will help them feel included and also provide other guests with avenues in which to engage with them as well.

The host/hostess should also attempt to subtly break the conversation in the event that one voice is dominating.

Toasting

If wine is served, it is a nice touch for the host to toast the guests early in the meal.

This means rising to speak and projecting sincere sentiment, praise, gratitude or even humor – while being brief. It's very flattering to be toasted and a great way to surprise and delight your guests. Give some thought beforehand to what you'd like to say and then be natural in your delivery. The purpose of a toast is to make someone happy and feel proud, and is a charming thing to do.

Traditionally, the host makes the first toast. But an inspired guest may do so if nothing has been done by mid-meal. When a toast is made, everyone at the table should raise their glass toward the person being toasted; repeat the name, *To Sam!* and then take a drink. If you do not drink wine, raise your water glass and sip from it.

Serving

Most small dinner parties (six to eight guests) are implemented without help. In this case your roles as the host/hostess is to simply and graciously rise and clear plates as necessary between courses, and then clear all serving pieces, dishes, and unused silver from the table before serving the dessert.

If time allows, it is nice to take a little break between dinner and dessert to give guests time to digest. A 20 to 30 minute breather not only allows the stomach to rest but clears the palate as well. I sometimes ask friends to help clear the dishes to the kitchen, or on a more formal evening I'll let guests visit and finish the wine while I tidy up just a bit before serving dessert - trying to be careful to not appear as if I'm "slaving away" in the kitchen and making guests uncomfortable.

To serve dessert, it is a nice touch to ask each guest how big or small a portion they would like in advance. Guests appreciate having a choice as to how much they want to eat, especially when the invitation for seconds is left open. When serving a dessert with whipped cream or another added garnish, consider passing this separately in a bowl. Then if your guests want to indulge or avoid altogether, again it is their choice.

When dessert is finished, invite guests to linger over coffee to avoid breaking up the mood by moving to another room or rushing to clean up. *If you are relaxed, your guests will be too.*

Conversation

Some people are just born being good conversationalists, but if that is not your story, fear not for it is an art that can be learned!

Some easy tips include: Be cheerful and avoid doom, gloom and crudeness; be informed; ask questions and contribute; and when in a pinch use subtle flattery and laugh in good fun. In other words, be the perfect date – attentive but not clingy, formal but not stiff, and a true lady or gentleman in every way!

When the conversation needs to be changed or livened up, toss out a piece of news that everyone will enjoy, or tell a funny story about something that happened recently.

Remember to also be a good listener and allow others to join in.

Buffet Service

When hosting large groups, family reunions and holidays, buffets are a graceful way to entertain with less fuss. Buffets also give the occasion a feeling of abundance and activity- which is fun and has a way of making everyone comfortable. Much more flexibility is enabled when serving buffet-style as well, and last minute guest additions, subtractions or latecomers become "no big deal."

A Buffet works for any meal, but can be especially useful for breakfast when hosting overnight guests who wake up at different times.

The secret to a good buffet is advance planning so that the serving line moves quickly and efficiently.

Help this along by arranging foods progressively and by placing condiments or sauces next to the foods they are to be used with. Moving the drinks and desserts to another location will also make it easier on everyone.

The Buffet Table

Use the same care to create an aesthetically pleasing buffet table as you would for a seated meal. Craft a clever centerpiece and use pretty serving pieces, then garnish dishes to add lots of color. Keep hot dishes covered until time to serve, and don't forget to use trivets and heat protectors under dishes to avoid scorching your table.

Step back from the buffet as you are arranging it and review the layout for balance, and check the placement of serving pieces to ensure all items are within easy reach. I like to also lay the dinner plates at both ends of the table to

expedite service, and often bundle the silverware in the napkins for quick and easy pick-up.

Create both visual interest and more room on the table's surface by using cake pedestals and other serving pieces of varying heights.

This can also be accomplished by turning soup bowls upside down to create an array of levels for serving platters to sit upon. Then stagger the higher platters across the back of your buffet or in the center of the table.

Be both creative and practical with the foods being served. If serving baguettes or loaves of bread for example, slice the bread into pieces that are cut ¾ of the way through the loaf. This will give your presentation the drama and height of a whole baguette loaf while also making it easy for guests to tear off a single serving as they go through the line.

Likewise, if serving bagels, buns or other sandwich breads, pre-cut these horizontally, leaving just a hinge to keep both sides in place. This will make it much easier for your guests to fill sandwiches with one hand while they hold their plate in the other.

The same applies for serving cakes or other items that are served by the piece. Pre-cut a small section of cake, for example, to help guests get started and once the first few pieces have been taken, cut a few more.

Thinking through how guests will be able to navigate the buffet with ease will make all the difference in both their comfort and an expedient process.

Mix different foods on serving platters for visual appeal. For example, serve both the roast turkey and root vegetables on the same platter. *Remember that we feast first with our eyes, and visually dress-up your presentations with edible flowers and herbs, whole slices of lemons and limes, clusters of grapes, and pomegranates cut in half.*

Big juicy seasonal berries also make a wonderful addition to any dessert platter. And a mixture of desserts in different sizes, shapes and textures served together is visually appetizing in a subliminal way.

Service

Napkins for a buffet should be oversized with extras provided.

The host and hostess should encourage guests to serve themselves and be on hand to help carry plates as necessary. If possible, recruit helpers to refill drinks during the meal, gather up empty plates and bus them to the kitchen, and/or serve the desserts.

Foods

Keep in mind that guests will have their plate in their lap, and try to plan foods that don't require a knife to cut. It is also nice to have enough foods for second helpings.

Seating

Buffet suppers are informal as a rule and guests sit wherever they are relaxed. A successful buffet will ensure a place to sit for every guest with a place to set their drink.

So think ahead when planning a buffet, assess how many guests can comfortably fit into your home or gathering space, consider what side tables and other pieces of furniture can be called into service, and resist the temptation to exceed the limit.

The gracious host/hostess will also plan to keep an eye on the serving line and invite guests to sit in places where they will be most comfortable.

As a side note, if you find yourself sitting next to someone you just can't seem to find anything in common with and are unable to get a conversation going, stick it out through the main course. In this more informal buffet setting it is then okay to switch to a new seat when you get up for dessert.

When to Begin

Unlike at a seated dinner when guests wait for the hostess to lift her fork and begin eating, with a buffet, as soon as guests have filled their plates and found a seat they can begin. There is no need to wait for everyone to be served in this setting.

Outdoor Entertaining

Entertaining in Mother Nature's backyard has a multitude of pluses that outweigh the threat of rain, mosquitoes or too much sun.

Here are a few tips to make your outdoor party an occasion to remember:

Place your buffet or serving table against a pretty backdrop in your lawn or garden, or facing a panoramic view of water or mountains.

Pick up the colors of your garden in the napkins, dishes and/or tablecloth, and try repeating landscape elements on the party table by matching groupings of flowers to those in the garden.

Be lavish with fresh blossoms, but use them naturally. Let arrangements be loose and flowing and incorporate as many plants from your garden as possible.

Use rustic pottery and stoneware – or paper plates and cups. For added color, wrap serving dishes in colorful kitchen towels. But avoid plastic forks, spoons and knives if you can, because they are so hard to work with. For an evening party, dress up your serving pieces a bit more, using bold-shaped glasses and cloth napkins.

When entertaining at night, use lighting to illuminate the buffet, light walkways and lead people to different areas in the garden. If using candles, be sure to protect them from any breeze or potential draft.

Keep drinks cold in an easily accessible cooler or large tub.

Use baskets and clever containers to hold silverware, napkins and other items needed in multiples.

Cover dishes with net "tents" before and after serving, and remove any dishes that may spoil in the heat to the refrigerator (or ice chest) once guests have been served.

If eating in the grass, *watch for anthills* and the like, and secure your tablecloth or blanket with something clever like potted plants.

Assemble all of the picnic items you will need the night before the party and check to make sure everything is clean and ready to use.

Buy twice as much ice as you think you'll need, and include extra plates, cups and silverware – especially if children will attend.

Make all food ahead of time, including cocktails if possible, to ensure a fuss free affair.

It is always a good idea to go outside a day or two before the party at the same time you plan to entertain. This is a good way to determine where shady spots will be, what kind of lighting you can expect and where furniture and tables will be the most advantageous.

When inviting guests, let them know the party will be informal and encourage them to wear comfortable clothes.

Keep a supply of summer wraps handy in case the weather turns cool.

Cluster pots of scented herbs of lavender and rosemary near the areas where guests will be sitting and take advantage of these natural bug deterrents. Or, have insect repellent on hand to keep mosquitos at bay.

Entertaining Children

If children have been invited, try having a few heathy snacks just for them, as it is often hard for kids to wait until the adults are ready to eat. Something as simple as a handful of frozen blueberries or seedless grapes, or my Lady Bug popsicles made from fresh fruit and honey, are all great choices.

Then have plenty of extra cups, plates and napkins on hand, as well as paper toweling to mop up spills.

It's nice to also organize a few games or swimming relays, with simple *prizes, to keep children occupied while adults mingle.

*IDEAS FOR KID'S PARTY GAME PRIZES

For kids under ten: Books, banks or a toy safe, magic tricks, hand puppets.

For Kids ten & older: Classic books, tickets to a play, concert or movie, sports equipment and/or memorabilia, money.

Balloons, sparklers and gum balls also work well.

Larger Occasions

Entertaining Groups of Ten or More • Successful Co-Hosting

Entertaining Groups of Ten or More

When formally entertaining large groups, don't be afraid to ask for help.

My rule of thumb is that for any formal dinner party with more than eight guests, help will be needed for the preparation and set-up, service and clean-up.

Co-Hosting

It is not only fun to throw a party with friends, but the process is often more creative and affordable. Consider asking friends who like to cook and entertain to co-create something special with you for your next big occasion. Then encourage everyone to help with the menu and décor planning, and things like providing party favors for guests to take home.

This is a good way to manage a large gathering, broaden your friendships and even learn something new from fellow hosts and hostesses.

Hiring Help

For large parties plan to hire or engage one helper for every eight to ten guests.

I've always had good luck with high school or college-age helpers. Young people who enjoy cooking and are eager to learn the art of entertaining are fun to mentor and have abundant energy. Another option is to engage an acquaintance with waiting experience.

Whoever you choose, be sure to be specific about expectations, including what to wear, how guests are to be served and treated, and duties while the party is underway.

Try asking helpers to assist before the party as well as the day of. This way expectations can be expressed in a more relaxed atmosphere and allow time to show assistants specifically how you expect things to be done. This also provides help with the pre-work and party set-up, which is where an eager novice wants to develop expertise and a seasoned server can offer advice – thus is a win-win either way.

Using a Time Line

Throughout Occasions, *time lines have been included with each menu to illustrate how meals can be broken down and prepared in advance, making the entertaining process more easily managed. Time lines are also a good place to designate tasks for each host and or helper.*

When building your own time lines, consider the steps involved in each dish on the menu. Look for every possible thing that can be done in advance, and how far in advance, so that you can stagger the preparation.

When you leave only the last minute tasks to the party, you also allow more time to enjoy your guests and the event you have worked to create.

Purchasing Prepared Dishes

Try patronizing specialty grocers for take-out options so you are familiar with what is available, good and affordable. It's okay to take advantage of a few time-savers when hosting large groups.

Successful Co-Hosting

Talk First – Commit Second

Before you engage in co-hosting talk through the event to make sure everyone is in agreement and thus also enjoys the co-hosting process. Consider:

Date and time (Be considerate to schedules of all hosts).

Number of guests (What can you manage, and how many each host will invite).

Budget (Dollar amount to be committed by each host).

Location (Best location for the number of guests and party theme being planned).

Whether or not to serve alcohol.

Kids or no kids.

Communicate Throughout

Openly communicate throughout the co-hosting process to ensure each host/hostess is pleased with the outcome and everyone enjoys the experience.

Divide Responsibilities

Don't leave details to the last minute. Instead plan together what needs to be done and divide tasks evenly.

Plan to keep large parties simple with buffet service and self-serve drink and dessert stations.

Then set a time line for the party together.

Consider each task involved, including the invitation preparation and mailing (2 to 3 weeks in advance) and who will manage replies.

Consider the menu and quantities needed and try to avoid foods that need last minute attention.

Arrive Early

Co-hosts should arrive early enough to help tidy the public areas as necessary. During this time, help stock the bathrooms with fresh towels and tissue, and make a plan for who will coordinate what during the actual party (like greeting each guest and pouring drinks). *Then turn down the temperature to accommodate extra body heat once guests arrive.*

Be sure to also determine a spot or room for coats and purses.

Being on point early will also help you be prepared in the event of early arrivals.

All Hands on Deck

During the party, each host should take ownership in the success of the gathering. This will allow each host/hostess to in turn be a guest at the party, relax and have fun.

It's also a good idea to set aside a few tasks in advance, like filling water glasses or garnishing platters, for eager yet unsolicited kitchen helpers.

People like to help at parties – it makes them feel like they are a part of the action. So don't let offers to help throw you off your game, but instead use them as an opportunity to allow guests to feel they are essential to the gathering and help you get everything together in a timely manner. You'll be surprised how essential extra help truly is at the last minute!

And if someone makes a sassy remark about your cooking, keep your cool and move on!

Pay Attention to Details

Enjoy the journey, and know that I am with you every step of the way!

Watch your party unfold "from the balcony" so you are aware of how the event is progressing. Watch how guests are feeling and if the dessert station, bar or other aspect of the event needs attending.

This does not mean fretting and forgoing time with your friends, but simply means learning to keep a quiet eye on the details so that everyone in turn will feel at home.

Share in the Clean-up

After the guests have gone home, co-hosts should help put away foods, wash dishes and restore the home or location.

This is a fun time to re-live the highlights of your gathering and discuss what worked well and what did not – and maybe even plan your next party!

Wines

Choosing a Wine • Opening Wine • How to Pour Wine
Serving Wines • Calculating the Amount You Will Need
& *Glossary of Recommended Wines & Liqueurs*

Choosing a Wine

Choosing the right wine for dinner can be daunting. To help simplify the process, keep three things in mind. First, match the color, or choose the type of grape most apt to complement your main course. Second, consider the weight of the wine with regard to the weight of your entrée. Finally, consider what you can afford.

*Grapes can be light, medium or heavy &
red, rosè or white in variety.*

Each variety will pair well with certain foods, as the following chart will simplify.

When deciphering variety, one of the most helpful ways to learn is to simply spend time in the store reading the winemaker's description on the backs of wine labels. This is a good way to get ideas of flavor, body and potential food pairings and is really helpful in understanding the pronounced flavors and characteristics of different wines.

Pair the weight of the meal with a wine of similar weight or body.

For example, a hearty roast beef is heavy and should be paired with a full-bodied wine. Likewise, grilled chicken is light, and will pair well with a light wine.

In other words, if you are serving a strongly flavored or rich entrée, you will want to match it with a full bodied wine. Wine and meat should complement each other, and a substantial meal requires a wine that can stand up to intense flavors with enough strength to cut and thus complement the foods being served.

When pairing wine with a meal of concentrated flavors look for descriptions like, deep, full-bodied, rich or complex.

If you are serving a lighter meal of grilled fish, pasta or vegetables look for wines described as, light, crisp or refreshing..

Now take this a step further -
Choose wines with the same flavors as the entrée.

For example a light citrusy wine will pair well with something like lemon chicken, and a smoky red will be perfect with barbecue. Envision the meal you are planning and then consider how the flavors described in different wines might complement or obscure.

Once you begin to get the hang of looking at varieties and finding complementary wines, try stepping out of the box and contrasting flavors.

Look for wines that are dissimilar to your entrée.

For example, when serving a salty Salade Niçoise with Toasted Anchovies, a good contrasting wine would be a soft and fruity Sauvignon Blanc.

Once you are comfortable with complementary flavors, you will be ready to go bold and try pairing hot or highly acidic foods with a citrusy Rosè, or pairing flavorful spicy dishes with light palate-cleansing wines.

Three Easy Rules of Thumb

Match sweet and fruity wines like a Riesling with spicy foods.

Match the woody flavors of Chardonnay with creamy sauces and strong herbs.

Match full-bodied Cabernet Sauvignons with heavy beef entrées.

When Choosing More Expensive Wines

Do some research first so that you are familiar with the ratings for both the wine and vintner (wine maker), and don't be afraid to ask questions.

I have always found the personnel in wine shops to be very willing and helpful. They appreciate being asked to share their expertise and can make recommendations within a certain price point and menu design. Finer restaurants often have a sommelier, or in-house wine expert, who can also be both helpful and informative.

Vintage and year are a little trickier, because all wines age differently. Some common traits of all wines include:

Younger wines are great as light, refreshing, easy drinking choices, because fruity wines tend to lessen in quality with age.

When shopping for something dense and complex, look for wines that have aged at least two or three years.

If the bitter taste of tannin bothers you, know that age will soften tannins and make them more agreeable.

In general, the flavor in wines intensifies with age – unless they have a "cocoon period" where they will instead mellow a bit before growing again in flavor. Doing research and asking questions is how you will learn to spot wines that have cocooning periods.

In summary, the best wines will always be the ones you love to drink.

Trust your instincts and become aware of what you really enjoy. Learn as you go by trying new things and making notes about how wines are made, the year they are made, and their flavors.

Choosing a Wine

Throughout Occasions, wines have been recommended with each menu.

A BASIC FORMULA FOR CHOOSING WINES:

	LIGHT WINES	MEDIUM WINES	HEAVY WINES
WHITES & ROSÉ	Chenin Blanc, Pinot Grigio, Gewürztraminer, Riesling, Rosé	Sauvignon Blanc, Fumé, Vernaccia	Chardonnay
REDS	Pinot Noir or Merlot	Merlot, Madeira, Sangiovese	Cabernet Sauvignon, Bordeaux, Chianti, Petite Sirah

TYPE OF GRAPE

Match Color	Poultry & Pork are best served with white wine. Beef & lamb work better with reds.
Consider weight	Choose a rich white wine with a rich white sauce. Serve a full-body red with a flavorful beef and/or hearty sauce.
Take into account what you can afford	Expressions like "blend" and "table wine" are typically cheaper, but also can be bland in taste and poorly balanced because they are made from grapes from an array of regions and varieties. These can make fine drinking wine, but are not always a good choice for a special occasion.

WINE CHOICE FOR FOOD TYPE
Choose a grape that will complement your main course

	LIGHT WINES	MEDIUM WINES	HEAVY WINES
White Meat	Ham	Chicken, pork, veal	
Red Meat		Roasted wild meats	Beef, steak, lamb
Seafood	Lighter fish – Sole or shrimp	Heavier fish – Salmon, tuna	
Cheese	Lighter cheeses	Fuller cheeses like Goat or Pecorino	
Vegetables	Soft vegetables – Asparagus, lettuce	Carrots, beans, bell peppers	Root vegetables: Turnips, beets, etc.
Grains	Couscous, rices	Rice, risotto	Bulgar wheat
Sauces	Lemon/citrus, Vinaigrettes	Olive oil, cream, butter	Meat or spicy sauces, tomatoes
Fruits	Melons, berries	Apples, pears	Dense fruits like banana

Wines also have an "influence" of fruit or oak, for example, which will likewise complement your meal. As you explore wine choices on your own, ask questions, read labels and try new varieties

Opening Wine

With a Winged Corkscrew

Use a knife to cut off the foil just under the lip of the wine bottle, then pull off the foil cap and throw it away. The foil can change the taste of the wine and should be cut just below the lip of the wine bottle to prevent any wine from touching it.

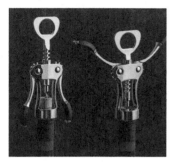

Set the corkscrew in place in the center of the cork and push down gently. The metal cap that surrounds the screw should be resting on the top of the cork, with the butterfly wings down, or lowered against the neck of the bottle.

Turn the handle at the top of the corkscrew. Hold the metal cap in place with your left hand and use your right (or dominate) hand to turn the handle and screw the corkscrew down into the cork. As you twist, the wings will begin lifting upward.

There is no need to apply pressure, but simply continue turning the handle until the wings have lifted to an upright position. Then use both hands to push down the two wings. As you push down the wings, the cork will lift up and out on its own. Continue pushing until the wings are flat against the bottle's neck and the cork has been freed from the bottle.

How to Pour Wine

Remove Foil from Neck of Bottle

The foil protecting the cork can contain lead. If left in place, it can leach into the wine as it is poured. Removing the foil will also help avoid drips.

Wipe the Bottle Opening

Use a clean bar towel to wipe away any dust or cork debris before pouring.

Ensure Glasses are Clean & Dust Free

Check glasses for dust or smudges before pouring wine into them, and store glasses upside down to avoid dust build up between uses.

Use Both Hands

Properly pouring wine means cradling the bottle with both hands and then carefully pouring four to five ounces into the glass. *An easy way to eye-ball this amount is to pour the wine just to the breaking point in the shape of the glass.*

Another thing to remember is to leave the glass on the table while pouring, and to hold the bottle six to ten inches above the glass. This allows the wine to aerate and improves the flavor by softening the tannins in the wine as it is poured.

After each pour, twist the bottle gently to prevent dripping.

Wipe the Neck Between Each Pour

Keep the remaining wine in the bottle from drying on the lip by wiping the neck between each pour.

That Extra Touch

Pour wine with the label facing your guests so that they can see the vintage and vineyard.

Pour white wines wrapped in a thick bar towel to avoid warming the wines with the heat of your hands.

Consider pouring just a taste for an honored guest or wine enthusiast to approve before pouring the first glass.

Serving wines

Red wine should not be chilled, but served slightly below room temperature (53 to 69 degrees) with Pinot Noir at the cooler end of this range. *Reds should also be opened at least 30 minutes prior to serving.*

White wine should be well-chilled to 45 to 50 degrees, slightly warmer (50 to 55 degrees) for a chardonnay.

Sparkling wine should be chilled the most, or 38 to 45 degrees. Higher quality sparkling wines are served at the higher end of temperature range.

Calculating the Amount Needed

A 750 milligram bottle contains five to six glasses or servings of wine.

Calculate the number of guests multiplied by the estimated number of glasses each guest will potentially consume to determine how many bottles to purchase for the occasion.

Glossary of Recommended Wines & Liqueurs

Bordeaux – A wine produced in the Bordeaux region of France that can be a red, claret, sweet white, dry white or rosé. Good with meats, chicken, mushrooms and strong cheese.

Cabernet Franc – An earthy, spicy and rich red wine, known for having notes of blueberry and violet or coffee. Full bodied with a touch of bitterness, Cabernet Franc is good with stews, red meats and smoky dishes.

Cabernet Sauvignon – A classic and very popular red wine with a dense color and complex aroma. Full to soft-bodied; high in tannin and noticeably acid. Flavors of black currant, cherry and other dark fruits to savory herbs, cedar and oak. *Cabs are best from Napa Valley in California.* Because Cabernet grapes are easy to grow, these wines are often an inexpensive yet very good choice. Especially good with rich and hearty dishes like grilled or roasted beef.

Calvados – French cider brandy. Good with after dinner sweets.

Champagne – A sparkling wine made from a second fermentation that creates carbonation. Made primarily from pinot noir or chardonnay grapes blended with dark fruits or crisp apples and citrus. A celebration wine.

Chardonnay – A barrel-aged, okay to citrus-flavored white wine that gives a crisp buttery mouthful and is very drinkable. Chardonnay grapes are grown all over the world and wines can be crisp to sharp - sometimes sparkling. Good with poultry, rich seafood, sweet corn. *Chardonnay is a good value on a budget.*

Chenin Blanc – A white sparkling or dessert wine that is full-bodied and sometimes fruity with honey and floral characteristics. Good with fish.

Chianti – A strong Italian wine from central Tuscany. Made with 80% Sangiovese grapes and typically aged for 38 months. High alcohol and dry. Good with hearty beef, strong cheeses, tomato sauces and pasta dishes.

Fumé – A French wine grape with crisp and aromatic herbs flavors. Good with fish and chicken.

Pouilly Fumé – From the Loire Valley and often thought to have a gun flint smell. A good balance to dishes high in acidity, as well good with scallops, shellfish and many appetizers.

Gewürztraminer – An aromatic dry white wine made from a pink grape with a sweet flamboyant bouquet of rose, passion fruit or other florals. Good with ham, also good with spicy foods, Asian food and fish.

Madeira – A dry sweet Portuguese wine that is very robust and boasts a long life after opening. Good with sweets.

Malbec – A red wine with deep aromas and soft tannins that is bold and spicy. Made in France and Argentina. Good with tuna steaks, lamb, hamburgers, pizza and barbecue.

Marc – A French brandy made from the residue of wine grapes. Good with desserts.

Merlot – A popular red that is dark blue in color. Merlot is full-bodied, high alcohol with velvety tannins and a lingering finish. Often has a big, intense dark fruit flavor like plum or blackberry, and/or vanilla and coffee. Merlots are aged with oak and often have a smoky taste. *Merlots are best from France and Northern America.* Merlots are the easiest wines to pair with food. This agreeable choice is very good with fatty salmon or beef.

Pastis – A popular drink in the south of France with a licorice or anise flavor, served diluted with cool water. Good with small bites and appetizers.

Petite Sirah – (AKA: Durif) A variety of red wine made from the Durif grape with a spicy, plummy and full-bodied flavor. Good with spicy foods.

Pinot Grigio – Refreshing and summery. Honey, lavender and stone fruit flavors, often with heavy notes of pear. Good with Thai food, salads, seafood and roasted chicken, and easily drinkable.

Pinot Noir – High priced and extravagant, pinot noir is a red wine grape grown all over the world, and *especially good from the state of Oregon in the USA.* Light colored, medium bodied and low in tannin; it has a fruity aroma of cherry, raspberry and/or strawberry and often has an earthy influence. Good with complex dishes like pasta, grilled salmon, baked ham and beef, and equally good with a decadent chocolate dessert. Because the pinot noir grape is hard to grow, a good pinot is expensive. But when made well, this wine is complex, rich and nuanced. *Spend at least $20 a bottle to get your money's worth; cheaper pinots are not worth it.*

Riesling (Johannisberg) – A white grape variety from the Rhine region of Germany. Flowery and/or fruity, aromatic, dry and semi-sweet. This powerful white wine can also be a sparkling or dessert wine. Rieslings are good with eggs, shellfish, spicy Asian foods, salads and poultry.

Rosè – A wine that incorporates some of the color from the red skin of the grape. The flavors can be sweet to bone dry with fruit, rose and/or peony influences, and can also be sparkling. Good with almost anything. These *very drinkable wines* are light, often fruity and mild enough to pair well with most any dish. Go with a Côte-du-Rhône red blend from the south of France when looking for a great Rosè. Côte-du-Rhône wines are also very affordable.

Sangiovese – A deep ruby red wine with a bright and acidic taste made from grapes grown in central Italy (Tuscany). Often peppered with hints of spice, cherry and even tobacco. Good with anything Italian.

Sauvignon Blanc – A white wine from green-skinned grapes with a grassy or herbal to tropical flavor. It is sometimes fruity/lemony or grassy, and always crisp, elegant and fresh. Good with chicken, tart cheese and vegetables, and a good pairing for lighter, softer dishes, casual drinking and appetizers. *Sauvignon Blanc is also the best choice for cooking because of its punch of acidity without an overpowering flavor.*

Shiraz – Similar to a cabernet sauvignon with fruity to chocolaty influence. Good with pizza, beef and heavy meats.

Sirah – Dense and peppery with a strong spicy flavor, Sirah is made from a peppery grape. Good with peppery foods.

Vernaccia – A white grape grown in central Italy that makes a light yellow wine with a deep and delicate bouquet and pleasant aftertaste. Often has hints of fresh fruits and wild flowers. Good with cold meats, eggs and fish.

Vino Santo – AKA: Holy Wine. A late harvest Italian dessert wine. Good with buttery but not too sweet desserts. (**Vendage** is a late harvest French dessert wine.)

Zinfandel – Similar to a pinot noir, Zinfandel is rich and berry-heavy with fruity and spicy flavors and fine tannins. Often have hints of raspberry, cherry and raisin. A great wine to drink on its own. Good with barbecue, chili and rich foods that can stand up to the hearty yet fruity taste.

TERMS

Full/medium/soft-bodied – The intensity of a wine's flavor.

Tannin – The chemical compounds in wine that affect color and texture. Tannins cannot be smelled or tasted, but are instead perceived by the dry sensation and sense of bitterness left in one's mouth. Wines high in tannins are good paired with red meat.

Varietal – A wine that has been made from a single named grape.

The Table

Setting a Formal Table • Folding Napkins • Caring for Linens

Setting a Formal Table

Table setting protocols are important for any host or hostess to know.

Even though table settings today are often informal, there are times – like when you are entertaining your mother-in-law, the boss, or the Dowager Countess is coming to dinner – when you will want to set your table according to established standards.

The standards listed below were developed and designed with the comfort of the diner in mind. For example, the fork is always placed on the left and the knife on the right. This is for the ease of a right-handed diner who will naturally hold the knife and cut meat or vegetables with their dominate hand.

The same applies for placing drinks to the right of the plate as they too will most naturally be lifted with the dominate hand. As well, the edge of the knife points toward the plate to keep sharp edges from being brushed accidently as plates are cleared.

When the table is set properly, the dining experience is more efficient for the diner and is visually balanced and appealing. From placing flatware to using place cards, everything you need to know for your table setting repertoire is covered in this guide when planning something formal. For everyday meals and informal get-togethers you may choose to not fuss and have fun using your creativity – that's okay too.

The Overall Table

Each element on the table should be coordinated for an overall effect. This does not necessarily mean everything must match, but rather be complementary in feel and color. If rooms other than the dining room are called into service for the meal, set the tables in these rooms with the same care you would in the dining room, and try to coordinate these tables and centerpieces with the furnishings.

PLATES

If you want to be formal, you should use a salad plate and plan to clear it before the entrée is served. If you do not have help with the service of your meal, then preset the salad on its plate just before guests are seated, and plan to clear this plate for your guests between courses.

If you do not want to clear plates between courses then dispense with a salad plate entirely and serve the salad with the main course, all on one plate.

The exception to this rule would be if your main course is something very runny or gooey. Then a separate salad plate is recommended regardless.

DINNER PLATES

One inch from the table's edge

Be sure to consider if you dinner plate is large enough for the meal you are planning.

If your meat or entrée, salad, vegetable and bread or roll are all on one plate, it should be 12-inches in diameter. Otherwise, give guests a smaller plate for either the salad and/or the bread or roll.

BREAD & BUTTER PLATES

Above the forks

If you are serving bread or rolls, I recommend using a bread and butter plate. It is nice to also have a butter knife placed across the top of the plates, with the blade toward the user.

A pat or round of butter can be placed on each butter plate and alleviate the need for passing a butter dish.

FLATWARE

Placed in the order they will be used

Set your table uniformly by placing flatware one-inch from the edge of the table at place settings that are equal in distance from one another on the table.

The base of all flatware should align evenly across the bottom of each place setting. While this may sound over-the-top, it really does make a pleasing overall presentation, and also helps prevent silver from accidentally being toppled off the table because it has been set too close to the edge.

The basic rule of thumb is to set your table with whatever silverware is needed for the meal.

Traditionally, the pieces that will be needed first, or in the first course, are placed farthest right and left of the plate, working from the outside to the center. It is not necessary to place silver that will not be used.

FLATWARE – KNIVES & SPOONS

On the right

The knife is usually just one – unless you are serving an appetizer at the table that requires a knife. If so, provide one knife for the appetizer, and one for the meat. *Sometimes a steak knife is used, and in this case the steak knife should take the place of the dinner/ meat knife.*

Today, most appetizers are served reception-style and consumed before guests are seated. This is a much easier approach and also makes one knife on the table enough.

If salad is to be served with cheese or contains an item that will need to be cut, a salad knife is needed and placed to the right of the dinner knife. The blade of the knife faces the plate.

Spoons are on the table, to the right of the knives. Soup spoons, because they will be used in the first course, are placed to the right of the dinner spoon.

FLATWARE – THE FORKS

On the left

Usually two forks are placed at a formal setting, one for salad and one for the meat; occasionally one more for the appetizer, but never more than three beside the plate at once.

The salad fork is placed to the outside of the meat (or entrée) fork, only when the salad is served as a first course.

If only one course is being served, only provide one fork.

The dessert fork and spoon, when part of the setting, are placed above the plate.

The dessert spoon is placed above the dessert fork (if there is a need for both). The spoon handle faces right, the fork handle faces left, corresponding with the silverware placement beside the plate.

When clearing plates between courses, be sure to also clear the silver used with that course.

GLASSES & GOBLETS

Above the knife

Glasses are placed on a diagonal, starting with the water glass above the knife, and leading to the lower left. The white wine glass is used for the first course. The middle, red wine glass, is used during the remaining courses. As follows, if serving only one course and/or one wine, use only one wine glass.

It's nice to keep a pitcher of ice water on or near the table to refill water glasses during the meal. *When doing so, use my friend Julia's trick to avoid dripping between pours by rubbing a tiny bit of butter just under the rim of the pitcher's lip!*

WINE GLASSES

To the right of the water goblet

The white wine glass is used for the first course. The middle, red wine glass, is used during the remaining courses.

The wineglass should be filled just under halfway, or to the point where the glass (shape) breaks.

If you are wearing lipstick and it gets on your glass, subtly use the inside of your thumb to wipe it away.

NAPKINS & LINENS

The napkin can be placed on the plate, unless the first course is in place, in which case it should be placed to the left of the forks, as a rule.

Napkins come in two sizes, with smaller choices (approximately 11 to 12 inches) designed for luncheon and larger napkins used for dinner.

Decorative napkin rings can be used to hold rolled and folded napkins and can be anything from a fine engraved antique silver ring to a simple piece of felt crafted for a Christmas table. Try creatively wrapping each napkin with fresh flowers or tucking in tiny fruits or whole spices, just for fun!

Pretty trimmings attached to individual rings can also be charming. I love tucking a pretty rose into a tapestry ribbon, cinnamon sticks into raffia, or tying napkins with a ribbon that holds a miniature bouquet of fresh flowers. These home-spun rings also make delightful gifts to send home with each guest (if you think they would like to have them). Clever rings can complement the occasion and are a great way to incorporate your imagination by adding tiny treasures to delight your guests in their napkin bundle.

When using a tablecloth, keep in mind that it will determine the mood of your table and establish the degree of formality.

A formal linen cloth should generously overhang the table on all four sides. Napkins, tablecloths and linens on a formal table should always be pressed.

If using place mats, remember that the entire place setting should fit on one mat.

THE CENTERPIECE

Centerpieces and table decorations should be low enough (or tall enough) for all guests to be seen.

When using flowers, keep in mind that heavily scented flowers like gardenias can sometimes spoil the appetite, especially in the summer months when the air is warm.

Flowers are a customary centerpiece, but found objects, a platter of fruits and vegetables, and other decorations make clever centerpieces as well.

Focus on beauty when setting the table – the little details will make all the difference.

SERVING BUTTER

An individual pat of butter on each butter plate is my preferred method of service.

If you wish to have butter on the table to pass around Family Style, make it look pretty by placing it on an earthenware or porcelain plate, and be sure to include a butter knife.

The same applies for presenting salt and pepper, if individual sets cannot be provided at place settings.

SALT & PEPPER SERVICE

At a large table, a salt and pepper set should be placed for every two guests at the table. If you wish to pass salt and pepper Family Style, use shakers that coordinate with your dishes.

COFFEE SERVICE

If coffee is to be served, place a cup and saucer to the right of the dinner plate with a spoon placed on the right side of each saucer.

CANDLES

Candles are technically a lighting source and should be used as such. *Candlesticks therefore, would not belong on the luncheon table, as daylight will suffice.*

Candlesticks, when used for dinner, should always be lit, and candles should be above or below eye level to avoid glare in guests' eyes.

An abundance of candles makes such a gracious table and gives an intimate feeling to the meal.

Candlesticks can be uniform or not, and an individual-sized votive at each setting can also be enchanting.

Always use unscented candles at the table to avoid a scented candle competing with the aromas of your meal. Candles made of beeswax are a good choice because they drip less.

PLACE CARDS

Place cards are used for formal dinner parties and display only the guest's name.

Place cards allow the host/hostess to strategically seat guests around the table to ensure everyone enjoys the conversation and celebration.

Pretty cards can be purchased and most can be printed with home computers enabling the use of elegant or clever fonts.

As a guest, do not ask your host to change the seating arrangement unless you have a very good reason to do so.

If you have guests with limited mobility, place cards will also ensure these friends have easy access to and from the table.

Be creative with place cards when entertaining close friends and family.

Consider using tiny framed photos of each guest instead of a card with their name on it. Or use mementos that speak to each guests and that will be meaningful to them, like a tiny Eiffel Tower, ceramic garden wheelbarrow or miniature football. This is also a great way to get dinner conversation started as each guest will get a kick out of explaining why their "place card" has been chosen for them.

MENU CARDS

Each chapter cover page for the menus in Occasions *has been designed in a menu card format.*

Menu Cards are an easy way to make your evening elegant and showcase the meal.

Be sure to make one card for each guest, and tuck them into napkins or place one on the plate of each guest. Approximately 4 x 6-inches is a nice size.

Place the date at the upper right and "Dinner" or "Lunch" in the upper center.

Leave a bit of space between courses so that your guests will know how the meal is being served. If your party is a special celebration, indicate this on the top of card.

Italian Night

ANTIPASTI
Gamberi Alla Griglia Avvolti in Pancetta & Basilico
VINO
Vernaccia

SECONDI PIATTI
Spinaci & Ravioli di Ricotta con Salsa
di Burro Prosciutto Tostato
Con Aceto Balsamico Glassa
VINO
Red Sangiovese
& Acqua

FRUTTA - DESSERT
Limone Lavanda Shortbread
CAFFE'- LIQUORI
Caffe'
Vino Santo

If you are an accomplished hostess, it is fun to write your menus in French or Italian, or as appropriate to your menu.

Computers can easily translate documents, and while every nuance of the language may not be perfectly correct in its translation, your friends will get a kick out of the effort and have a keepsake of the meal!

Shown above is the menu for Italian Night in the Autumn section of Occasions.

Above all, setting the table should be a satisfying and creative endeavor. Don't fret if you don't have enough matching plates for the entire party, but mix coordinating choices and craft the kind of table that showcases your personality. It is fun to see how many different tables can be created by mixing things up!

Folding Napkins

There are many imaginative ways to fold napkins. Here are three favorites:

Embroidered or Monogrammed Napkins

To show off a pretty monogrammed or embroidered napkin, start by folding it in half lengthwise and then crosswise.

Place the loose edges upward to form a diamond shape. Fold over the loose edge at top to form a small triangle, with the tip just above the monogram or embroidery.

Now fold under the two side points of the napkin from the edges of top triangle. This will create a slight flair from the top triangle to the bottom (triangle) of napkin.

Place folded napkins directly on the service plates with the triangle points – and monogram toward the diner.

Large Dinner Napkins

Fold the square napkin in two with the loose edges down. Then fold to the left, with the edges on the left once, and then twice.

This rectangle now has all of the loose edges at the left and bottom, which will allow the diner to then pick up the napkin by the right hand corner and neatly place it in their lap.

A large dinner napkin should not be completely unfolded when in use, but merely spread across one's lap folded in half.

Napkin Rosettes

Fold a large square napkin in two to make a triangle with pointed end away from you.

Roll the napkin tightly toward the pointed end, stopping 3 to 5 inches from point. Then roll the rolled napkin from end to end, stopping 3 to 5 inches from the end of the roll.

Secure the remaining 3 to 5 inches into the roll, or rose, by tucking this piece into the fold of the roll. Use a knife to tuck the edges in and keep "rose" roll tight and secure. Then carefully separate the top two triangles that are sticking up.

Fold these down on opposite sides of the "rose" and invert them to form a "leaf " on both sides of the blossom. Set roses leaf side down at place settings.

Caring for Linens

After guests have gone home, use a pre-treating laundry spray on used napkins, being careful to hit any wine or chocolate stains as well as lipstick. Then wash linens overnight.

For stubborn stains and lipstick you have not pre-treated, try removing stains with scalding water.

Heirloom linens should be washed by hand in warm water using a mild detergent.

Avoid using bleach, but instead hang freshly laundered linens in the sun to dry. Sunlight will naturally brighten whites.

To iron, spray linens with water to moisten, and use a steam iron with starch.

Embroidered napkins should be ironed on a heavy cotton towel or spongy surface.

This will raise the initial or design and really make it stand out.

Store table linens flat in acid-free tissue to prevent yellowing. Avoid hangers and plastic bags to prolong life.

USE THE SAME CARE WITH FINE CHINA, SILVER & CRYSTAL

Fine china is best washed by hand, especially if it has gold or silver trim. Most dishwashers today have a china setting though, which helps save time in clean-up - but be sure to use a detergent that has no citrus additives as these can be abrasive.

When washing china and crystal by hand, use a large plastic tub or line your sink with rubber pads. This will keep your pieces safe from accidentally chipping while swishing in the water.

Sterling should always be washed by hand and dried immediately, but I've had no problem putting crystal in the dishwasher, as long as it is stacked securely and any lipstick is removed in advance.

Utilizing Time Lines • Good Cooking Habits• Stocking the
Pantry & Freezer • Kitchen Essentials • How Long Will It Keep?

Utilizing Time Lines

Each menu in Occasions *has a time line for your use.*

Entertaining is made easy via the pre-work, and time lines are a great way to help organize tasks. Once the invitation has been issued, plan your menu, wines and décor, then backtrack. Consider each step of each task and determine how much can be done before the actual event.

When you are still in the kitchen working throughout your own party it takes all the fun out of entertaining – not to mention that it makes your guests uncomfortable. So plan ahead to ensure your occasions are always fun, and your food is served just as it is meant to be.

To build a time line, start by considering what aspects of your meal might be prepared early, like the dessert. Then consider what parts will take the longest and determine what time the preparation should start, reading each recipe carefully in advance.

If there are unfamiliar techniques involved, immerse yourself in the material to ensure an understanding before you begin.

Many foods can be prepared weeks in advance and frozen.

Likewise, the table can be set days ahead, leaving only fresh flowers to be added the day of the event.

There is no rule that says an entire dish must be made all at one time. I often break the preparation down for complicated dishes, and hold prepared foods when possible, to make things easier on myself once the guests arrive.

In summary, take the time to do as much before the party as you possibly can (down to even having the ice bucket full) leaving only the last minute heat-and-eat tasks for the actual event - then enjoy!

Good Cooking Habits

Before you start your mixer or turn on the stove, read through recipes from start to finish.

Think about what you are supposed to be doing and why. Consider the time it will take and give yourself a bit of leeway so you don't get flustered. If unfamiliar terms are used in recipes, consult the glossary and never assume.

Then, set all of your ingredients on the counter to ensure you have what is called for and pre-measure and prepare ingredients before beginning.

There's nothing worse than trying to hold a delicate meringue because you do not have the other ingredients ready, or getting half way through a recipe to discover you are missing a key ingredient.

*The secret to a great meal
is to time all dishes to finish cooking at the same time.*

Again, a simple time line will help you think through the timing of each dish so that everything in your meal is enjoyed as it is meant to be served.

For example, if you are serving a roast that will take 2 hours to cook and 20 minutes to rest, and potatoes that will take 20 minutes from start to finish, the potatoes should not even be peeled until the roast has finished cooking.

No matter the skill level, good timing is the true secret to being a good cook!

Practice, Practice, Practice

Try practicing more complicated dishes on the weekend when you have more time to attempt unfamiliar recipes, and make notes on recipes to document the tacit knowledge you have picked-up from trying new things.

Always make an unfamiliar dish exactly as directed the first time, then experiment with new ideas and personal preferences the next time around. And don't be discouraged if a dish does not come out exactly right the first time. Go back and review what you did and did not do to determine where things went wrong, and then try again – *you'll get it!*

Stocking the Pantry & Freezer

The Pantry

Build a pantry that is full of "staples." This will make both preparing home-cooked and healthy meals on busy nights easier and entertaining guests more doable because fewer things will need to be purchased in advance of the party.

When planning menus, consider what is in season and what is on special in the market. *Ingredients always taste better when they are at their peak of freshness.*

Don't skimp on essentials like extra-virgin/good quality olive oil, pure vanilla extract, fresh herbs and the like.

Be flexible when planning your menus and prepare dishes that take advantage of nature's natural timetable.

The Freezer

Try to keep an array of "quick" foods on hand for unexpected guests by doubling recipes when you can and keeping as assortment of good homemade dishes in the freezer. You will find that many homemade foods are just as easy to double as to making only a single recipe.

Try making two lasagnas or two recipes of tomato sauce for example. Most all foods freeze well and will keep in the freezer for two weeks to two months or more. Make entertaining easy by experimenting with multiples.

I have also found that most desserts are too large to be consumed in one meal, and make a practice of setting aside half of most desserts to freeze for another occasion. Cookies are easy to divide in half and freeze; pies can be made into two 5-inch pies instead of one 9-inch; and cakes can often be made into cupcakes so half of them can be frozen. This avoids having tempting calorie-laden foods in the kitchen as well!

Kitchen Essentials

Over time, try to collect kitchen essentials. Treat yourself to good cake pans and a cooling rack as your budget allows and buy spices as you need them for new dishes. Purchase these items gradually and replace them as necessary. Before you know it, your kitchen will be well stocked.

KITCHEN STAPLES

Bacon
Baking Powder & Baking Soda
Beans (black, cannellini, kidney)
Bouillon Cubes
Fresh Herbs
Bread Crumbs
Broth (beef & chicken)
Butter
Buttermilk
Cheese
Chocolate (a variety including cocoa)
Coconut
Cream & Milk
Cream of Tartar
Eggs (large)
Crisco Shortening
Flour (all-purpose & cake)
Fresh Garlic
Honey
Ketchup
Lemons, Limes

Maple Syrup
Mayonnaise
Molasses
Mustard (Dijon & brown)
Nuts
Oils (a variety, along with olive oil)
Onions
Pastas & Lasagna
Preserves
Rice
Salt (kosher & table)
Sour Cream
Soy Sauce
Spices
Sugar (granulated, brown & powdered)
Syrup
Cornstarch
Vinegars
Wines & Liquors
Yeast
Vanilla Extract (pure)

OTHER STAPLES INCLUDE:

Anchovies
Chipotle Chilies
Condensed Milk
Tomato Paste
Tomatoes (fresh & canned)
Plastic Containers

Aluminum Foil
Plastic Wrap & Plastic Baggies
Waxed Paper & Parchment Paper
Paper Towels
Cheesecloth
String

ESSENTIAL KITCHEN EQUIPMENT

Measuring cups (one set for wet ingredients & one for dry)

Measuring Spoons

Kitchen Scales

Instant-Read Meat Thermometer & Candy/Frying Thermometer

Kitchen Timer (in addition to the one on your stove)

Mixing/Prep Bowls (all sizes)

Cutting/Chopping Board

*Good Knives (these are expensive and can be collected one at a time if necessary)

Kitchen Shears & Twine

Vegetable Parer

Can Opener

Pepper Grinder

Funnel

Nut Grinder

Grater

Colander

Fine-Mesh Strainer

Salad Spinner

Ruler

Whisk

I ALSO RECOMMEND:

Grapefruit Knife

Micro Plane Zester/Grater
Melon Baller

Mortar & Pestle
Meat Tenderizer

Immersion Blender

Food Processor

Powerful Blender

Winged Wine Corkscrew

Citrus Juicer

Squeeze Bottle(s)

Stand Mixer

Tongs

*KNIVES:

8 or 10-inch Chef's Knife

3 or 4-inch Paring Knife

10 or 12-inch Serrated Bread Knife

6-inch Boning Knife

A good heavy Cleaver

10-inch Honing Steel

FOR COOKING YOU'LL NEED:

Pots/Skillets/Saucepans

Kettle

Wooden Spoons
Rubber Spatulas (stiff and small offset)

Metal Utensils (slotted spoons, tongs, whisks, skewers)

Basting Brushes (one for cooking & one for baking)

Slotted Flexible Metal Spatula

Saltcellar & Pepper Mill

Pizza Brick

Skewers

Bulb Baster

Brush

Griddle

FOR BAKING YOU'LL NEED:

Hand Mixer
Pastry Blender
Rolling Pin
Flour Sifter
Cake Pans
Loaf Pans
Bundt Pan

Cookie Sheets
Jelly Roll Pan
Muffin Tins
Pie Pans
Pie Shield
Pie Crust Shield/Ring
Cooling Rack(s)

I ALSO RECOMMEND:
Pasta Machine
Pastry/Bench Scraper
Pastry/Biscuit/Cookie Cutters
Pizza Cutter
Spring Form Pan

Small Tart Tin(s)
Custard Cups
Pastry Bag & Tips
Ice Cream Maker
Slow Cooker (crock pot)

How Long Will It Keep?

ITEM	3 to 4 mos.	6 mos.	8 mos.	Up to 1 yr.	1 to 2 yrs.	Indefinitely	Notes
Baking Powder		■					Test by placing 1 teaspoon in a bowl & adding 1 teaspoon of water. It should bubble & fizz vigorously.
Baking Soda			■				
Cornstarch						■	
Cocoa					■		
Flour (all-purpose & bread)				■			In a sealed container.
Gelatin (powdered)						■	
Brown Sugar	■						In airtight container. If sugar hardens, microwave for 30 seconds.
Granulated Sugar						■	In airtight container.
Vanilla Extract					■		
Yeast (instant)						■	In airtight container in the freezer.

The Right Cocktail Glass

THE GLASS	USE & SIZE
OLD FASHION GLASS	A short tumbler that holds 6 to 8 ounces.
HIGHBALL GLASS	A tall glass that holds 8 to 10 ounces.
PILSNER GLASS	A tall, slender glass used for beer that holds up to 1 pint.
CHAMPAGNE FLUTE	A stem glass with a tall, narrow bowl that holds 6 to 10 ounces.
COCKTAIL GLASS	Often called a martini glass, a stem with inverted cone bowl; holds 4 to 5 ounces.
SNIFTER	A short, stemmed glass with a vessel that has a wide bottom and relatively narrow top. Used for dark liquors like bourbon, brandy & whiskey.
JULEP CUP	A silver or pewter straight-sided metal tumbler.
WINE GLASSES *Larger bowls are used to serve reds* *&* *Small narrower bowls for whites*	Stemware with a bowl, stem and foot. *When drinking chilled white wine, hold the glass by the stem to prevent body temperatures from warming the wine, and avoid stemless wine glasses for white wines.*
JIGGER	A measuring cup for alcoholic beverage, holds 1.5 ounces or 3 Tablespoons.

GLASSES L TO R: OLD FASHION, HIGHBALL, PILSNER, CHAMPAGNE FLUTE, COCKTAIL, SNIFTER, JULEP CUP, WINE-RED, WINE-WHITE, JIGGER.

Utilizing Flowers

Basic Flower Arranging • The Meaning of Flowers • Other
Symbolic Herbs & Flowers • Edible Flowers & Herbs
Chilling with Style • Tussie Mussies

Basic Flower Arranging

*Today it is easy to find beautiful cut flowers
in supermarkets, health food stores and
at farmer's markets. Crafting your own
centerpiece is not only fun to do, but saves a
bit of money as well.*

The Basics

Start with an under layer of large leaves or
fern to create a base.

Then position your tallest and largest
flowers, in odd numbers, creating a
triangular shape with the tallest point at the
top of the arrangement.

Fill between the larger flowers with smaller
ones and more greenery throughout.

*Just like in the landscape, you want to work in odd
numbers when arranging flowers in a vase.*

Consider contrasting colors and texture
when selecting flowers, then make the most
of each choice in your arrangement.

Trim stems liberally to be in accordance
with the height of the vase.

And create hot pops of color by positioning
varied but similar colored blossoms close
together.

Also:

> Remove the majority of the leaves on the parts of stems that will be under water, as these leaves will cause the water in your vase to become cloudy very quickly.

> If packets of fertilizer come with your bouquet, mix it into the water before beginning to ensure blossoms have long life.

> Use garden pruning shears or scissors to cut stems.

> If using a shallow vase, insert a "frog" or green florist brick into the vessel and secure with strips of florist tape by making a cross and attaching to the sides of the vessel. This will hold the frog down in the water. *When using a frog, soak it in water for a few hours before beginning. This will saturate the frog, keep it stable and prevent it from floating in the water.*

> Then cover the tape with flowers as you build your arrangement.

> *Be careful to not make a table arrangement that is too high or you will obstruct your guest's view of one another.*

The Deconstructed Bouquet

Use a cluster of small vases (like silver baby cups or small pitchers) on your table with just one type of flower in each vase – lilies in one, roses in another, daisies in the next. Deconstructed bouquets can also be placed at each place setting to create a more intimate table.

The Clustered Bouquet

Prepare the under layer as outlined earlier, then cluster groups of like flowers as shown above. A clustered bouquet produces large patches of color and texture and can be very dramatic. A group of tall flowers, like lilies or sunflowers could be at the top/center of your bouquet, with bunches of pretty roses below until every kind of flower has been incorporated in big bunches.

The Uniform Arrangement

March three to five uniform vases down the center of your table (as shown at right) all holding the same type of flower.

Also try using hydrangeas and poppies, or roses and olive tree branches.

The Vase – Get Creative!

Sugar bowls, julep cups, soup tureens and even old coffee cans can all be called into service and used to complement the occasion. Pumpkins, coconuts, watermelons, lemons and other fruits and vegetables can also be hollowed out and used to hold flowers.

Keep in mind that the centerpiece, the container and the flowers, will be seen close up and give special attention to their overall harmony with the entire table scape.

Use pieces of china or pottery that enhance the table setting, and then try filling them with river rocks and pebbles, cherry tomatoes, lime or lemon slices, or kumquats.

Drama can also be created effectively by contrasting colors and using vivid red flowers with a green malachite vase, for example. To really showcase your container, use only one variety of flowers like a cluster of raspberry orchids tucked into a coconut.

A clever and more natural vase can be crafted by wrapping a simple cylinder with stalks of asparagus, cinnamon sticks or the long green leaves of lilies. To make a more natural looking vase from a simple cylinder, or to dress up a large candle, start by encircling the container/candle with a large rubber band. Then tuck cinnamon sticks, large leaves (magnolia, bay, or hydrangea) behind the band until the entire vase or candle surface is covered. Then cover the rubber band with a pretty ribbon, raffia or long leaf from your garden, like a lily.

For a really large clear glass vase, slip in a gold fish to delight your guests throughout the meal as it swims and flirts amongst the stems! *If you choose a very tall vase or topiary, ensure the base is also thin enough for guests to see around.*

Set your chosen container on the table before you begin to assess its height and width. This will give you a better idea of the space you need to fill and tell you right away if your guests will be able to see around the arrangement during the meal.

Nosegays

If you are creating a bouquet to take to a friend, build it in a vase first. Once you are happy with the arrangement, carefully remove it from the vase as is, and wrap with florist wire to secure everything in place.

Then cover the wire with florist tape and make a 2 to 3-inch wide taped area to hold and carry the arrangement.

Tidy the stems once secured by shaving off the bottoms at an angle leaving the short sheared stems on the outer edge. Wrap the nosegay in a piece of tissue paper leaving the tops of the flowers showing at one open end and secure the base with a pretty ribbon - your friend will be delighted.

Outside Tables

When dining out of doors, formal flower arrangements can sometimes be too fussy. Try experimenting with potted plants instead, or a basket of apples and pears. Window boxes can also be a terrific choice – inside or out.

The Meaning of Flowers

Make your arrangement or gift of flowers even more expressive by considering the meaning behind each blossom.

THE MEANING OF THE BLOSSOM

Bamboo	Thought to bring good luck (actually means peace)
Daisy	For faith (gold)
Easter Lily	Symbolizes purity, hope, and life (white)
Jasmine	For bringing love, increasing sexual desire, promoting optimism
Job's Tears	For luck (seeds)
Lavender	Helps with grief and guilt, and/or aches and pains
Lily of the Valley	Helps with cardiac issues
Marigolds	Increases positive energy
Narcissus	Helps with insomnia
Nasturtium	Ease symptoms of nausea
Paper White	For passion
Poinsettia	Flower of the Holy Night, AKA: Christmas Stars
Rose	Ultimate gentle healing herb of love
Snapdragons	Natural reducer of anger
Violets	Ease symptoms of nausea, helps with dizziness

THE MEANING OF THE COLOR

Orange	A gentle energizer
Purple	For banishing the past - positive energy
White	Promotes healing of spirit, a natural pain reliever
Yellow	Stimulates the nervous system – balance emotions

THE MEANING OF THE ARRANGEMENT

Long stemmed is not formal – a gift of the moment.

Flowers in a vase demonstrate that more thought went into the gift.

Other Symbolic Herbs & Flowers

TWO MINIATURE ROSES –
Symbolizes two sweethearts

PARSLEY – To "perk" the appetite

OREGANO – A cure for baldness

BASIL – To procure a cheerful and
merry heart

MINT – To stir desire

VIOLET (flower and leaves) –
The ancient flowers of love and
faithfulness

CHIVE – A valuable antidote (for
what ails you)

CARNATION – Symbolic of the engagement of hearts, minds and hands

PANSEY – The happy "face"

PHLOX (flower and leaves) – Stateliness

Edible Flowers & Herbs

*Nothing brings more joy to
the table scape than fresh
flowers.*

*I love using fresh, in-
season blossoms as a
centerpiece, and using
flowers and herbs to
decorate baked goods and
entrées.*

When using flowers in creative ways be sure to learn which varieties are safe to consume. Not all flowers are edible, and plants should not be consumed if they've been sprayed with pesticide.

Incorporate flowers that are at their peak of bloom and collect them in the early part of the day.

Try to avoid unopened blossoms as they can be bitter.

Some Flowers Safe to Consume		
Anise Hyssop	Hollyhock	Peony
Bachelor's Button	Honeysuckle	Phlox
Begonia	Jasmine	Redbud
Borage	Johnny Jump-up	Rose
Carnation	Lavender	Scented Geranium
Chrysanthemum	Lilac	Snapdragon
Clover	Marigold	Sunflower
Dandelion	Nasturtium	Squash
Day Lily	Okra	Tulip Petals
Hardy Hibiscus	Pansy	Violet

Some Edible Herb Blossoms		
Basil	Lemon Verbena	Oregano
Chive	Marjoram	Rosemary
Fennel	Mint	Sage
Garlic	Onion	Thyme

WHEN THE OCCASION CALLS FOR FLOWERS, TRY USING:

Chive blossoms and stalks to garnish a pâté or egg dish,

Nasturtiums for a peppery accent in soups,

Pansies to decorate cakes,

Rose petals in drinks like champagne and iced tea,

Saffron flavored marigolds with poultry or rice,

Blue borage flowers in fruit cups and salads.

Tussie Mussies

From the earliest times Tussie Mussies have been associated with ritual and were a widespread Victorian tradition. Created with herbs and flowers, each with their own story to tell, these precious individualized bouquets convey your best wishes. As my friend Rosemary would say, giving a Tussie Mussie to someone is like presenting her with a love letter. These tiny treasures make wonderful gifts for young women and brides.

This "recipe" is for a Tussie Mussie I received from Rosemary as a young bride.

ROSE – Symbolizing beauty, youth and love
ROSEMARY – For devotion and loyalty, as well as remembrance

SAGE – To ensure domestic virtues

ARTIMESIA – The Chinese symbol for dignity

BORAGE LEAVES – For courage

MONEY PLANT – Ensures money in your pocket

LAVENDER – For purity and cleanliness

STRAWFLOWER and/or COREOPSIS – To say, "Always Yours"

BRIDE'S BUTTONS – For loyal love

CARAWAY – To call a straying husband back to hearth and home (if ever needed)

MUGWORT – To keep witches away (in the hard-to-imagine possibility that a mother-in-law acts like one!)

YELLOW JASMINE – For genius (added for my Todd)

Arrange all foliage into a small nosegay.
Bind with affection, best wishes, a doily and a ribbon tied in a bow.

Chilling with Style - Flower Cubes

Dress up your buffet table by chilling wine and other beverages — in style! You'll need:

Seasonal flower buds, blossoms & petals

Mint leaves and/or other herbs

Ice cube trays & water

Place rinsed blossoms, buds or petals and herbs at the bottom of each compartment of filled ice-cube trays.

Place trays in the freezer and allow water to freeze.

Then, in lieu of a traditional ice bucket, choose a pretty bowl or tin bucket large enough to chill a couple bottles.

When the cubes are set, fill the bowl, and add a bottle(s) of lemonade, wine or champagne.

Chill elegantly until ready to serve!

If you would like to use these ice cubes in drinks, be sure to use edible flowers.

Greeting & Managing Guests

Greeting, Seating & Managing • Introductions

Greeting Guests Who Visit Your Home

Make every effort to personally greet each guest upon their arrival and make them feel at home. Offer to take coats and stow handbags, and see that everyone is offered something to drink.

Thank your guests for coming right away and make an effort to introduce them to other guests, mentioning things in common to help get a conversation going. This will encourage mingling and the making of new friends after you have moved on.

And just for fun - if greeting in the French manner with a kiss on each cheek, remember to kiss the left cheek first, then the right, then the left again --- if you really like them!

Seating Guests at the Table

Consider guests that may have trouble getting to and from the table and seat on the end or a spot with the easiest access.

Alternate male and female guests and separate couples to give everyone someone new to visit with.

Try to seat guests next to others with whom they have things in common.

Managing Large Guest Lists

For a Sip and See or reception with a large guest list and no specially planned program, consider staggering your guest list.

For example, the invitation for an afternoon party from 2 to 4 pm with 60 guests could be staggered to accommodate such a large number of guests. Here's how it works:

The invitation for the first 15 guests reads:

> Please join us from 2 to 2:30 pm

Invitation for the next 15 reads:

> Please join us from 2:30 to 3 pm

And so on for the remaining hour and 30 guests, staggering each group 30 minutes apart.

Introductions

You will always make guests more comfortable by introducing them to others so they can talk with ease.

Here's how it's done:

>   A younger person is always introduced to an older person.
>
>   A person is introduced to someone in a higher position, or higher rank.
>
>   A young woman is introduced to an older man.
>
>   A young man is introduced to a young woman.

In other words, think quick before making introductions, and use the general rule that the elder or out-ranking person has the younger or lesser-ranked person introduced to them – regardless of sex.

This gesture is simply a very nice way of demonstrating respect to those who have earned it.

Here's an example - If you are introducing a young mayor to a middle-aged woman, you would introduce the woman to the mayor. The exception to this scenario would be if the woman were quite elderly, say 80 years. Then out of respect for her longevity the mayor would be introduced to the lady. You would say:

>   Mayor Wheeler, I'd like for you to meet Mrs. Julie Adams.
>
>   ***-or-***
>
>   Michael, I'd like for you to meet Julie Adams. Julie, this is Michael Wheeler.
>
>   ***-or, to your host-***
>
>   Charlotte, I would like to introduce you to my husband, Ashton Monroe. Ash, this is our hostess, Charlotte.
>
>   Then proceed to mention something the two may have in common.

Your response when introduced to another is:

Hello do you do Bobby.

-or-

Very nice to meet you Meredith.

-or-

Hello, how are you? (Response: Fine, thank you. And how are you?)

If seated, stand when being introduced to another.

Then proceed to shake hands after the introduction.

Shake hands by using a firm grip, but not a bone crusher, and by looking your new acquaintance in the eye. If you happen to be wearing gloves, it's more personable to remove them first.

FORMAL INTRODUCTIONS AT A BANQUET, BUSINESS FUNCTION OR RECEPTION:

Use full names and titles when introducing others.

Stand up when you are being introduced.

As a spouse, try to always make a point of introducing your partner to everyone in the room.

In the Role of Host or Hostess

It is a nice touch for the host/hostess to take newly arrived guests around and introduce them to four to five people before moving on to greet other guests. When you are the guest and your host is unable to do this for you, take the initiative to introduce yourself to as many folks as you are able, being careful to not interrupt earnest conversations.

If approaching a group and someone is talking, just wait until they take pause and then introduce yourself: *Hello, I'm Robin Peters, and I don't know anyone here except the hostess. Will you allow me to join in your conversation? Who would say "no" to such a sweet request?*

If You Forget a Name

While it's embarrassing, it happens to us all. If you suddenly can't recall the name of an acquaintance, bluff your way through.

For example, you bump into an old neighbor and longtime friend at a gathering. You remember your neighbor's name but haven't seen your friend in years and for the life of you can't remember her name. Just say,

Mrs. Wilson I'd like to introduce you to an old college friend. She was the only one I knew at UK who earned top grades while playing on the golf team and leading our sorority.

Then your college friend can chime in by saying,
Hi, I'm Mary Margaret, offering her name and hand to shake.

But if she does not and you are pressed for a name, just admit you've had a lapse in memory, and laugh about it – it's not the end of the world!

When you are paid a compliment:

A sincere *thank you* will suffice. Compliments should be made graciously and often, even to strangers.

I have always held that a person who gives and takes compliments with ease demonstrates self-assurance.

At Ease at the Table

Having and using good table manners will do more to boost your social life, your career & your relationships than anything else you can do!

Protocols at the table have stood the test of time because they were developed to make the dining experience comfortable and pleasant for everyone. Table manners remind us to slow down and enjoy both the meal and our companions in a mutually considerate way. Demonstrating poise and refinement at the table speaks to your respectfulness of others and ability to interact in any circle. Here are the basics:

Serving – Who is First

When the host or hostess is serving part of the meal from their place at the table, the guest of honor is served first, then other guests going counterclockwise around the table from that person. The co-host is served next to last and the hostess is served last. This places the emphasis on your guests and provides an order that everyone understands and can follow.

When to Begin
When the hostess picks up her fork to begin, you begin.

Knives & Forks

The American style is for the fork to be held in the right hand while the knife rests on the top right edge of the plate (when not in use) and the left hand rests in your lap.

At no time during the meal should dirty silverware, knives especially, be placed on the table or place mat.

When finished eating, the knife and fork should be placed at an angle in the center of the plate with the handles at the lower right, the blade of the knife facing into the center with the tongs of the fork down. Unused silver should be left on the table.

Beverages

Empty your mouth of food and wipe with a napkin before taking a sip of water or wine. This will both keep your glass clean and avoid the appearance of "washing down" your food.

Napkins

Place napkins in your lap. Place your napkin when the hostess sits and places hers. Dinner napkins should be left folded in half and placed horizontally across your lap in a simple demonstration of refinement.

When the meal and dessert are over, re-fold your napkin and place it next to the left of your plate. If you need to leave the table during the meal, neatly place your napkin on your chair while you are away to signal that you will return, especially when wait staff are employed.

Too Hot to Handle

If you take a large sip or bite of something hot, don't spit it out! Take a quick drink of water to cool your mouth, and then power through until you are able to swallow and move on.

Token Portions

If the entrée or another dish is not to your liking, simply move it about on your plate subtly and fill up on other choices. Don't risk embarrassing your host/hostess by mentioning this, especially in front of the other guests.

Take single portions of everything passed to ensure all are served, and ask for assistance if you need it with large platters and the like. Fellow diners are always happy to help hold large platters when needed.

Seasoning

Remember that it is insulting to your host to season food without first tasting it.

Bread and Butter

Demonstrate your finesse by buttering only one bite of bread at a time, and not using your bread as a sauce-sopper.

Tipping

It is okay to tip soup or dessert dishes. Just remember to tip the dish away from you, not toward.

When Accidents Happen

Accidents at the table happen to all of us. When they do, simply try to be as inconspicuous as possible and try not to be upset about it.

If you spill a food item, quietly retrieve it with any convenient utensil and place it on the side of your plate.

If you spill food or drip onto your clothing, use a clean knife or spoon to lift it off, or dip a corner of your napkin into your water glass and then lightly rub the spot.

If you drop a piece of chicken or food on the floor while trying to serve yourself, pick it up quickly with your napkin and put it on your plate. You should also eat this piece as well, for otherwise there may not be enough to go around.

If you take something into your mouth by accident, such as a piece of gristle, remove it from your mouth just like you would a watermelon seed. Roll it forward with your tongue into your spoon or fork. Then place it on your plate and hide it under a piece of food. In the unlikely chance that you find a bug or dirt in your salad, ignore its presence and leave your salad unfinished.

If you swallow wrong, choke or sneeze at the table, cover your mouth and nose with your napkin – but never blow into it and spoil the appetite of fellow diners! If you must, excuse yourself quickly with a simple, *Excuse me one second please,* directed to your host. When you return to the table murmur a quick apology and then forget about it.

Likewise, your dinner companions should refrain from staring while you struggle and make an effort to keep the conversation in play.

If anyone directs a question to you and your mouth is full, chew and swallow as much as you can before replying and hold any remaining food in the side of your mouth. It is possible to speak with a bit of food in your mouth and not be offensive - but not without tucking it to one side before speaking!

Likewise, dinner companions should make every effort to fill in the conversation while you prepare to answer.

Other good things to know:

Make an effort to keep the conversation flowing and include everyone.
When passing salt and pepper, pass as a pair.
Ask for dishes to be passed to you rather than making an enormous stretch across the table to help yourself.

Keep elbows off the table while eating, stow your phone, and sit up straight.

These simple gestures will speak volumes to fellow diners and let them know you are pleased to be in their company.

In summary, think of how you like for people to engage with you, give you their attention, and show interest in what you have to say – then return the favor.

WHEN HOSTING OVERNIGHT GUESTS, PREPARE A TRAY WITH A HANDWRITTEN "WELCOME" NOTE ALONG WITH A GLASS AND CARAFE FILLED WITH ICE WATER, A SMALL BOUQUET OF SWEET-SMELLING FLOWERS FROM YOUR OWN GARDEN, A SCENTED CANDLE OF LAVENDER, FIR OR EUCALYPTUS, A BAR OF GOOD QUALITY CHOCOLATE, A KEY TO YOUR HOME TIED WITH A PRETTY RIBBON, READING GLASSES (IF GUESTS ARE OVER 40), A SMALL PAD OF PRETTY PAPER AND A PEN, A SELECTION OF GOOD QUICK-READ BOOKS AND A SMALL BED SIDE CLOCK.

Weekend Entertaining

The Invitation

Plan to issue invitations for overnight visits well in advance – a month or two is not too far out.

Consider the personalities of your guests, and try to invite couples and/ or families that will enjoy each other and have things in common if you intend to mix groups.

Be specific about:

When to arrive and when to leave.

The best route to your home (include a map if no GPS is available) along with navigation tips for air travel, cabs, etc.

What clothes to bring for planned activities or events.

The Welcoming Host/Hostess

Remember the little things to make your guests feel welcome and be comfortable.

It's nice to plan a few activities/excursions for your guests, and announce their times (and/or the hours of operation for tourist sites) on the first night. Be sure to mention what your guests might need such as green fees, bike helmets or museum admission cards.

Make a plan for the morning that includes who will make the coffee and other arrangements for breakfast the night before, so guests will be comfortable if they rise first.

Breakfast can be a great meal for employing a buffet, and much of the set up can be done the night before. I like to have bowls of fruits, sweet breads and cereals all ready to set out as guests wake up, and serve lots of hot coffee and fresh juice. I lay the buffet with plates and napkins before going to bed and have all the food on serving platters or in carafes so they are ready to just set out – by the first one who wakes up!

Have plenty of food, an assortment of drinks, and set out snacks between meals.

It is also a good idea to sketch out a menu for each of the meals you plan to serve at home when entertaining overnight guests. This helps you consider what to shop for and make in advance to freeze, like cupcakes or a quiche.

It is nice to have the things on hand to put together the various meals efficiently. Even if you are just planning to have cereals and fruit for breakfast and make-your-own sandwiches for lunch, everything needed to put these meals together is in the kitchen when you plan ahead, allowing you and your loved ones to maximize your time together.

Leave snacks out for guests to munch on, and bring the outside in by adding fresh flowers to guest rooms and common areas.

In the winter months, it's neat to use evergreen and holly for seasonal color and the wonderful scent of fir. And don't forget to straighten, shine and sweep each room.

In short, consider what is enjoyable for you and what makes you comfortable when away from home, and then provide this for your friends.

The Gracious Guest

Things to remember when visiting friends at a lake side cottage, mountain ski lodge or a primary residence overnight.

DO arrange your own transportation and organize your luggage well in advance to ensure you have everything needed.

DO plan to bring a small gift for the host/hostess like a set of pretty guest towels, box of fragrant soaps, place card holders and a set of place cards, paper dinner napkins, or a gift they can use on holiday.

DO help in the kitchen.

DO NOT bring your pet (or) bring your children unless specifically invited, criticize or discipline the host's children, leave your room a mess and bed unmade, ignore something you break, be late or too informal, or stay too long.

DO cancel your visit if you are ill.

DO write a warm letter of thanks when you get home.

The Guest Room

When overnight guests are expected, take a moment to freshen your guest room with little things that will make them feel appreciated & comfortable.

In addition to your welcoming tray, be sure that all bed linens have been freshly laundered and are sweet smelling, and check the guest room lighting to ensure no bulbs have gone bad.

Set out fresh towels in the guest bath with a selection of small shampoos and soaps, and check to make sure there is plenty of toilet paper and tissue!

These thoughtful touches will make your guests feel pampered and keep you from running up and down and all around for things at the last minute and missing out on the fun. Anticipating the needs of your guests will also help ensure your time together is all the more memorable because everyone is comfortable.

Hostess Gifts & Party Favors

Hostess Gifts • Party Favors for Guests
Gifts for the New Baby & Sweet Sixteen • Traditional Wedding
Anniversary Gifts

While the act of entertaining friends is a gift in and of itself, providing an optional party favor is an added generosity. As a guest, presenting a small gift to the host/ hostess upon arrival demonstrates your appreciation for being invited to the soiree.

Gift giving is one of the nicest and warmest of customs, with the size or expense of the gift being irrelevant to the manner in which it is given. Whatever you choose, present it unself-consciously and with enthusiasm. It's that personal touch that will bring meaning to both the giver and receiver.

For you see, gift giving is actually a selfish act when done well. Giving a charming present with spot-on timing and in a true spirit, will bring far more to the giver than receiver!

Hostess Gifts

The ultimate goal of gift giving should be to give pleasure. When you are invited to someone's home for dinner or an overnight stay, consider what your host/hostess might want, or what he/she does not have. This could be anything from a good bottle of wine, a carefully selected bouquet of fresh flowers, a box of unscented white candles for the table, or an item for the kitchen or bar. Then attach a simple hand-written note and tie with a bow and your appreciation will long be remembered!

THESE KITCHEN TOWELS WERE GIVEN TO ME RECENTLY WHEN MY LONG-TIME FRIEND SUZANNE CAME TO DINNER. SHE KNEW I WAS WORKING ON A NEW BOOK AND HER GIFT CHOICE COULD NOT HAVE BEEN MORE DELIGHTFUL.

Many people send flowers after the dinner party to say thank you, but it's sometimes nicer to send the bouquet beforehand.

If you choose to do this, arrange to send the flowers the night before the party or morning of, so that your hosts can have time to place your gift in an optimal spot and not go to the expense of purchasing too many flowers themselves.

If you bring cut flowers to an informal diner, ask for a vase and arrange them for your host yourself, then ask where they should be placed. This will allow your host to tend to the bar and other logistics. Don't ever fret over the kind of flowers given or the expense. All flowers bring beauty to any interior.

Party Favors for Guests

Sending a small treat home with guests can be a memorable way to end your gathering. This can be as simple as a plant for the garden, a small box of homemade cookies or a wrapped piece of cake.

For a birthday party with a circus theme, a little bag of peanuts or popcorn is an easy and clever choice.

Focus on a favor that will both surprise and delight, and be unexpected. And remember that the old adage, "It's the thought that counts" is really true.

Gifts for the New Baby

It's always fun to shop for a new baby! Tiny articles of clothing and diapers are always welcome. But if you'd like your gift to become a special keepsake, consider an engraved item like a tiny mug or silver frame with the baby's name and birthday. A music box could also become an heirloom over generations, and a monogrammed blanket or bib are both items that will be treasured for years to come because of the personalization.

Gifts for the Sweet Sixteen

Gifts ideas for a special sixteen-year-old can be a simple and sentimental Tussie Mussie, or something more substantial commemorating this turning-point year. *A dressing table set; a special piece of jewelry or a charm; or a box of monogrammed notepaper.*

Traditional Wedding Anniversary Gifts

Eros, Agape, Philia, Storge…

Traditions weather the test of time because ancient wisdom knew the importance of taking pause when selecting a gift. When we slow down to thoughtfully honor an occasion in a traditional way, we put extra thought into the gift and/or occasion and remember its significance. Here are the traditional gifts that celebrate

…Romantic, Spiritual, Friendship and Familial love.

Anniversary Year	Traditional Gift
First	Paper or clock
Second	China
Third	Crystal or glass
Fourth	Electrical appliances
Fifth	Silverware
Sixth	Wood
Seventh	Desk set or computer
Eighth	Linen or lace
Ninth	Leather
Tenth	Diamond jewelry
Eleventh	Fashion accessories
Twelfth	Pearls
Thirteenth	Textiles or furs
Fourteenth	Gold
Fifteenth	Watches
Twentieth	Platinum
Twenty-Fifth	Sterling Silver Jubilee
Thirtieth	Diamonds
Thirty-Fifth	Jade
Fortieth	Rubies
Forty-Fifth	Sapphire
Fiftieth	Golden Jubilee
Sixtieth	Diamond Jubilee

The Occasions
Menus Featuring What's in Season

Spring
Mexican Fiesta
Breakfast in Bed
Easter Whimsy
A Ladies' Spring Luncheon
Kentucky Derby Buffet
A Young Lady's Sweet Sixteen Luncheon

Summer
A French Provincial Picnic
Garden Party
Independence Day Lawn Party
Bride's Maids Luncheon
Wedding Rehearsal Dinner
Anniversary Candle Light Dinner

Autumn
Italian Night
Indian Summer Tailgate Picnic
German Oktoberfest
Baby's Welcoming Brunch
Thanksgiving
Travelers' Night

Winter
Christmas Eve Dinner
New Year's Eve Buffet
De-Light-ful Dinner
Powder Day
Alpine Feast
Formal Birthday Dinner Party

Occasions

Spring

Seasonal Fruits & Vegetables

FRUITS & NUTS

Pineapple
Rhubarb
Strawberries

VEGETABLES & HERBS

Arugula
Asparagus
Carrots
Endive
Fava Beans
Garlic
Greens
Leeks
Lettuce
Mushrooms, Morel
Onions, Vidalia
Oranges, Navel
Peas
Radicchio
Radishes
Redbud Blossoms
Spinach
Tomatoes, Heirloom
Watercress
Zucchini Blossoms

Tex Mex cuisine is a staple for those of us living in the Southwest, and the recipes in this menu are tried and true.

In your home, a Mexican Fiesta should be centered on fun and be relaxed - with good food that is easy to prepare along with plenty of spice!

A SATURDAY IN MARCH
Mexican Fiesta
FOR 8

Black Cherry Mojitos
Fire-Roasted Salsa with Corn Chips

Chili Chicken
Spanish Basmati Rice
Re-fried Black Beans

Decadent Chocolate Layer Cake

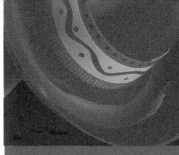

RECIPES

BLACK CHERRY MOJITOS

FIRE-ROASTED SALSA

CHILI CHICKEN

SPANISH BASMATI RICE

RE-FRIED BLACK BEANS

DECADENT CHOCOLATE LAYER CAKE

Serve a Sauvignon Blanc *with a lemon or herbal influence with the chicken, or a peppery* Sirah.

MAKING CHOCOLATE CURLS

TIME LINE
Welcome Amigos!

This dinner for eight can be served two ways. Either Family Style with the dishes on the table and passed, or with dishes set on a buffet (or kitchen island) so guests can fill their plates and then return to the dining table for the meal.

For entertaining secrets see Menus: Feasting with the Five Senses, *p. 2.*

ONE WEEK BEFORE THE PARTY

Make salsa and refrigerate.

TWO DAYS BEFORE

Do grocery shopping; be sure to purchase corn chips. Set the table and arrange centerpiece.

Make place cards.

ONE DAY BEFORE

Bake and frost cake. Seal and keep refrigerated.

Marinate chicken. Chill wine.

TWO HOURS BEFORE SERVING

Prepare and assemble rice, and prepare beans. Cover and hold at room temperature.

ONE HOUR BEFORE SERVING

Prepare ingredients for mojitos and assemble everything needed for the bar.

Remove cake from refrigerator, but leave covered.

ONE HALF-HOUR BEFORE SERVING

Grill chicken and cover to keep warm.

Bake rice and keep warm. Heat beans and keep warm.

WHEN GUESTS ARRIVE

Make and serve mojitos.

Set out chips and salsa with cocktail napkins.

WHEN TIME TO SERVE

Pour wine.

Set warm chicken, rice and beans on table or buffet and enjoy. After dinner, serve the cake.

Black Cherry Mojitos

A classic mojito showcases rum and the revitalizing flavor of mint. This cocktail takes it up a notch by incorporating the woodsy fruit flavor of black cherries.

PRONOUNCED: MOW-HEE -TEAU

YIELD: TWO MOJITOS

3½ jiggers black cherry rum
12 to 15 fresh mint leaves
4½ Tablespoons super fine sugar
6 Tablespoons tart black cherry juice
Juice of ½ fresh lime
1 cup club soda, chilled
Crushed ice
Lime wedges
Mint leaves

Superfine Sugar is a very fine form of sugar (not powdered) used for candied fruits and flowers and in drinks.
If you do not have superfine sugar in your pantry, you can easily make it.
Simply pulse granulated sugar in a blender until it becomes powder-like in texture.
Do not try to substitute granulated sugar if recipes call for superfine.

Fill two highball glasses halfway with crushed ice. Add 12 leaves of mint and stir to crush leaves and bring up their flavor.

In a cocktail shaker, add sugar, cherry juice, lime juice and rum. Shake well to combine and chill, approximately **30 seconds.**

Pour cherry rum mixture over crushed ice in glasses, dividing evenly.

Add soda to top off the glasses, swirl and garnish with remaining mint and/or wedges of lime.

Fire-Roasted Salsa

Roasting coaxes a delicious soft and smoky flavor from the tomatoes and onions in this salsa. It can be made hot, medium or mild, depending on the amount of jalapeño.

YIELD: ONE QUART

3 cups ripe tomatoes
4 large cloves garlic
1 yellow onion
1 Tablespoon olive oil
Kosher salt and freshly ground black pepper
6 tomatillos
¼ cup fresh cilantro
1 8-ounce can green chilies, minced
1 teaspoon kosher salt
2 jalapeño peppers, minced
⅓ cup scallions, chopped (including green parts)

Preheat oven to 425 degrees.

Cut tomatoes and onions into wedges, add garlic cloves and place in a jelly roll pan lined with foil. Drizzle with olive oil and sprinkle with salt and pepper; toss to coat. Roast for 15 to 20 minutes or until browned and tender. Cool slightly.

Meanwhile, remove the husks from tomatillos and roast in a dry skillet over high heat. When tomatillos are nearly roasted and charred on all sides, add a small amount of water to the pan and cover to steam and finish cooking.

In a food processor, place roasted vegetables, tomatillos and cilantro. Process until smooth.

In a large mixing bowl, combine processed vegetables with chilies and salt. Stir gently to combine.

Add jalapenos (to taste) and scallions; mix to combine.

Chili Chicken

This chicken is marinated overnight in chilies, spice and citrus, then grilled and topped with more chilies before serving.

SERVES: EIGHT

CHILI MARINADE

4 chicken breasts
½ cup olive oil
Juice of 2 limes
Juice of ½ lemon
1 anaheim chili pepper, seeded & minced
1 jalapeño chili pepper, seeded & minced
3 cloves garlic, roughly chopped
1 teaspoon ground cumin
1 teaspoon kosher salt
¼ teaspoon freshly ground black pepper

Add all ingredients to a food processor, except chicken, and purée.

Place chicken in a large casserole dish and pour marinade over top.

Seal with plastic wrap and marinate in refrigerator **overnight** to ensure the flavors get all the way into the center of the chicken.

TO GRILL

Marinated chicken
1 8-ounce can green chilies
Large edible leaves
Limes or lemons

Grill chicken over medium-high heat for 4 minutes on each side, flipping only once. After flipping chicken, top each breast with additional green chillies for remaining 4 minutes on the grill.

Carefully remove chicken breasts from the grill, ensuring chilies are not disturbed. Serve chicken with the chili side up on a platter lined with large edible leaves and/or slices of lime and lemon between the pieces of chicken to garnish.

See Oils & Other Fats, *p. 379.*

Spanish Basmati Rice

Chilies and cumin flavor this cheesy rice — that's also really easy to make!

SERVES: EIGHT

2 cups basmati rice
2 Tablespoons canola oil
½ yellow onion, chopped fine
3 to 4 cloves garlic, minced
1 10-ounce can green chilies & tomatoes
1 8-ounce can whole tomatoes
2¼ cups chicken broth, divided
1½ teaspoons cumin
1 teaspoon kosher salt
8 to 10 ounces cheddar cheese, grated

Preheat oven to 325 degrees.

In a large skillet over medium heat, warm oil. Add onions and cook for 3 to 4 minutes, or until soft.

Reduce heat to low and add rice and garlic. Cook for approximately 3 minutes, stirring constantly to avoid burning.

Add green chilies and tomatoes and cook another 2 minutes.

Add 2 cups broth.

Season with cumin and salt and bring to a boil.

Transfer to a buttered baking dish; smooth mixture to create an even top, then pour an additional ¼ cup of the broth over the rice.

Top casserole with cheese and bake for 20 to 30 minutes, or until brown and bubbly. Garnish with fresh cilantro before serving.

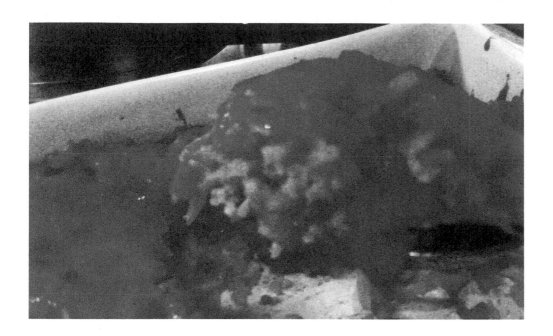

Re-Fried Black Beans

This black bean twist on re-fried pinto beans is an unexpected treat.

SERVES: EIGHT

1 15-ounce can black beans, rinsed
2 teaspoons canola oil
¼ yellow onion, chopped fine
2 to 3 cloves garlic, minced
1 teaspoon cumin
2 teaspoons kosher salt
½ teaspoon freshly ground black pepper

Heat oil in a large skillet over medium heat. Add onions and sauté until tender.

Add garlic and cook until soft, approximately 1 minute. Stir in spices.

Add beans. Using a wooden spoon, crush approximately half of the beans, leaving the remaining beans whole for added texture and visual appeal.

Melt cheddar cheese over the beans before serving by placing skillet into a 350 degree oven for 5 to 7 minutes.

Serve hot.

Decadent Chocolate Layer Cake

This decadent three-layer cake combines dark cocoa for an intense chocolatey cake with a filling of sweet whipped almond cream. Instant espresso powder gives the frosting a character boost. The combination of flavors is unbeatable!

To help ensure your success, see Light & Airy Cakes, p. 361.

SERVES: EIGHTEEN

CAKE

1 cup unsweetened dark cocoa

2 cups boiling water

2¾ cups all-purpose flour

2 teaspoons baking soda

½ teaspoon salt

½ teaspoon baking powder

1 cup unsalted butter, softened

2½ cups granulated sugar

4 large eggs

1½ teaspoons pure vanilla extract

Preheat oven to 350 degrees. Butter and lightly dust with cocoa three 8-inch cake pans.

Combine 1 cup cocoa and boiling water and beat until smooth. Cool completely.

Sift together the flour, salt, soda and baking powder onto a sheet of waxed paper; set aside.

In a large bowl with an electric mixer, cream butter, sugar, eggs and vanilla until light and fluffy, approximately 3 to 4 minutes.

Add flour mixture alternately with cocoa mixture, beginning and ending with flour mixture and mixing just to combine between batches. *Do not over beat or your batter will be tough.*

Divide cake batter evenly between the three prepared pans. Bake for 25 to 30 minutes, or until toothpick inserted into center of cakes comes out clean. Cool in pans for 5 to 7 minutes, then remove by carefully loosening the sides of each cake with a knife and removing cakes to a cooling rack to cool completely.

-more-

Good quality chocolate is essential when baking. I recommend the European made Lindt or Tobler, or the San Francisco made Ghirardelli.

Cakes tend to stick to pans if left in too long after removing from the oven. Unless otherwise instructed, cool cakes for only the first 5 to 7 minutes in the cake pans, and then remove to a wire rack to cool completely.

FILLING

1 cup heavy cream, chilled

¼ cup powdered sugar

1 teaspoon almond extract

Whip cream until soft peaks form. Beat in sugar and almond to combine. Refrigerate until ready to fill cakes.

FROSTING

1 6-ounce package semi-sweet chocolate chips

½ cup Half and Half cream

1 cup unsalted butter

1 Tablespoon instant espresso coffee powder

2½ cups powdered sugar, sifted

Sift powdered sugar to avoid lumps in the frosting, then combine chocolate chips, cream and butter in a saucepan. Stir over medium heat until melted and smooth. Remove from heat and whisk in espresso powder and powdered sugar.

Then place pan over a bowl of ice and beat with an electric mixer until the frosting thickens and holds its shape, at least 5 minutes.

ASSEMBLY

Place one cake layer topside down on a cake plate.

The bottom of the cake will absorb the cream better, and by placing the stickier top of the cake down first you prevent this very tall cake from slipping off the plate.

Spread half of the cream filling over the bottom cake layer. Repeat with the second layer and remaining filling.

Place the third layer on top with the topside up.

Frost entire cake as instructed on page 365.

Keep cake refrigerated until party time, then allow to come to room temperature before slicing. Store leftover cake in the refrigerator.

Chocolate cake tops are especially pretty when sprinkled with purple sugar crystals, white or dark chocolate curls and silver French dragées!

Draw a vegetable peeler across the sides of a chocolate bar, applying steady pressure. If your chocolate is brittle and breaks before it curls, warm it in your apron pocket or between your hands for a few minutes. If chocolate seems too soft to curl, then pop the chocolate bar in the refrigerator and try again in a few minutes.

Melt two ounces of chocolate over a double boiler (2 ounces will make 8 to 10 curls). When just melted, spread a thin layer onto the bottom of a glass baking dish using a spatula. When the chocolate is just firm but not hard, place the blade of a metal spatula at a 45 degree angle onto chocolate and apply gentle, steady pressure as you push the spatula forward in half-circles.

Control the tightness or looseness of curls with the angle of your spatula. A 30 degree angle will create a looser cone-shaped fan of curls.

Use excess shards of chocolate as accents to the curls, or placed like a rope around the bottom of the cake as shown below.
Transfer the curls to cakes with a spatula, not warm hands (which will quickly melt and distort curls) and refrigerate until ready to use.

Chocolate curls are pretty mounded atop cakes.

BREAKFAST IN BED IS FOR TRAVELERS
WHO'VE GOTTEN IN LATE AND
THOSE IN NEED OF PAMPERING.

SERVE ON A TRAY THAT BECOMES A TABLE, AND BE
SURE TO INCLUDE
HOT TEA AND COFFEE TO SPARE.

A LAZY MORNING IN MARCH

Breakfast in Bed

FOR 2

Hot Tea & Coffee

Pumpkin Pancakes with Ricotta "Butter"
Sage Butter Maple Syrup
Fresh Fruit in Season

or

Almond Redbud Cake with Honey Glaze
Fresh Fruit in Season

RECIPES
Pumpkin Pancakes with
Ricotta "Butter"
Sage Butter Maple Syrup

Almond Redbud Cake
with Honey Glaze

Choose either the pancakes or redbud cake as the main dish, and serve fresh fruit with both.

TIME LINE
S'il Vous Plait

Breakfast in bed is designed to be prepared entirely in the kitchen then served in the guest room on a tray that holds everything needed for the meal. *For entertaining secrets see Hosting Overnight Guests, p. 59.*

THE NIGHT BEFORE

Prepare tray(s) with linens, cups and saucers, plates and napkins.

Make pancake batter; refrigerate.

Or, make Redbud cake; refrigerate.

ONE HALF-HOUR BEFORE BREAKFAST

Bring redbud cake to room temperature -or-

Bring ricotta to room temperature; then stir vigorously.

Prepare fruits in individual bowls, cover and keep refrigerated.

FIFTEEN MINUTES BEFORE SERVING

Cook pancakes on a hot griddle. While cakes are cooking, make the maple syrup.

Place cream and sugar on the tray with fruit bowls and a small tub of ricotta, along with a butter knife.

FIVE MINUTES BEFORE BREAKFAST

Make a fresh pot of tea and/or coffee.

Plate pancakes (or redbud cake) while coffee is brewing.

Put hot syrup into a small pitcher (for pancakes).

WHEN TIME TO SERVE

Carry filled tray with a carafe of hot coffee or pot of tea to the guest room.

Pumpkin Pancakes with Ricotta "Butter"

These buttermilk pancakes have an intense pumpkin flavor that is enhanced when rich and velvety ricotta cheese is sandwiched between the cakes in each stack. Sage Butter Maple Syrup provides a woodsy balance to these decadent breakfast delights.

YIELD: EIGHT PANCAKES

2 cups all-purpose flour
1 teaspoon baking soda
1 teaspoon baking powder
1 teaspoon pumpkin pie spice
1 teaspoon kosher salt
1¼ cups buttermilk
4 Tablespoons unsalted butter, melted and cooled slightly
½ cup pure pumpkin purée
3 Tablespoons pure maple syrup
2 large eggs, separated
1 teaspoon pure vanilla extract
Ricotta cheese

Test the griddle before pouring on the batter with a few drops of water. If the water sizzles and pops, your griddle is hot enough to begin cooking

Preheat griddle; coat with butter just before adding the batter to avoid scorching the butter.

Separate eggs and whip egg whites until they resemble sea foam.

Sift dry ingredients together into a large bowl. Add 1 cup of buttermilk, melted butter, pumpkin purée, syrup, eggs **yolks** and vanilla; whisk to incorporate.

Gently fold in the beaten egg **whites** to ensure pancakes are feather light. Add additional buttermilk to batter as desired for thinner consistency.

Spoon onto griddle and cook until the cakes start to bubble on top – *that's when you know your cakes are ready to flip.*

Flip and cook second side until lightly browned.

Bring ricotta to room temperature and stir to encourage a creamy texture, then spread between pancakes before adding syrup.

Canned pumpkin is preferred for this recipe.

Serve with fresh ricotta cheese (instead of butter) between each cake.
A fresh and velvety ricotta adds a scrumptious richness to these cakes.

Sage Butter Maple Syrup

This rich buttery syrup is laced with dense caramel flavors and has a hint of the forest from its infusion with the sage. It is the perfect accompaniment to pumpkin pancakes.

YIELD: ONE AND ONE-HALF CUPS

4 Tablespoons unsalted butter
20 fresh sage leaves, rinsed
1½ cups pure maple syrup

In a small saucepan, melt butter over medium low heat.

Add fresh sage and simmer until the leaves are just crisp and browning around the edges, approximately 10 minutes. When the butter is infused with sage flavor and has browned slightly, remove from heat.

Remove the sage leaves and discard. Add the maple syrup and heat to warm. Serve warm.

I like to use Waterfall Farm Pure Maple Syrup *made by my new daughter-in-law's family in Warrensville, North Carolina.*

Shown here are Lurline and Michael in Sugar Season.

Almond Redbud Cake
with Honey Glaze

This gluten free cake has the tart nutty flavor of redbud blossoms and is gently sweetened with a honey glaze.

SERVES: EIGHT

ALMOND REDBUD CAKE

2 cups almond flour, sifted
1 teaspoon baking powder
½ teaspoon baking soda
1 teaspoon salt
4 eggs, lightly beaten
⅔ cup honey
¼ cup vegetable oil
1 teaspoon pure vanilla extract
Zest of 1 lemon
¾ cup redbud blossoms, rinsed

Redbud blossoms have a slightly nutty flavor and their pink magenta color will add striking beauty to any dish. Watch for redbud blossoms in early spring.
See p. 383 for more.

Preheat oven to 325 degrees. Coat bottom of a 9-inch spring form cake pan with butter and dust with almond flour. Sift 2 cups of flour with the powder, soda and salt onto a sheet of waxed paper; set aside.

In a large bowl with an electric mixer, beat eggs with honey and oil. Add lemon zest and vanilla; mix to incorporate. Gradually add flour mixture to egg mixture, mixing by hand, just enough to incorporate. Fold in Redbud blossoms.

Pour batter into prepared pan and spread top to create an even surface.

Bake 30 to 40 minutes, or until golden brown and toothpick inserted into the center of the cake comes out clean.

LEMON HONEY GLAZE

3 Tablespoons honey
Juice of 2 fresh lemons
2 teaspoons pure vanilla extract

In a small saucepan over low heat, warm honey. Add lemon juice and butter, stir to combine. Remove from heat and set aside.

Prick hot cake with a toothpick across the entire top surface, inserting the pick into the full thickness of the cake. Pour glaze over top surface of cake slowly, allowing glaze to soak in as you go; let stand for 15 to 20 minutes.

Remove the cake from the pan and allow to cool completely before slicing. Garnish top of cooled and glazed cake with additional Redbud blossoms and enjoy.

Thanks to Emily for contributing this recipe.

EASTER IS MY FAVORITE HOLIDAY.

IT IS A HAPPY CELEBRATION SET IN THE GLORIOUS SPRINGTIME WHEN FLOWERS AND TREES ARE BURSTING TO LIFE.

I LIKE TO MAKE A BIG FUSS ABOUT THE EASTER BUNNY AND DECORATE THE TABLE WITH WHIMSICAL TRINKETS AND CERAMIC EGGS FROM EASTERS PAST.

IT'S FUN TO EMPLOY BASKETS AND RIBBONS AND HOMEMADE GOODIES AT INDIVIDUAL PLACE SETTINGS, AND BE A KID FULL OF ANTICIPATION ALL OVER AGAIN!

EASTER SUNDAY
Easter Whimsy
FOR 6

Honeyed Fresh Carrot Soup

Poulet avec les Champignons
Mâche, Endive, Pear & Raspberry Salad

Classic White Bunny Cake
Buttercream or **Coco's Cocoa Frosting**
French Strawberry Glacé Pie

RECIPES

HONEYED FRESH
CARROT SOUP

POULET AVEC LES
CHAMPIGNONS

MÂCHE, ENDIVE, PEAR
& RASPBERRY SALAD

CLASSIC WHITE BUNNY
CAKE

BUTTERCREAM
FROSTING

COCO'S COCOA
FROSTING

FRENCH STRAWBERRY
GLACÉ PIE

Serve a Chardonnay,
or a Pinot Grigio
with a citrus and/or
buttery influence, with the
poultry.

HOW TO MAKE A
BUNNY!

USING CHAMPAGNE
TO KEEP CAKES MOIST

"DOCTORING"

TIME LINE
...Hoppin' on his way!

This dinner for six should be served in three courses. Serve the soup first, then serve the chicken and salad. Then the desserts.

For entertaining secrets see The Thank You Note, *p. 7.*

TWO DAYS BEFORE

Set a whimsical Easter table.

Make carrot soup and refrigerate.

THE DAY BEFORE

Make pie dough; refrigerate.

Bake cake, cool and seal with plastic wrap; refrigerate.

Make buttercream and cocoa frosting; refrigerate.

Chill wine.

Prepare all vegetables for chicken and salad, wrap in a damp paper towel and refrigerate in a sealed container.

Prepare vinaigrette; refrigerate.

EASTER MORNING

Assemble salads on individual plates; wrap in plastic and refrigerate.

Assemble and bake pie.

Decorate bunny cake, cover and refrigerate.

THIRTY MINUTES BEFORE SERVING

Prepare chicken from start to finish.

TEN MINUTES BEFORE SERVING

Dress salads; place on individual serving plates. Set aside.

Ladle soup into individual bowls and garnish.

Fill water and wine glasses.

FOR THE FIRST COURSE

Place soup bowls directly onto preset dinner plates and invite everyone to partake in the first course.

When first course is complete, remove soups bowls and set salad plates to the right of each place setting.

FOR THE ENTREE

While in the kitchen, plate the chicken and serve hot with the salad.

Set out Bunny cake and pie to come to room temperature during the second course.

FOR THE THIRD COURSE

Serve the Bunny cake and pie, asking guests prior to serving which they would prefer.

AFTER EASTER

Write a warm note of thanks to host/hostess, or others who helped with the occasion.

Honeyed Fresh Carrot Soup

This sweet purée of fresh spring carrots, cream and honey is brightened by pure carrot juice, which adds back the carroty flavor that can be lost when carrots are cooked. This garden-fresh soup is good served hot or cold.

SERVES: SIX

2 cups fresh carrots, peeled and sliced

2 Tablespoons unsalted butter

1 large shallot, minced

1 quart pure carrot juice

½ cup heavy cream

2 to 3 teaspoons sourwood honey

2 teaspoons kosher salt

Olive oil

Freshly ground nutmeg

In a large stock pot, melt butter.

Add shallots and carrots and cook/stir approximately 15 minutes, or until tender.

Add 1 cup of the carrot juice, stir, and continue to cook another 20 minutes.

Add the cream, stir, and reduce heat; cook 5 minutes.

Add remaining carrot juice, honey and salt. Remove from heat.

Using an immersion blender, purée the mixture until smooth.

Ladle into bowls and top each bowl of soup with fresh parsley, or a few drops of olive oil and a dusting of nutmeg.

Poulet avec les Champignons

This succulent chicken with wild mushrooms is flavored with herbs and a savory wine sauce.

PRONOUNCED: POO-LAY AH-VEC LEZ CHA –PING-YONG

SERVES: SIX

4 large, skinless chicken breasts
1 teaspoon kosher salt
½ teaspoon freshly ground black pepper
1 Tablespoon fresh marjoram, minced
2 Tablespoons fresh thyme leaves, minced
2 Tablespoons butter
2 small shallots, minced
2 cups wild cremini mushrooms, quartered
2 large cloves garlic, minced
1 Tablespoon all-purpose flour
1 cup chicken broth
½ cup sauvignon blanc wine

See Herbs, *p. 375.*

See p. 221, Balsamic Vinegar Glaze.

Preheat oven to 400 degrees. Season chicken breasts on both sides with salt and pepper; rub with marjoram and thyme.

In a large, oven proof skillet, heat butter. Add chicken and sear over medium heat on both sides until browned; 3 to 4 minutes per side.

Place skillet in hot oven, cover and bake chicken for 15 minutes, or until cooked through. Remove skillet from the oven and then remove chicken from the skillet. Cover cooked chicken to keep warm; set aside.

In the hot skillet, add shallots and garlic and cook for approximately 3 minutes. Add mushrooms and cook another 1 to 2 minutes.

Add flour to skillet and stir to incorporate the flavor packed brown bits from the bottom of the pan. Add broth and then wine to deglaze the pan; cook and stir until bubbly and slightly thick. Spoon mushroom sauce over chicken to serve; garnish with additional fresh marjoram and thyme.

Mâche, Endive, Pear & Raspberry Salad

The harmonious tangy flavors of mâche and endive make for a refreshing salad when paired with fresh fruits and the "Holy Grail" of cheeses - Swiss Mountain Gruyère.

PRONOUNCED: MA-CHEY

SERVES: SIX TO EIGHT

1 bunch mâche leaves
1 bunch endive leaves
2 pears, sliced lengthwise
4 ounces gruyère cheese
1 cup walnuts, toasted
1 cup fresh raspberries
Lemony vinaigrette

Wash mâche and endive leaves well; spin dry and set aside. Core and slice pears with skin on.

If fresh pears are not available, use canned.

Toast walnuts. Rinse raspberries and allow to dry. Cut cheese into 1-inch wedges. Prepare Vinaigrette.

Assemble salad by placing whole endive leaves onto 6 to 8 individual salad plates. Cluster 3 to 4 slices of pear to one side, with 1 to 2 wedges of cheese below the pears. Then sprinkle salads with walnuts and raspberries, dividing evenly between salad plates. Place a cluster of mâche on top of all salads in the center of each plate. Drizzle with lemony vinaigrette. Serve chilled.

Mâche leaves are mild and slightly nutty with a subtle tang. See p. 377.

See p. 103, Light & Lemony Vinaigrette.

Bunny Cake

This cute little six-inch cake makes a fluffy bunny and is so fun to make with children. It can also be altered in a number of flavorful ways with different frostings and candies.

If you are baking a cake that needs to be held for more than one day, use champagne rather than water or milk and it will keep your cake moist much longer.

SERVES: TWELVE

CLASSIC WHITE CAKE

12 Tablespoons unsalted butter, softened
1½ cups granulated sugar
2 cups all-purpose flour
2 teaspoons baking powder
½ teaspoon salt
2 teaspoons pure vanilla extract
¾ cup whole milk
6 egg whites

Preheat oven to 350 degrees. Prepare three **6-inch** cake pans by buttering and lining each pan with parchment paper cut to fit the bottom of the pan.

Sift flour with baking powder and salt onto a sheet of waxed paper; set aside. Combine vanilla with milk; separate eggs.

In a large bowl with an electric mixer, combine butter with sugar and beat until light yellow in color and fluffy, approximately 3 minutes.

With the mixer running, add egg whites slowly and mix to combine. Then add flour mixture alternately with the milk and vanilla mixture, beginning and ending with flour. Fold batter by hand just to combine.

Pour batter into cake pans; bake 10 to 15 minutes, or until a toothpick inserted into the center of each pan comes out clean.

"DOCTORING"

Replace 1 teaspoon pure vanilla extract with coconut extract for *Bunny Cake*.

Replace 1 teaspoon pure vanilla extract with 1 teaspoon lemon zest to add a citrus tang.

Replace 1 teaspoon pure vanilla extract with flavored liqueur of choice.

Replace milk with ¾ cup champagne for a cake that needs to be held longer than one day.

DECORATING BUNNY – THE FROSTING

1 recipe Buttercream Frosting
Pink food coloring (for ears)
Green food coloring (for bow tie)

Reserve ½ cup frosting; color ⅔ green and ⅓ pink.

Place one cake round in the center of an oblong platter (or cookie sheet lined with foil); ice the top. Place a second cake round on top.

Now, frost the three pieces by holding in your palm and then placing on the plate once frosted. Then frost between the three added pieces and the center round to adhere all of the pieces together.

Frost the entire bunny with the white frosting. Frost the bow tie with green frosting.

Add a section of pink frosting to the center of both ears. Add remaining pink frosting as "polka dots" on the green bow tie.

DECORATING BUNNY - OTHER INGREDIENTS

14-ounces angle flake coconut
2 chocolate candies (for eyes)
1 pink candy (for the nose)
2 white macadamia nuts (for the teeth)
6 strands dried pasta or thin licorice (for whiskers)

Gently press the coconut into the white frosting - this is the bunny's fur.

Now decorate the bunny's face with candies and pasta.

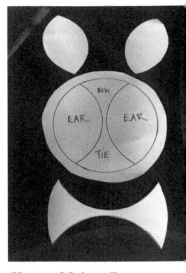

How to Make a Bunny
Using a serrated knife, cut the third cake round into three pieces per diagram above. Start by carving two half circles from each side of the round. Then place these above the stacked rounds - these will be Bunny's ears. Place the remaining middle piece below the stacked rounds - this will be Bunny's bow tie.

Buttercream Frosting

The basic recipe for this easy frosting can be flavored many ways using flavored liqueurs and fresh berries.

YIELD: FROSTING FOR ONE LAYER CAKE OR EIGHTEEN CUPCAKES

1 cup unsalted butter
3 cups powdered sugar
2 teaspoons pure vanilla extract
⅛ teaspoon salt

In a large bowl with an electric mixer, beat butter until creamy.

Add powdered sugar, extract and salt and continue to cream until well incorporated and fluffy.

GRAND MARNIER BUTTERCREAM

Substitute one teaspoon of vanilla with Grand Marnier liqueur. The orange flavor is great when serving chocolate especially, and can be made even more pronounced by shaving orange curls on top of frosted cakes!

BLACKBERRY BUTTERCREAM

Substitute one teaspoon of vanilla with blackberry liqueur. Then add one cup fresh blackberries, crushed, with an additional ¼ cup of powdered sugar to the frosting.

Coco's Cocoa Frosting

When using cocoa frosting, dye coconut pink with red food coloring mixed with just a bit of water. Stir in coconut until desired color of pink is reached, then remove from water and allow coconut to dry on paper toweling.

If you prefer a little chocolate bunny, use Coco's Frosting. Decorate chocolate bow tie with jelly beans to make it stand out, and put pink coconut (instead of frosting) inside bunny's ears.

YIELD: FROSTING FOR ONE LAYER CAKE OR EIGHTEEN CUPCAKES

3 Tablespoons unsalted butter, softened

¼ cup Ghirardelli sweet ground chocolate & cocoa

2⅓ cups powdered sugar, sifted

2 Tablespoons whole milk

1½ teaspoons Godiva liqueur

In a large bowl with an electric mixer at medium speed, cream butter with cocoa until thoroughly combined and crumbly, approximately 3 minutes

Add the sifted powdered sugar and beat (another 2 to 3 minutes).

Add the milk and liqueur and whip until light and fluffy (another 3 to 4 minutes).

French Strawberry Glacé Pie

This fresh strawberry pie has a layer of cream cheese lining the bottom crust, and a light glazed (glacé) filling that complements the bright flavor of a favorite spring time fruit. To help ensure your success see Baking Secrets, Rolling & Baking Pies, p. 358.

PRONOUNCED: GLAE-SAY

SERVES: EIGHT

PASTRY

1 recipe Butter Pastry
(See p. 146.)

1 3-ounce package cream cheese, softened

FILLING

1 quart fresh strawberries (4 cups)

⅔ cup water

1 cup granulated sugar

3 Tablespoons cornstarch

Do not use a perforated pie plate for this pie. When spreading the cream cheese onto the baked crust, it sometimes cracks. If you have a perforated pie plate, the filling will run out!

Bake pastry shell at 375 degrees for 12 to 15 minutes, or until golden brown; cool. Spread softened cream cheese over the bottom of shell.

Wash and hull strawberries, reserving ½ cup of choice berries.

In a medium saucepan, simmer 1 cup of strawberries with ⅔ cup water for approximately 3 minutes. Blend sugar with cornstarch and add to the boiling mixture; cook for 1 minute, stirring constantly. Cool mixture.

Place remaining 2 ½ cups strawberries in pie shell and cover with cooked sugar mixture. Garnish top of pie with reserved berries.

Refrigerate until firm, approximately 2 hours.

Serve with sweetened whipped cream.

It is always fun for me to have my girlfriends in for a special luncheon. Even though we all have busy schedules, when the arrival of spring is just around the corner, it annually provides an excuse to get together.

When preparing a luncheon for ladies, I like to make everything as pretty as possible and use fresh flowers on the table and with the food. The menu is light yet filling, and always includes a petite sweet to end the meal.

AN APRIL AFTERNOON
A Ladies Spring Luncheon
FOR 4

Parmesan Cheese Cups with Chèvre, Tequila Currants & Espresso

Crème Vichyssoise Glacée

Salade Niçoise with Toasted Anchovies
Vinaigrette Dressing
French Baguette & Butter

Almond Petit Fours with Candied Violets

RECIPES
PARMESAN CHEESE CUPS WITH CHÈVRE, TEQUILA CURRANTS & ESPRESSO

CRÈME VICHYSSOISE GLACÉE

SALADE NIÇOISE WITH TOASTED ANCHOVIES

VINAIGRETTE DRESSING

ALMOND PETIT FOURS WITH CANDIED VIOLETS

Serve a Fume *or* Sauvignon Blanc *to balance the acidity of the vinaigrette.*

BLANCHING VEGETABLES

MAKING WINE SPRITZERS

COOKING & BAKING WITH CITRUS

CANDIED VIOLETS & OTHER EDIBLE FLOWERS

TIME LINE
Lovely Girls…

This lady's luncheon for four is designed to be served in four courses with appetizers passed beforehand and the luncheon dishes plated before serving. Dishes should be cleared between courses.

For entertaining secrets, see Edible Herbs, *p. 49-50, and* Basic Flower Arranging, *p. 44-47.*

TWO DAYS BEFORE
Set a pretty spring table with china and linens.
Prepare parmesan cups (just the cups); cool and refrigerate in a seal container.
Plump currants; remove from liquid and refrigerate.
Prepare Vichyssoise; refrigerate.
Candy the violets; place in a sealed container.

THE DAY BEFORE
Bake cakes, cool, glaze and seal with plastic wrap; refrigerate. Chill wine and soda water.
Prepare vinaigrette; refrigerate.
Be sure to *purchase* a baguette and butter.

LUNCHEON MORNING
Pick as assortment of spring blossoms and tie to napkins. Arrange centerpiece.
Prepare all ingredients for the salad and refrigerate separately.
Set out wine glasses, appetizer plates and cocktail napkins in the area where the first course is to be served.
Add violets to each petit fours and place cakes on a serving platter.

THIRTY MINUTES BEFORE THE LADIES ARRIVE
Toast anchovies. Assemble everything needed for wine spritzers.
Assemble salads on individual serving plates; cover and refrigerate.
Mix currants and cheese; assemble parmesan cups and place on pretty serving platter.

UPON ARRIVAL
Serve parmesan cups as a passed appetizer.
Make and serve spritzers.

JUST BEFORE THE FIRST COURSE
Fill water and wine glasses at the table.
Serve soup in individual bowls and garnish.
Clear soup bowls when first course is finished.

JUST BEFORE THE SECOND COURSE
Toast baguette, slice and put on the table with butter.
Dress salads and top with anchovies; place on the table.
Clear salad plates and bread/butter when second course is finished.

FOR THE DESSERT COURSE
Serve petit fours.
Make and serve coffee upon request.

Parmesan Cheese Cups with Chèvre, Tequila Currants & Espresso

These little cups are made from pure parmesan cheese and filled with tequila infused currants then dusted with espresso powder.

YIELD: SIXTEEN CUPS

PARMESAN CUPS

1 cup parmesan cheese, grated

Preheat oven to 325 degrees. Line a baking sheet with parchment paper.

Mound parmesan cheese into rounds approximately 2-inches in diameter and ¼ to ½-inch deep. Space mounds at least 1 inch apart.

Bake for 8 minutes, or until golden brown, flattened and bubbly.

Immediately remove from the baking sheet with a metal spatula and place/form into miniature muffin tins to create 16 individual "cups" in a hollowed tulip shape, working quickly while cheese is warm and pliable.

Once cooled, remove from tins and fill.

CHÈVRE & CURRANT FILLING

4 ounces chèvre

⅛ cup currants, plumped

½ cup tequila

Instant espresso coffee powder

Plump currants by soaking in tequila until soft and swollen, approximately 20 to 30 minutes. Discard tequila.

Combine cheese with plumped currants, and then fill parmesan cheese cups. Dust each cup with a pinch of espresso powder.

Refrigerate until ready to serve.

Try serving cheese cups with slices of apple that have been soaked for a few minutes in water spiked with lemon juice. The lemon will keep the apple from turning brown, and the fresh fruit is great with these treats.

Crème Vichyssoise Glacée

Vichyssoise is the finest of all cold soups. Made with potatoes, leeks, onions and cream, this classic will not disappoint.

PRONOUNCED: VEE-CHEE-SWAZ GLAE-SEI

SERVES: SIX

When serving a dish cold, wait to taste for seasoning until the dish is cold.

2 large potatoes, peeled and diced
4 Tablespoons unsalted butter
2 leeks, cleaned and cut
into 1-inch pieces
½ yellow onion, chopped
3 cups chicken broth
2 teaspoons kosher salt
1 teaspoon freshly ground black
pepper
¼ teaspoon freshly ground nutmeg
1 cup Half and Half cream
½ cup sour cream
Fresh chives & chive blossoms

See Leeks, *p. 376*
and
Onions, *p. 381.*

In a large saucepan, cover potatoes with salted water and cook until fork-tender.

In a stock pot, melt butter and cook leeks and onion for 3 to 5 minutes, stirring frequently.

Add broth and bring to a boil. Then reduce heat and simmer until leeks and onions are tender.

Drain potatoes and add to the leek mixture; season with salt and pepper.

Using an immersion blender, blend all ingredients until smooth, about 1 minute. Chill for **3 to 4 hours.**

When cool, whisk in nutmeg, cream and sour cream; taste for seasoning; adjust. Serve cold, garnished with fresh chopped chives and chive blossoms.

Salade Niçoise & Toasted Anchovies

Salade Niçoise comes from the French, and is a cold salad that includes an assortment of fresh vegetables, briny capers and boiled potatoes. Traditionally served with tuna, salty toasted anchovies are used in this recipe.

PRONOUNCED: SALAD NEE-SWA-Z

SERVES: SIX

8 ounces fresh green beans, blanched

4 hard-boiled eggs, sliced

6 to 8 artichoke hearts, quartered

½ pint cherry tomatoes, halved

¼ red onion, sliced paper thin

6 to 8 ounces black and/or green olives, pitted

4 to 6 new potatoes, boiled with skins on and quartered

3 to 4 ounces capers, drained

4 to 6 anchovy fillets

1 bunch field greens

Kosher salt and freshly ground black pepper

Vinaigrette Dressing

Prepare Vinaigrette as per following recipe; set aside.

Blanch beans per instructions that follow.

Hard boil eggs.

Boil potatoes until fork tender in salted water. Cool and cut into quarters.

Prepare all remaining ingredients as directed.

In a small skillet, toast anchovies in just a teaspoon of olive oil and butter (after draining from can liquids) until toasty. Set aside on a paper towel to drain.

Wash and spin dry field greens and arrange on a platter, or individual serving plates, as desired.

Artfully mound all ingredients (except anchovies) in the center of the platter/plate and lightly salt and pepper beans, potatoes and eggs; drizzle with vinaigrette. Top with toasted anchovies.

Served chilled.

See p. 372, Perfect Hard Boiled Eggs.

Blanching green beans or other vegetables will bring out their natural sweetness and transform them into a brilliant, deep (green) color. Blanching also keeps vegetables from getting soft and losing their nutritional value.

Bring a large pot of salted water to a boil, using approximately one gallon of water per one pound of vegetables.

Once the water reaches a rolling boil, carefully add vegetables and allow water to return to a boil. Then let the vegetables cook for just 3 minutes.

With tongs, remove vegetables quickly from the water to a colander and run under very cold water to stop the cooking.

Refrigerate, wrapped in a damp paper towel, until ready to use.

Wine Spritzers

Made by mixing half wine with half soda water, and can be made with any kind of wine.

If using a white or rosé wine, be sure to chill both the wine and the soda water.

Serve spritzers over ice and garnish with lime and/or fresh mint or other fruits and herbs as appropriate to the wine being used.

Vinaigrette Dressing

A well-made vinaigrette can transform assorted greens into salads of distinction. Vinaigrettes can be adapted to your own tastes and made in an array of ways. Just stick to the basic formula of two parts fat to one part acid, then spice and flavor as per your preference. Be sure to always use the highest quality olive oil and good-quality vinegar.

YIELD: ONE-HALF CUP VINAIGRETTE, APPROXIMATELY

	CLASSIC FRENCH	MY GO-TO HOUSE	LIGHT 'N' LEMONY	
	½ cup olive oil	¼ cup olive oil	⅓ cup olive oil	*Olive oil is the classic choice. Infused oils add even more flavor. Oils from nuts add an earthy flavor. Vegetable oil yields a milder taste.*
	1½ teaspoons Dijon-style mustard	1 teaspoon Dijon-style mustard	1 teaspoon honey	*Dijon mustard adds flavor and creamy body.*
	2 Tablespoons red wine vinegar	⅛ cup white vinegar	Juice of 1 lemon *Citrus juices like lemon make excellent substitutions for vinegar.*	*Experiment with sweet & complex balsamic, rich & woodsy sherry wine, sprightly champagne, or sharp and clean-tasting rice vinegars.*
	1 shallot, minced	1 clove garlic, minced	2 to 3 Tablespoons fresh chives, minced	*Stir in chopped or dried herbs, minced garlic, shallot or onion.*
	¾ teaspoon kosher salt	¾ teaspoon kosher salt	¾ teaspoon kosher salt	*Dissolve salt or sugar in vinegar before mixing in the oil.*
	¼ teaspoon fresh ground black pepper	¼ teaspoon fresh ground black pepper	¼ teaspoon fresh ground black pepper	
	1 Tablespoon fresh herbs, minced	½ to 1 teaspoon zest of lemon	Zest of 1 lemon	*Minced or crushed dried chilies, roasted peppers and ground spices are other good choices.*

Always start with room temperature lemons, limes and oranges when cooking or baking.

Before squeezing the juice, use the palm of your hand to press down firmly on each (lemon) as you roll it back and forth on the counter two or three times. This will break open the juice sacs.

Whisk all ingredients in small bowl until well incorporated.

Drizzle over salad, or use as a marinade for grilled chicken or shrimp.

Almond Petit Fours
with Candied Violets

Petit Fours are individual servings of cake that are frosted on the top and all four sides. They are extra sweet and perfect for special celebrations. These tiny moist almond petit fours are filled with fruit preserves then lightly glazed and infused with sugar. Topped with a candied flower, they are the perfect ending to a springtime luncheon with fashionable friends.

PRONOUNCED: PET-TI FOURS

YIELD: THIRTY INDIVIDUAL CAKES

6 Tablespoons unsalted butter, softened

1¼ cups cake flour

¾ teaspoon baking powder

¼ teaspoon baking soda

¼ teaspoon salt

1 cup granulated sugar

½ cup almond paste

4 large eggs, separated

1½ teaspoons pure vanilla extract

½ cup whole milk

½ to 1 cup seedless blackberry *preserves, at room temperature

Sugar glaze

30 candied violets

What's the difference? All fruit spreads are made with fruits, sugar and pectin. ***Preserves*** *are made with chunks of fruit stored in its own juice or syrup.* ***Jelly*** *is made from fruit pulp and crushed fruit.* ***Jam*** *is a transparent gel in which the fruit comes from fruit juice.*

Preheat oven to 350 degrees.

Butter a 12 x 18-inch jelly roll pan; line with parchment paper. Butter parchment paper; dust with flour and set aside.

Sift flour with powder, soda and salt onto a sheet of waxed paper; set aside.

In a large bowl with an electric mixer, combine ¾ cup of sugar with almond paste. Mix on low until this resembles a coarse meal, about 2 minutes.

Raise speed to medium high and add butter. Mix until pale yellow and fluffy, about 2 minutes. Mix in egg yolks and vanilla. Add flour in 2 batches, alternating with the milk. Transfere to a large bowl; set aside.

In a clean bowl with an electric mixer (and clean beaters), whisk egg whites on high until foamy. Gradually add remaining ¼ cup of sugar and continue beating until soft peaks form.

Fold ⅓ of the egg **whites** into batter by hand, then gently fold in the remaining whites, being careful to not deflate.

Spread batter evenly into prepared pan. Bake 15 to 20 minutes, or until toothpick inserted into the center of the cake comes out clean. Transfer sheet cake to a wire rack and let cool completely. Unmold and gently remove parchment paper.

Carefully cut cake in half vertically, and then each half horizontally using a serrated knife. *This will give you two smaller cakes to work with and is much easier to manage. Use the largest pancake flipper spatula you have to help lift and separate the cake layers so they do not crack or break apart.*

Cake flour is soft wheat flour blended with a little cornstarch, and makes a lighter, more crumbly cake.

Spread bottom half of cakes with preserves; top with remaining cake halves. *You may not need an entire cup of preserves, but use a generous amount and enough to seal the top and bottom cakes together.*

If a recipe calls for cake flour and you do not have it on hand, use 2 Tablespoons less all-purpose flour for each cup of cake flour specified. Then replace the 2 Tablespoons of flour removed with 2 Tablespoons of cornstarch and sift with the remaining flour.

Refrigerate filled cakes for **1 hour.**

Cut filled cake into 1½-inch squares, and transfer to a wire rack set over a jelly roll pan (to catch the glaze drippings). Prepare sugar glaze.

Pour glaze over each petit four, gently spooning the glaze first over each side of each cake while you hold the pieces in your hand. Then spoon glaze over the top once the cakes are set onto the rack. Coat each cake completely on all four sides and the top.

Reuse glaze as needed, removing any small bits of cake that might have fallen into the glaze while working. Refrigerate until glaze is set, approximately 20 minutes.

Top each petit four with a candied violet and small leaf of fresh mint just before serving.

Keep cakes refrigerated until party time, then allow to come to room temperature before serving. Store leftover cakes in the refrigerator where they will keep for 2 to 3 days.

SUGAR GLAZE

4 cups powdered sugar

½ to ¾ cup milk

In a large bowl, whisk just enough milk into powdered sugar to create the consistency of a light drizzle-able glaze. Start with just a small amount of milk and experiment. It is easier to add more milk if needed.

The cake in this recipe is easy to work with but the glaze is a bit tricky because it needs to be thin enough to spoon and drizzle, but heavy enough to cover the cakes. Keep in mind that this is a thin glaze, not a frosting.

It is nice to match the preserves with the type of flower you plan to place on top of petit fours. For instance, because I planned to use candied violets for this spring luncheon, I used blackberry (violet-colored) preserves. If you make these cakes in the summer and use a yellow flower, try peach preserves. If using a bright pink flower, raspberry preserves, and so on.

Occasions   **Almond Petit Fours with Candied Violets**

Candied Violets &
Other Edible Flowers

Flowers can be stored in an airtight container between layers of waxed paper for up to two weeks before losing their color.

1 cup wild violets	Rinsed in cool water and allowed to air dry naturally on paper toweling
1 egg white	Beaten lightly until foamy
½ cup superfine sugar	
1 small, clean artist's paintbrush	Suitable for detailed work
Toothpicks	Enough for each flower
Styrofoam board	Approximately 18 inches, square and 1-inch thick

If you do not have superfine sugar in your pantry, you can easily make it. See p. 388.

Carefully hold each violet by the stem on the underside of the blossom.

Using a paint brush, lightly coat the entire surface of each petal, top and bottom with a thin coating of egg white.

While petals are still moist, with your fingers lightly sprinkle the sugar on all surfaces. Then gently swirl the stem between your fingers to shake off excess sugar.

Lay violets on a sheet of waxed paper so air can circulate around all sides of the flowers and it can dry naturally. Pinch off the stem as you lay each violet down.

Do not try to re-use sugar as you work; it will be too moist to cover evenly.

If you are candying larger blossoms like roses, spear the bottom center of the blossom with a toothpick, then paint. Stick the toothpicks into a piece of Styrofoam so that the flowers can be elevated and dry thoroughly.

Allow flowers to dry completely, uncovered, before using; approximately 4 to 8 hours depending on humidity.

Use flowers to garnish baked goods as soon as possible for best results.

A BUFFET SERVICE IS AN EFFICIENT WAY TO MANAGE A LARGE PARTY LIKE DERBY DAY.

WITH SIXTEEN GUESTS, A MAIN SERVING TABLE SHOULD BE LAID, ALONG WITH SEPARATE STATIONS FOR BOTH DRINKS AND DESSERTS TO AVOID BOTTLENECKS.

IT'S NICE TO HAVE MINT JULEPS FOR GUESTS UPON ARRIVAL, AS THESE TRADITIONAL DERBY COCKTAILS WILL SET THE TONE FOR THE HORSE RACE AND CELEBRATION.

WE LIKE TO BROADCAST THE RACE AT CHURCH HILL DOWNS ON TELEVISIONS THROUGHOUT THE PARTY, INSIDE AND OUT, AND SERVE BACON CHIPS AND BEER CHEESE WHILE WAITING FOR THE RACE TO BEGIN.

ONCE THE RUN FOR THE ROSES IS COMPLETE, INVITE EVERYONE TO GO THROUGH THE BUFFET LINE AND SELF-SERVE DESSERT STATION AS THEY SETTLE BETS AND COUNT WINNINGS.

THE FIRST SATURDAY IN MAY

Kentucky Derby Buffet

FOR 16

Kentucky Mint Juleps
Bacon Chips with Beer Cheese & Melba Toast

No Burgoo Beef Stew
Country Ham
Sweet Potato Biscuits
Spring Fruit Salad with Creamy Citrus
Dressing
Spinach Peas & Pesto

National Red Velvet Torte with Blueberries
Chocolate Almond Thumbprint Cookies
Run-for-the-Roses Derby Pie

RECIPES

KENTUCKY MINT JULEPS
BACON CHIPS
NO BURGOO BEEF
STEW
SWEET POTATO
BISCUITS
SPRING FRUIT SALAD
WITH CREAMY CITRUS
DRESSING
SPINACH PEAS & PESTO
PESTO
NATIONAL RED
VELVET TORTE WITH
BLUEBERRIES
CHOCOLATE ALMOND
THUMBPRINT COOKIES
RUN-FOR-THE-ROSES
DERBY PIE

Serve a dry sweet **Gewürztraminer** *wine, or a dark fruity* **Pinot Noir** *with the ham.*
Serve a **Cabernet Franc** *with the stew.*

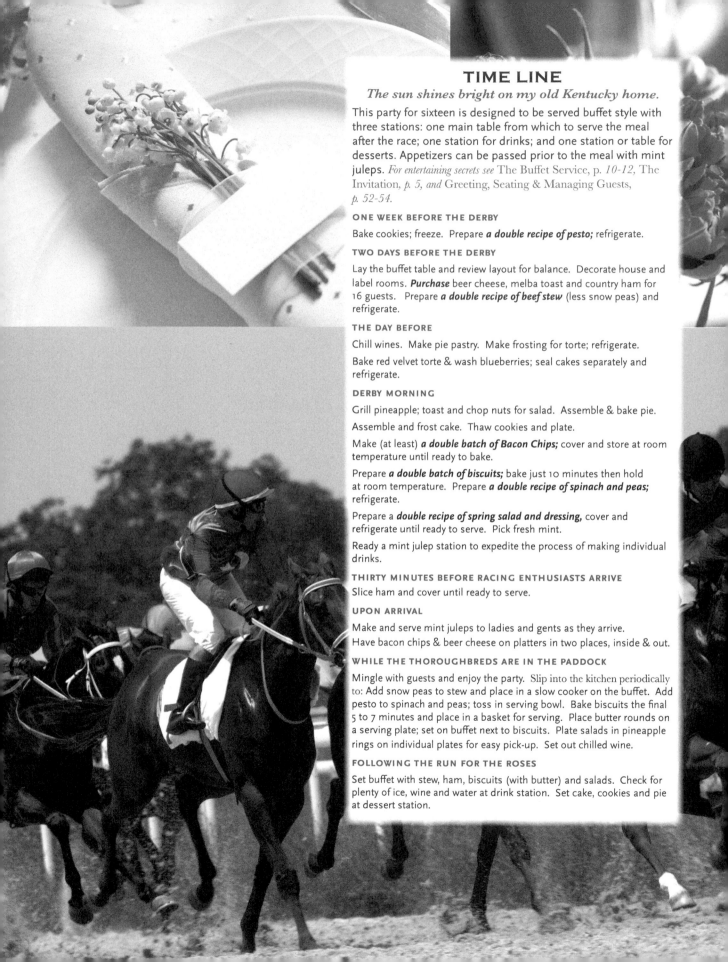

TIME LINE

The sun shines bright on my old Kentucky home.

This party for sixteen is designed to be served buffet style with three stations: one main table from which to serve the meal after the race; one station for drinks; and one station or table for desserts. Appetizers can be passed prior to the meal with mint juleps. *For entertaining secrets see* The Buffet Service, p. *10-12,* The Invitation, p. *5, and* Greeting, Seating & Managing Guests, p. *52-54.*

ONE WEEK BEFORE THE DERBY

Bake cookies; freeze. Prepare *a double recipe of pesto;* refrigerate.

TWO DAYS BEFORE THE DERBY

Lay the buffet table and review layout for balance. Decorate house and label rooms. **Purchase** beer cheese, melba toast and country ham for 16 guests. Prepare *a double recipe of beef stew* (less snow peas) and refrigerate.

THE DAY BEFORE

Chill wines. Make pie pastry. Make frosting for torte; refrigerate.

Bake red velvet torte & wash blueberries; seal cakes separately and refrigerate.

DERBY MORNING

Grill pineapple; toast and chop nuts for salad. Assemble & bake pie.

Assemble and frost cake. Thaw cookies and plate.

Make (at least) *a double batch of Bacon Chips;* cover and store at room temperature until ready to bake.

Prepare *a double batch of biscuits;* bake just 10 minutes then hold at room temperature. Prepare *a double recipe of spinach and peas;* refrigerate.

Prepare a *double recipe of spring salad and dressing,* cover and refrigerate until ready to serve. Pick fresh mint.

Ready a mint julep station to expedite the process of making individual drinks.

THIRTY MINUTES BEFORE RACING ENTHUSIASTS ARRIVE

Slice ham and cover until ready to serve.

UPON ARRIVAL

Make and serve mint juleps to ladies and gents as they arrive.
Have bacon chips & beer cheese on platters in two places, inside & out.

WHILE THE THOROUGHBREDS ARE IN THE PADDOCK

Mingle with guests and enjoy the party. Slip into the kitchen periodically to: Add snow peas to stew and place in a slow cooker on the buffet. Add pesto to spinach and peas; toss in serving bowl. Bake biscuits the final 5 to 7 minutes and place in a basket for serving. Place butter rounds on a serving plate; set on buffet next to biscuits. Plate salads in pineapple rings on individual plates for easy pick-up. Set out chilled wine.

FOLLOWING THE RUN FOR THE ROSES

Set buffet with stew, ham, biscuits (with butter) and salads. Check for plenty of ice, wine and water at drink station. Set cake, cookies and pie at dessert station.

Kentucky Mint Juleps

If you distill the essence of southern hospitality down to beverage form you will find the Mint Julep! This is the traditional drink of the Kentucky Derby. In my undergraduate years at the University of Kentucky in Lexington, I learned to appreciate the traditions and trappings of horse racing, and this is how I was taught to make a julep while living in the Bluegrass state. Mint Juleps are a must-have on the first Saturday of May!

YIELD: ONE JULEP

1 silver julep cup
1 jigger good Kentucky bourbon
Finely crushed ice
Fresh mint leaves
1 teaspoon granulated sugar

Take a silver cup – only a silver cup!

Fill it with ice crushed to the fineness of snow.

Bruise one spring leaf of mint to extract its tender essence and add it to the ice.

Then dissolve a teaspoon of sugar in a "Kentucky" jigger of good Bourbon whiskey and pour it over the ice.

Let the fluid filter through the ice to the bottom of the tumbler.

Then swirl the julep cup slowly until a coating of thick white frost forms on its outside.

Garnish cocktails with a sprig of mint and hand to an appreciative lady or gentleman.

A traditional mint julep is served in silver or pewter cups, and is held only by the bottom and top edges, allowing frost to form on the outside of the cup.

This straight-sided metal tumbler readily conducts cold from the ice, causing condensation on the outside of the cup and making the julep all the more refreshing on a sultry southern day.

Bacon Chips

These crunchy chips of bacon infused with maple syrup and toasted nuts are wonderful! Chips can be prepared early in the day and stored at room temperature until ready to serve.

YIELD: SIXTEEN HORS D'OEUVRES

½ **pound applewood-smoked bacon, sliced thick**

¼ **cup pecans, chopped fine**

4 **Tablespoons maple syrup**

¼ **cup brown sugar, packed**

2 **teaspoons dijon-style mustard**

¼ **teaspoon cayenne pepper**

1½ **teaspoons kosher salt**

½ **teaspoon freshly ground black pepper**

Preheat oven to 400 degrees.

Combine pecans, syrup, brown sugar, mustard and spices in a small bowl.

Cut each strip of bacon in half and lay slices on a metal baking rack placed in a jelly roll pan that has been lined with foil.

Be sure to line your pan with foil for easy clean-up!

Brush/spoon ¾ of the syrup mixture onto the bacon strips, using approximately one teaspoon of syrup to each half-piece of bacon.

Bake 15 to 20 minutes, or until bacon is crisp.

Time will be dependent on the thickness of the bacon.

Brush bacon with remaining syrup before the last five minutes of cooking time; finish cooking.

Transfer to a plate lined with paper toweling to drain, syrup side up.

No Burgoo Beef Stew

Although Kentucky Burgoo is typically served at horse races, I prefer this lighter stew with whole baby carrots and mushrooms that give it a fresh yet rustic look. The stew can be made ahead and kept warm during the buffet in a slow cooker.

SERVES: TEN

3 pounds beef chuck roast

¼ cup all-purpose flour

2 Tablespoons kosher salt, divided

2 teaspoons freshly ground black pepper

4 Tablespoons canola oil, divided

2 Tablespoons tomato paste

1 28-ounce can whole tomatoes

*1 bottle dry red wine

2½ cups beef broth

4 cloves garlic, chopped roughly

2 cups heirloom carrots

1 large parsnip, chopped

4 celery stalks, coarsely chopped

10 ounces pearl onions, peeled

5 baby golden potatoes, halved

1½ cups wild cremini mushrooms

4 sprigs fresh thyme

4 sprigs fresh rosemary

1½ cups sugar snap peas

Made like a classic French daube (beef braised in red wine) the chunky pieces of meat in this no-burgoo-stew are incredibly flavorful and tender.

Preheat oven to 350 degrees.

*Pour one glass of wine for the cook, then reserve remaining wine for the stew!

Cube roast into 1 to 1½-inch cubes and remove any fat.

In a large bowl, combine flour, 1 Tablespoon salt and the pepper. Add beef cubes and fold to coat each piece well with the flour mixture.

In a large Dutch oven, heat 2 Tablespoons canola oil over medium heat. In two batches, brown beef chunks on all sides. Transfer the first batch to a plate and add remaining oil before adding the second batch.

Reduce heat to medium; add tomato paste and incorporate by stirring constantly for 1 minute, scraping up any flavor packed brown bits from the bottom of the pan in the process.

Add tomatoes and break into halves with a spoon. Then add wine, broth and garlic to the pot. Bring to a boil over high heat. Boil for 10 minutes.

Cover pot and place in oven to bake for **1 hour and 15 minutes.**

Clean carrots and remove all but ½-inch of the leafy stem. Clean mushrooms by rubbing off any dirt with a kitchen towel and then trimming off the tips of the stems, leaving mushrooms whole.

Prepare all other vegetables as directed, then lightly steam the snap peas and set aside. *Snap peas can sometimes be hard to find. If so, use frozen peas.*

Remove the pot from the oven and add carrots, parsnips, celery, onions, mushrooms and potatoes.

Leave thyme and rosemary on their stems and bundle together with kitchen string; add to the pot.

Return pot to the oven and bake an additional **50 minutes.**

Finally, add remaining 1 Tablespoon kosher salt and the snap peas.

Bake another 10 minutes. Remove herb bundle and serve hot.

Sweet Potato Biscuits

These Southern-style biscuits are moist, delicious and a beautiful rusty-orange color.

YIELD: TWELVE TWO AND ONE HALF-INCH ROUNDS

¾ cup sweet potato, baked

1¾ cups all-purpose flour

1 Tablespoon baking powder

½ teaspoon baking soda

1 teaspoon kosher salt

2 Tablespoons golden brown sugar, packed

7 Tablespoons unsalted butter, cold

⅓ cup buttermilk

3 Tablespoons scallions, sliced thin (including green parts)

Preheat oven to 375 degrees. Pierce sweet potato and then bake until fork tender, approximately 45 minutes. Peel and mash potato, measure and set aside to cool.

Raise oven temperature to 425 degrees.

In a large bowl, add flour, baking powder, baking soda, salt and brown sugar. Mix to combine.

Dice butter into small cubes and add. Using a pastry cutter, cut in butter just until the batter begins to resemble a course meal.

Add the buttermilk and cooled sweet potato and mix just until the dough comes together. Add scallions (sliced very thin on the diagonal) and fold in to combine, being careful to not overwork the dough.

On a lightly flour surface, turn out the dough and knead 2 to 3 times to coat with flour. *The dough should be smooth and soft.*

Now roll the dough to ½-inch thickness and cut into 2-inch rounds. Gather scraps and re-roll until you have 12 rounds and all the dough has been used.

On a baking sheet lined with parchment paper, place biscuit rounds, allowing at least one inch between rounds. Bake 12 to 15 minutes, or until golden brown.

Biscuits are best served hot - with lots of butter!

Spring Fruit Salad with Creamy Citrus Dressing

A creamy citrus dressing with tart in-season fruits makes this salad a delightful springtime choice. Serve plated as individual salads for quick and easy pick-up in the buffet line.

SERVES: TEN

FRUIT SALAD

10 grilled pineapple rings
2 cups fresh strawberries, sliced
¼ cup fresh rhubarb, sliced thin
2 crisp celery stalks, sliced diagonally
Juice of 1 fresh lemon

Slice and grill pineapple rings just long enough to get blackened grill marks; then cover and refrigerate until ready to plate.

Combine strawberries and rhubarb with celery; sprinkle with fresh lemon juice and gently mix to combine; set aside.

CREAMY CITRUS DRESSING

1 cup yogurt
½ cup light mayonnaise
½ cup brown sugar, packed
½ cup fresh orange juice
Juice of 1 fresh lime
2 jiggers brandy
1½ cups pistachios, toasted and chopped
Cinnamon

Whisk yogurt, mayonnaise, sugar, juices and brandy until creamy.

Add to strawberry and rhubarb mixture and refrigerate for **1 to 2 hours** to infuse flavors and chill well.

Plate salads by placing a pineapple ring in the center of individual salad plates and filling the centers with a scoop of the strawberry mixture.

Sprinkle with pistachios and a dusting of freshly ground cinnamon just before serving.

Spinach, Peas & Pesto

This symphony of melodious greens and musical textures band together in perfect three-part harmony!

SERVES: TEN

1 bunch fresh spinach, cleaned and stemmed
1 12-ounce bag frozen peas
2 to 3 Tablespoons pesto
½ cup pine nuts, toasted
Kosher salt and freshly ground black pepper to taste
Parmesan cheese

Rinse frozen peas briefly under very hot water to thaw; drain and set aside.

Clean spinach; toast pine nuts.

Just before ready to serve, assemble all ingredients in large bowl and toss with pesto to coat.

Dust finished salad with freshly grated parmesan cheese.

This salad is tricky to season, because if you add the salt or pesto too early it will wilt the greens. So be sure to wait until just ready to serve to finish this salad.

Pesto

This sauce of fresh basil, pine nuts and parmesan cheese is blended to perfection with just a hint of good olive oil.

YIELD: APPROXIMATELY ONE CUP

When making pesto in bulk at summer's end, store in ice cube trays and freeze.
Each cube will equal approximately 2 Tablespoons of pesto, making the cubes easy to use "pre-measured" in recipes and pastas throughout the winter months.

2 cups fresh basil leaves, packed
¼ cup pine nuts
2 Tablespoons walnuts
2 cloves garlic, peeled
1 teaspoon Himalayan pink salt
½ teaspoon freshly ground black pepper
⅔ cup good quality olive oil
¼ cup fresh parmesan cheese
¼ cup pecorino cheese
Juice of ½ fresh lemon

Toast nuts. Grind cheeses in food processor; remove and set aside.

In a food processor bowl, combine basil, toasted nuts, garlic, salt and pepper. Pulse to finely chop and combine all ingredients.

With the processor running, gradually add enough oil to form a smooth and thick sauce. Taste and adjust seasoning as needed.

Transfer to a mixing bowl, add cheeses and lemon juice, stir to combine.

National Red Velvet Torte with Blueberries

This cake is named after one of my favorite childhood movies, *National Velvet, and is sure to win the trifecta at any Derby party! Don't be alarmed by the beets in the batter as they will become sugary sweet when roasted.

SERVES: EIGHTEEN

RED VELVET CAKE

3 ounces unsweetened chocolate

2 cups granulated sugar

4 large eggs

1½ cups vegetable oil

2 teaspoons pure vanilla extract

2 cups all-purpose flour

2¼ teaspoons baking soda

¼ teaspoon salt

1½ pounds beets, roasted and puréed

Pre-heat oven to 350 degrees. Butter three 8-inch round cake pans and line with parchment paper.

Roast beets for 20 to 30 minutes in the oven. Cool and purée until smooth.

Using a double boiler, break in chocolate and melt; set aside.

Sift the flour, baking soda and salt onto a sheet of waxed paper; set aside.

In a large bowl with an electric mixer, combine sugar, eggs, oil and vanilla on low speed for 3 minutes.

Add the sifted dry ingredients to the sugar and egg mixture and continue to mix on low speed, scraping down the sides of the bowl with a spatula as necessary until well incorporated.

Add melted chocolate and continue to mix on low speed until just combined.

Add puréed beets, and fold in by hand until thoroughly combined.

Evenly divide the batter between the three prepared pans and bake on the middle rack of oven for 20 to 25 minutes or until toothpick comes out clean.

Remove the pans from the oven and transfer to a cooling rack after 5 minutes, letting cakes cool for only the first few minutes in the pans, then turning the layers out onto the rack and let cool completely.

CREAM CHEESE & MASCARPONE FROSTING

2 cups heavy cream
12 ounces American cream cheese, softened
12 ounces Italian mascarpone cheese, softened
1 teaspoon almond extract
2 cups powdered sugar, sifted

In a small bowl, whip cream to soft peaks. Set aside in refrigerator.

In a large bowl with an electric mixer, blend cream cheese on low speed until it is soft and smooth. Add the mascarpone and continue to mix on low speed until the cheeses are well combined.

Add extract and powdered sugar and mix until just combined.

Then turn off the mixer and fold in the whipped cream by hand with a spatula. Keep mixture refrigerated until ready to assemble.

ASSEMBLY

Using a serrated knife, slice each cake layer in two horizontally.

Place the first half layer on a cake plate with top side down and frost the top of the layer. Repeat until all of the layers have been stacked with frosting between each layer. Then place the top layer top side up and frost. Leave the sides of the cakes un-frosted, like a torte.

Keep torte refrigerated until party time, then allow to come to room temperature before slicing. Store leftover torte in the refrigerator.

On Derby Day, top cake with a triple row of fresh blueberries in the shape of a horse shoe, across the top layer.

Chocolate Almond Thumbprint Cookies

Preserves and dried fruits are terrific with chocolate, and this chewy almond cookie filled with fruit preserves is taken up a notch when drizzled with bittersweet chocolate! Cookies can be kept in an airtight container for one week or frozen. To freeze, place finished cookies on a cookie sheet and freeze until chocolate is solid. Then remove to a container to avoid crushing chocolate drizzles when stacked.

To help ensure your success, see Baking Secrets, Cookies, p. 356.

YIELD: THIRTY-SIX COOKIES

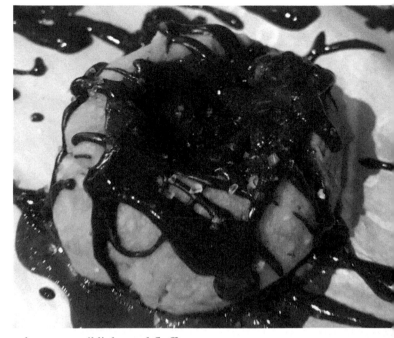

1 cup unsalted butter, softened

½ cup golden brown sugar, packed

2 cups all-purpose flour

1 cup almonds, toasted and chopped fine

1 teaspoon salt

2 teaspoons pure vanilla extract

¼ cup black cherry jam

¼ cup apricot jam

4 ounces bittersweet chocolate

2 teaspoons light corn syrup

1 Tablespoon unsalted butter

Fleur de sel

Preheat oven to 350 degrees. Line two cookie sheets with parchment; set aside. Measure, toast and then chop almonds.

In a large bowl with an electric mixer, beat butter and sugar until light and fluffy, approximately 4 minutes.

Whisk together the flour, almonds and salt; gradually add to butter mixture. Mix until incorporated; stir in vanilla.

Pinch out 36 uniform pieces of dough and pat them together gently. Then roll into balls by swirling between your two palms, and replace onto the cookie sheets.

Using the handle of a wooden spoon, make an indentation in the center of each ball; repair cracks in dough as necessary. **Bake 7 minutes.**

Remove cookies from the oven and spoon ½ to 1 teaspoon of jam into the center of each cookie, filling half of the cookies with apricot jam and half with black cherry.

Return to the oven and bake another 7 minutes, or until cookies are brown around the edges.

Let cookies cool by sliding, while still on the parchment paper, onto a wire rack while you prepare the chocolate.

In a double boiler, melt chocolate. Stir in corn syrup and butter.

Drizzle chocolate mixture over each cookie first one direction and then the other while chocolate is warm. Then sprinkle lightly with sea salt.

Let cool completely.

Run-for-the-Roses Derby Pie

Derby pie is a nutty chocolate chess that has been a Kentucky Derby Day tradition since the 1950s. Run-for-the-Roses Derby Pie is made with butter pastry and almonds, incorporating the traditional derby pie flavors with unique ingredients and plenty of delectable milk chocolate.

SERVES: EIGHT TO TEN

PASTRY

1 recipe Butter Pastry

(See p. 146.)

Prepare pastry and chill dough as directed.

Roll pastry to ⅛–inch thick and fit into 9-inch pie plate. Chill an additional 30 minutes before filling and baking.

CHOCOLATE FILLING

1¼ cups almonds, chopped

1¼ cups Ghirardelli milk chocolate chips

1 cup light corn syrup

½ cup granulated sugar

½ cup dark brown sugar, packed

¼ cup good Kentucky bourbon

4 large eggs

¼ cup unsalted butter, melted and cooled

2 teaspoons cornmeal

2 teaspoons pure vanilla extract

½ teaspoon kosher salt

Preheat oven to 325 degrees. Toast almonds and cool. Place nuts and chocolate chips into prepared and well-chilled pie shell.

In a large saucepan, bring corn syrup, sugars and bourbon to a boil, then reduce heat and simmer for 3 minutes. Set aside to cool.

In a large bowl, whisk eggs, cooled butter, cornmeal, vanilla and salt until well combine and airy.

Add ¼ of the sugar mixture to the egg mixture and whisk together to temper the eggs. Then add remaining sugar mix and combine well.

Pour mixture over nuts and chips in pie shell. Cover crust with pie shield. Bake for 40 to 45 minutes with the shield, then rotate the pie and remove the shield. Bake an additional 5 to 10 minutes, or until pie is golden brown and set.

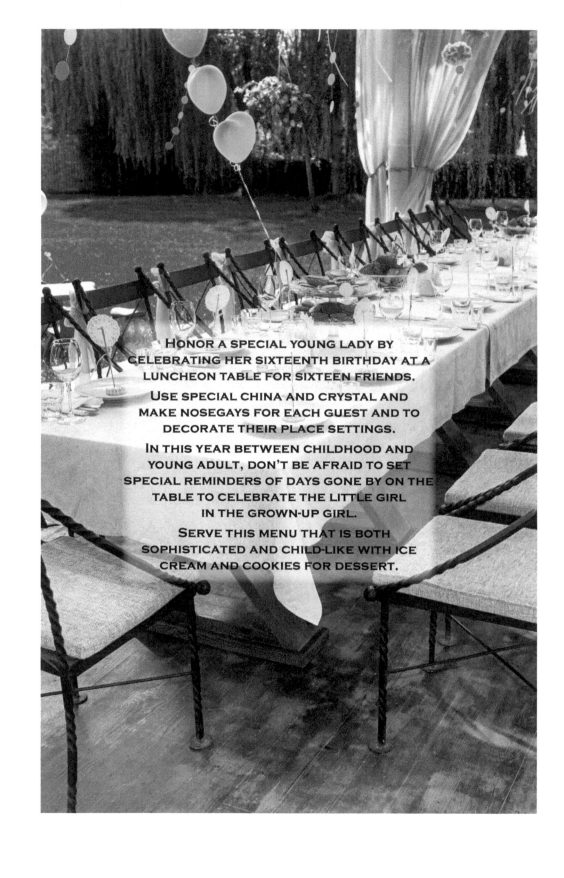

HONOR A SPECIAL YOUNG LADY BY
CELEBRATING HER SIXTEENTH BIRTHDAY AT A
LUNCHEON TABLE FOR SIXTEEN FRIENDS.

USE SPECIAL CHINA AND CRYSTAL AND
MAKE NOSEGAYS FOR EACH GUEST AND TO
DECORATE THEIR PLACE SETTINGS.

IN THIS YEAR BETWEEN CHILDHOOD AND
YOUNG ADULT, DON'T BE AFRAID TO SET
SPECIAL REMINDERS OF DAYS GONE BY ON THE
TABLE TO CELEBRATE THE LITTLE GIRL
IN THE GROWN-UP GIRL.

SERVE THIS MENU THAT IS BOTH
SOPHISTICATED AND CHILD-LIKE WITH ICE
CREAM AND COOKIES FOR DESSERT.

ON A SIXTEENTH BIRTHDAY IN MAY

A Young Lady's Sweet Sixteen

FOR 16

Georgia's Lavender Punch
Perfect Bites

Parmesan Chicken
Lemony Risotto with Spring Asparagus &
Snap Peas
Fava Beans & Spring Onions in Butter

Neapolitan Twist Ice Cream
Brown Butter Shortbread Cookies

LAVENDER SIMPLE SYRUP

TIME LINE
Sugar, Spice & Everything Nice

An easy way to manage this luncheon is to prepare individual plates of chicken, risotto and beans for each guest, then to clear the entrée plates before serving the dessert of cookies and ice cream.

And because all little girls adore their Daddy, why not ask the father of the birthday girl to do the serving – complete with a tuxedo jacket and bow tie? If the father is willing, this will both provide the necessary help for serving the meal and allow Dad to be a part of the celebration!

For entertaining secrets see Setting a Formal Table, *p. 28-34.* Tussie Mussies, *p. 51 and* Gift Ideas for Sweet Sixteens, *p. 63.*

TWO DAYS BEFORE

Set table, make place cards, decorate table with reminders of childhood.

THE DAY BEFORE

Make ice cream and freeze. Make and bake cookies; seal in plastic wrap on serving platter.

LUNCHEON MORNING

Make lavender punch; refrigerate. Make perfect bites but hold assembly of nuts and tomatoes until last minute.

Scoop ice cream into small bowls, cover and return bowls to the freezer.

ONE AND ONE HALF HOURS BEFORE THE YOUNG LADIES ARRIVE

Prepare **four recipes of chicken** and sprinkle with parmesan cheese, then hold in the pan to keep warm.

Prepare **double recipe of risotto** and hold in pan to keep warm.

Prepare **a double recipe of beans.** Sauté fava beans and onions and hold in the pan to keep warm.

Add fresh slices of lemon and lime with lavender flowers to the pitcher of punch.

UPON ARRIVAL

Add nuts and tomatoes to the bites and ready to serve. Serve punch over ice with Perfect Bites.

JUST BEFORE THE MEAL

Crisp chicken and melt cheese by heating just a few minutes in a 350 degree oven. Fill water glasses. Plate chicken, risotto and fava beans and place on the table at each place setting.

JUST BEFORE DESSERT

Add a cookie to each ice cream bowl and serve, and then,

Give *a Tussie Mussie to the Birthday Girl*.

Georgia's Lavender Punch

My long-time friend Georgia shared this refreshing citrus punch with me many years ago. The lavender is a recent addition that Georgia approves!

SERVES: SIXTEEN

2   1-liter bottles club soda, chilled
1   12-ounce can frozen lemonade
Juice of 1 lime
Juice of 2 lemons
1 cup lavender simple syrup

Combine all ingredients in a large pitcher and stir to combine.

Refrigerate until ready to serve.

To serve, fill a large pitcher with ice and pour in the punch.

Serve in chilled glasses filled with ice, fresh lemon and limes slices and buds of fresh lavender.

LAVENDER SIMPLE SYRUP

1 cup water
1 cup sugar
1 tablespoon fresh lavender blossoms

Bring lavender, sugar and water to a boil, and then simmer until the sugar dissolves (approximately 10 minutes). Let cool before using.

If desired, one 750-millilliter bottle of champagne can be substituted for one 1-liter bottle of club soda.

Perfect Bites

Sweet basil and goat cheese with pine nuts make a perfectly combined bite. Perfect Bites can be partially prepared one to two hours ahead of serving, and completed just before serving.

YIELD: TWENTY "PERFECT" BITES

Toasting brings out the essential oils in nuts and seeds, resulting in much more flavor.
Nuts absorb moisture readily and toasting will both dry them out and heighten their flavor. Go slowly and watch, as nuts burn easily. See p. 379.

When using pine nuts in recipes use care. Their flavor is strong and can dominate a dish if used too liberally.
Pine nuts are also fatty and luxurious; so always balance their flavor with a bit of salt or a tart herb.

4 ounces goat cheese, at room temperature
2 Tablespoons Half and Half cream
Kosher salt
Freshly ground black pepper
20 large unblemished basil leaves
2 medium plum tomatoes, finely chopped
½ cup pine nuts, lightly toasted
Extra-virgin olive oil (for drizzling)
Freshly ground black pepper

Toast pine nuts in a small skillet over medium heat, stirring occasionally, for approximately 3 minutes. Turn nuts as they roast and watch carefully to ensure they do not burn. Let cool.

Toasting is the best way to roast these buttery soft nuts and prevent burning.

Wash large (2 to 3-inch) basil leaves and allow to dry naturally on paper toweling. Finely chop tomatoes.

In a small bowl, mix the goat cheese with cream and season lightly with salt and pepper. Dollop one teaspoon of the cheese on each basil leaf; placing bites on the serving plate as you go.

Sprinkle the pine nuts evenly onto each dollop, lightly pressing nuts into the cheese to set.

Scatter the chopped tomatoes on each bite; pressing lightly to set as well.

Drizzle bites lightly with good quality olive oil. Top with a sprinkle of freshly ground black pepper.

Serve immediately.

Parmesan Chicken

Tangy Dijon, piney thyme and lemon zest give this crunchy breaded chicken a piquant flavor.

SERVES: FOUR

2 large chicken breasts
2½ Tablespoons canola oil, divided
¼ cup dijon-style mustard
¼ cup sauvignon blanc wine
2 Tablespoons olive oil
2 teaspoons zest of lemon
2 teaspoons fresh thyme leaves
½ cup panko bread crumbs
¼ cup course yellow corn meal
1 teaspoon kosher salt
Freshly ground black pepper
2 Tablespoons parmesan cheese, grated

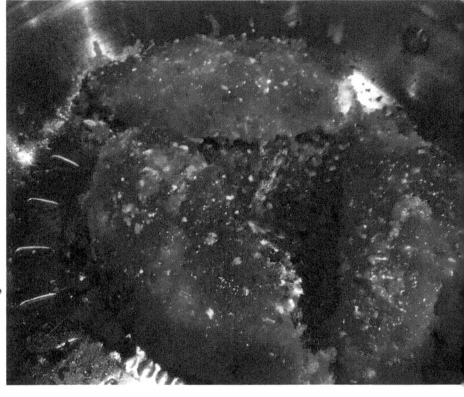

Preheat oven to 350 degrees.

Cut chicken breasts in two, and then pound the four pieces with a meat hammer until approximately ¼-inch thick.

In a medium-sized bowl, combine mustard, wine, olive oil, zest and thyme.

In a second bowl, combine bread crumbs, corn meal, salt and pepper.

Heat ½ of the canola oil in large skillet over medium-high heat.

Dip and coat chicken pieces in mustard and wine mixture, then dredge in bread crumb mixture and coat well.

Sauté chicken in hot oil just until golden brown on each side, approximately 4 minutes per side.

Add remaining canola oil as needed when browning second side, turning chicken pieces only once.

Then cover skillet and place it in the oven to finish cooking for approximately 15 minutes.

During the last 2 minutes of cooking time, sprinkle each breast with parmesan cheese and continue to bake to melt the cheese. Serve hot.

Lemony Risotto with Spring Asparagus & Snap Peas

Creamy rice with bites of mushroom, spring asparagus and snap peas is seasoned to perfection with fresh lemon. Be sure to use tender young in-season asparagus and peas because they are added at the last minute and cook a very short time.

SERVES: SIX

1½ cups arborio rice

4 Tablespoons unsalted butter

1 shallot, minced

1 cup morel mushrooms

1½ Tablespoons roasted garlic

½ cup sauvignon blanc wine

5 to 6 cups chicken broth

1 bunch fresh asparagus

1 cup snap peas

¼ cup fresh parmesan cheese, grated

Zest of ½ fresh lemon

¼ cup fresh chives, minced

Kosher salt & freshly ground black pepper to taste

Additional parmesan cheese &

Fresh parsley

See p. 374 Roasted Garlic.

To avoid sticky risotto, complete the process of incorporating all of the broth within 20 to 25 minutes.

Every item you add to a risotto must be timed. If you are adding something very delicate like spring asparagus, or a berry, add very late in the process so it will not break up. Likewise, if you are making a seafood risotto with something like shrimp, this should be added early so it has time to cook.

Clean mushrooms per instructions on p. 378-79.

Break off woody stems and slice asparagus on the diagonal into ½-inch pieces. Prepare other vegetables and herbs as directed.

Melt 3 Tablespoons butter in a medium saucepan and sauté the shallots over medium heat until soft but not brown. Add the rice and mushrooms and sauté evenly until the rice is translucent, approximately 3 minutes. Add the garlic, wine, ½ cup of the broth, and cook, stirring constantly, until the liquid is absorbed. Continue adding small amounts of the remaining broth and cooking in this manner until the rice is creamy and the center is firm, approximately 20 to 25 minutes.

When the risotto is done, stir in the remaining 1 Tablespoon of butter, fresh springtime asparagus and snap peas, cheese, zest and chives, and season with salt and pepper.

Serve in warm bowls garnished with fresh parsley and shaved lengths of parmesan cheese for a truly comforting treat.

If morel mushrooms are not available, substitute with shitake or another spring variety.

Fava Beans & Spring Onions in Butter

Fava beans have a great, delicate yet bitter flavor and are in season in the spring and summer months. Favas are delicious both raw or lightly sautéed.

SERVES: SIX

2 cups fava beans, shucked

2 spring onions, diced

2 teaspoons unsalted butter

2 Tablespoons olive oil

4 Tablespoons basil, sliced thin

Shuck favas twice by first removing beans from the pod and then by briefly blanching beans to easily remove the skin from each bean.

In a saucepan, sauté onions in butter until soft.

Add beans with a little water and olive oil; cover while they cook for approximately 3 to 5 minutes. At the last second, toss in the chopped basil. Serve immediately.

The bright green Fava beans need to be shucked twice. After popping them out of their larger pod, be sure to remove the individual skins.

By briefly blanching the individual beans, shucking the second, individual skin is made effortless with just a quick squeeze.

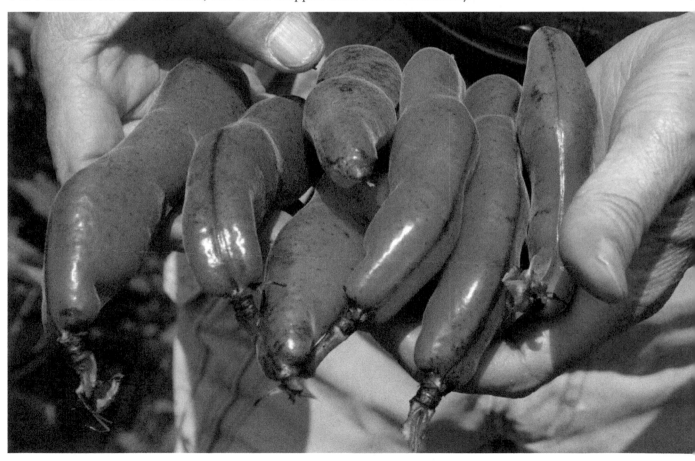

Neapolitan Twist Ice Cream

Creamy and light vanilla bean ice cream infused with fresh strawberries and crunchy chocolate covered almonds!

YIELD: ONE GALLON

1 pint Half and Half cream
Seeds from 2 vanilla bean pods
6 large eggs
2 cups granulated sugar
½ teaspoon salt
½ cup light corn syrup
1 Tablespoon pure vanilla extract
2½ to 3 cups milk
½ cup strawberries
½ cup dark chocolate covered almonds

Remove vanilla beans from pods; set aside.

Roughly chop chocolate almonds. Hull and quarter strawberries, Then sugar lightly to get the juices running and to soften the berries just a bit.

In a small saucepan, bring cream, vanilla beans and pods to a boil; turn down heat and let simmer 5 to 10 minutes. Remove pods; discard.

Whip eggs, sugar and salt for 10 minutes, or until light yellow in color.

Mix in syrup and add vanilla extract. Stir to combine well. Pour into ice cream freezer and fill to ½ full.

Stir in ¼ of the strawberries and ¼ of the almond pieces.

Fill remaining ½ of freezer with milk.

Freeze per instructions with freezer. When ice cream has frozen, fold in remaining strawberries and almonds; combine well.

Then freeze an additional 4 to 5 hours to harden.

Vanilla and vanilla bean have a cherry-like, woody flavor and should always be used as the star of the show.
Vanilla is to baking as salt is to cooking, and is especially good in dairy desserts.
See p. 388.

Brown Butter Shortbread Cookies

These chewy cookies of caramelized butter & fresh lemon make an irresistible shortbread.

YIELD: TWO DOZEN COOKIES

1 cup unsalted butter

¾ teaspoon juice of fresh lemon

¾ cup granulated sugar

2 Tablespoons milk

2 teaspoons pure vanilla extract

2 cups all-purpose flour

1 teaspoon baking powder

½ teaspoon salt

Prepare a pan of ice water.

Melt butter and continue cooking, stirring occasionally, until it smells like caramel and is almost ready to burn, approximately 10 minutes.

When butter suddenly turns amber, thrust the pan into ice water as shown above.

Stir lemon juice into the butter and let sit until solidified, approximately 15 minutes. Once butter is solid, Preheat oven to 300 degrees.

Remove butter to a large bowl with an electric mixer and beat with the sugar until fluffy, approximately 3 minutes.

Beat in the remaining ingredients, combining vanilla with milk and whisking flour with powder and salt before adding.

Knead on a clean, lightly floured surface 10 to 12 times until smooth.

In the palm of your hands, roll into small (1-inch diameter) balls.

Place balls on un-buttered baking sheet and flatten slightly with a fork, once horizontally and once vertically. *Flattened balls should be no less than ½-inch in height to ensure a chewy center (see above photograph).*

Lightly sprinkle each cookie with sugar. Bake 20 to 25 minutes, or until edges are golden brown. Remove to wire rack to cool.

Summer
Occasions

A French Provincial Picnic

Garden Party

Independence Day Lawn Party

Bride's Maids Luncheon

Wedding Rehearsal Dinner

Anniversary Candle Light Dinner

Summer

Seasonal Fruits & Vegetables

FRUITS & NUTS

Apricots
Berries
Cherries
Figs
Grapes
Limes
Melons
Nectarines
Peaches
Plums
Watermelon

VEGETABLES & HERBS

Avocado
Basil
Beans, Fava
Beans, Green
Cabbage
Cauliflower
Corn
Cucumbers
Eggplant
Flowers, edible
Garlic

Herbs
Lavender
Okra
Onion
Peas
Peppers, Bell
Peppers, Chili
Potatoes
Squash
Tomatoes
Zucchini

THE SOUTH OF FRANCE IS A CHARMING PLACE IN A MEDITERRANEAN CLIMATE. MY TIME IN INTOXICATING PROVENCE WITH ITS WARM STONE VILLAGES, ROMAN RUINS AND BRILLIANT SUNSHINE WILL ALWAYS BE SAVORED - AND HAS INSPIRED THIS MENU.

A PICNIC IN CELEBRATION OF PROVENCE SHOULD BE AN ADVENTURE WITH KNIFE, FORK AND CORK SCREW, AS AUTHOR PETER MAYLE SO APTLY ASSERTS. PACKED WITH DELECTABLE FRENCH DELIGHTS, THIS MENU CREATES A PROVENÇAL ADVENTURE FOR YOU TO ENJOY AT HOME IN AN AFTERNOON THAT IS CASUAL, RELAXED AND LONG — C'EST BON!

A JUNE AFTERNOON

A French Provincial Picnic

FOR 10

Foie Gras with Fig Chutney and Toasted Brioche

Poulet Rôti
Kickin' Deviled Eggs
Aïoli with
Roasted Asparagus & Garlic Chips
Fleurs de Courgettes

French Fruit Tart, Butter Pastry, Vanilla Cream
Classic French Macaroons – *Ooh la la!*

RECIPES

POULET RÔTI

KICKIN' DEVILED EGGS

AÏOLI

ROASTED ASPARAGUS

GARLIC CHIPS

FLEURS DE COURGETTES

FRENCH FRUIT TART

BUTTER PASTRY

VANILLA CREAM

CLASSIC FRENCH MACAROONS

In true Provincial style, serve Pastis *to start, then serve a* Rosè *from the Côtes-du-Rhône region in the South of France to complete this menu. A Fumé with crisp aromatic herb flavors would also be a good choice to complement the chicken.*

HOW TO TRUSS A BIRD

USING RAW EGG

SECRETS TO SUCCESSFUL MACAROONS

TIME LINE

Bonjour! Parlez-vous Francaise?

This outside party for ten is designed to be relaxed. Prepare a table that guests can come and go to and from throughout the afternoon.

For entertaining secrets see Outdoor Entertaining *p. 13 and* Introductions, *p. 53-4.*

TWO DAYS BEFORE

Purchase Foie Gras, fig chutney and brioche for 10 guests.

Assess picnic location by going outside at the same time the picnic will be held to determine good spots for tables, guest seating and food set up. Make butter pastry and refrigerate.

THE DAY BEFORE

Prepare **a double recipe of poulet rôti**; then refrigerate overnight to roast the next morning. Make deviled eggs; plate, cover and refrigerate. Make Aïoli and refrigerate. Prep asparagus; refrigerate wrapped in damp paper toweling to hold until ready to cook.

Complete fruit tart by preparing butter cream, assembling tart and baking. Then cool, cover tightly and refrigerate.

Set outdoor spaces and organize seating and service tables.

Chill wine, pastis & soda water.

PICNIC MORNING

Make macaroons; cool and **box for take-home treats.**

Set out table service, napkins and lots of sunflowers!

TWO HOURS BEFORE THE PICNIC BEGINS

Bring chickens to room temperature and roast. Set a kitchen timer for roasting time and remember to baste while preparing the rest of the meal.

ONE HOUR BEFORE THE PICNIC BEGINS

Roast asparagus; make garlic chips. Hold at room temperature. Prepare to serve pastis over ice with cool water by setting out glasses, ice bucket, etc.

ONE HALF-HOUR BEFORE THE PICNIC BEGINS

Fry zucchini flowers, drain and hold at room temperature. Slice and toast brioche. Plate Foie Gras, chutney and brioche; set out cocktail napkins.

UPON ARRIVAL

Serve pastis with chilled water and Foie Gras, chutney and toasted brioche.

JUST BEFORE THE MEAL

Carve chickens and plate. Plate deviled eggs. Plate fleurs de courgettes.

Arrange a small bowl of aioli on the platter with asparagus and garlic chips.

Set tart out to come to room temperature during the meal. Serve wine.

JUST BEFORE DESSERT

Slice tart and serve.

AS GUESTS DEPART

Give out boxes of macaroons as favors to take home.

Poulet Rôti

This classic method for roasting chicken employs spot-on French culinary technique coupled with a rustic farmhouse presentation and is just perfect for a Provincial picnic. Careful basting is the key to success.

PRONOUNCED: POO-LAY ROW-TEE

SERVES: SIX

1   3½-pound chicken
2 teaspoons kosher salt
1 teaspoon freshly ground black pepper
4 Tablespoons unsalted butter, divided
1 Tablespoon vegetable oil
4 to 6 carrots
1 yellow onion
4 medium sized potatoes
½ to 1 cup water
1 bunch watercress

Rinse chicken inside and out and dry with paper toweling. Sprinkle ¼ of the salt inside the cavity, along with a few grinds of pepper, and cut off the fat around the opening to the cavity; discard.

Using your hands, separate the skin from the meat of the bird by inserting one hand between the flap at the bottom of the breasts and working your way up, and the other from the neck, working your way down. *Be very careful to not tear the skin in the process.* Once skin has been separated, rub the meat with a small amount of butter, salt and pepper. Truss the chicken as per instructions that follow.

In a large skillet, melt **2 Tablespoons** of butter with the vegetable oil. When hot (but not smoking) brown the chicken, breast side down. Then turn the chicken as it browns until all sides have been toasted nicely and the entire bird is golden brown. *It will take approximately **20 minutes** to brown entirely.*

Regulate the heat as necessary during this process to prevent scorching the skin. When completely browned, remove to a large roasting pan with a metal cooking rack.

Meanwhile, peel and slice carrots; peel and chop onion. Peel potatoes and cut into uniform-sized quarters. Place vegetables in a large bowl and season with remaining salt and pepper and toss gently to coat.

Place the vegetable mixture into the same skillet the chicken was browned in and

Separating the skin from the meat will result in a much crispier cooked skin because the process allows the rendered fat to escape easier.

Thanks to Robby for teaching me this method!

Bon Appetit!

stir/heat for approximately 5 minutes to coat the vegetable with the remaining fats from the chicken.

Now deglaze the skillet by pouring ⅓ cup of boiling water over the vegetables and stirring and scraping up the flavor packed brown bits from the bottom of the pan as you go.

Preheat oven to 350 degrees.

In the roasting pan, surround chicken with the vegetables and the glaze. *Use care to not overcrowd pan with potatoes and other vegetables or the chicken with stew rather than roast.*

Roast for **1½ hours**, basting every 15 minutes with liquids from the pan while also gently tossing the vegetables.

During the first two bastings, add an additional ¼ cup of water. Then add only enough additional water to keep approximately 1 cup of liquid in the roasting pan throughout the cooking time.

Let it rest! Resting 10 to 15 minutes is essential when roasting any bird or large cut of meat. Resting allows time for the meat to relax and the internal juices to redistribute evenly throughout the meat, which also makes it tastier.

Transfer the chicken to a cutting board and carve.

Bring the juice in the roasting pan to a boil for 30 seconds, then turn off the heat. Whisk the hot juices with remaining Tablespoon of butter, and pour this sauce over the chicken to serve.

Garnish serving platter with the bittersweet flavor of fresh watercress to lift the roasted flavors of the bird.

HOW TO TRUSS A BIRD

A whole bird should be trussed before it is roasted or braised to keep it from drying out during the cooking time. This also ensures an attractive presentation and makes carving much easier.

1) Place the bird, breast side up, in front of you. With a 3-foot long piece of kitchen string, wrap the center of the string under the chicken tail and cross the string securely over the top of the tail.

2) Then press the string under the ends of the drumsticks and cross the string over them tightly. Now catch the string under the pointed end of the breastbone and bring the string over each thigh where it meets the body; hold securely in place.

3) Turn the bird over and bring the two ends of string together at the center of the upper back, capturing the wings and tying them tightly to the body of the bird as you go. Make a knot to secure the truss and trim away any remaining string.

Kickin' Deviled Eggs

A classic with a kick!

SERVES: EIGHT TO TWELVE

8 hard-boiled eggs
½ cup good mayonnaise
½ teaspoon apple cider vinegar
2 teaspoons horseradish mustard
¼ teaspoon kosher salt
⅛ teaspoon freshly ground black pepper

Place eggs in a saucepan or pot large enough to allow only one layer of eggs, then cover with cold water to one inch above the eggs.

Cook over high heat until the water begins to boil, then cover the pan and remove from heat.

Allow eggs to sit covered in hot water for 17 minutes.

Then drain eggs from hot water and place into an ice bath.

To remove shells from eggs, crack under cool running water and carefully peel. Gently dry peeled eggs with paper toweling and slice in half lengthwise. Then pop out the yellow yolk centers into a separate medium-sized bowl.

Place whites of eggs, hollow-side up, onto a serving platter lined with leaf lettuce (to prevent eggs from sliding across the plate).

In a medium-sized bowl, mash the yolks with a fork until crumbly. Add mayonnaise, vinegar, horseradish mustard, salt and pepper; mix well.

Evenly divide yolk mixture into the hollow centers of cooked egg whites by dropping a heaping teaspoon into the center of each half slice.

Sprinkle filled eggs with paprika; serve chilled.

Deviled eggs are good with smoked fish.

For a change of pace try topping eggs with a small piece of either smoked salmon or trout.

Aïoli

No French picnic is complete without "Provençal Butter" AKA: Aïoli! This rich and garlicy mayonnaise is a creamy-smooth sauce when made with a thin drizzle of oil and a whisk. Avoid the temptation to make Aïoli in a food processor, or your sauce will turn into glue. Fresh asparagus is especially good with Aïoli — and very French.

PRONOUNCED: EYE-OH-LEE

Aïoli is made by constant whisking.

To keep your mixing bowl from slipping as you whisk, start by placing a kitchen towel over a small saucepan and setting a metal mixing bowl over the towel. This will allow you to use both hands — one to whisk and one to pour.

Je ne sais quio?

YIELD: ONE-HALF CUP

1 large egg yolk, organically grown

3 cloves garlic, ground

½ teaspoon kosher salt, divided

½ cup good olive oil

¼ teaspoon cayenne pepper

Juice of ½ fresh lemon

¼ teaspoon freshly ground black pepper

Rub garlic cloves against the tip of the tines of a fork to release, then grind the cloves into a paste using a mortar and pestle.

Vigorously whisk egg **yolk,** garlic paste, half of the salt and 2 teaspoons of water to blend.

Continue whisking as you slowly drizzle the oil into this egg mixture, one teaspoonful at a time.

Whisk constantly until the sauce is thick and emulsified.

Stir in the cayenne, then taste.

Season with lemon juice, additional salt and black pepper as necessary to taste.

Consuming raw or undercooked eggs is not advisable for young children, pregnant women or those with certain medical conditions.

Use flash pasteurized raw eggs to avoid salmonella concerns.

ROASTING ASPARAGUS ON THE GRILL

From asparagus to peaches, seasonal fruits & vegetables roasted on the grill have a delicious smoky flavor with an exterior that is crisp and just slightly charred. But the intense heat of the grill can also burn tender veggies.

To protect grilled produce, mix ¼ cup mayonnaise with 1 to 2 teaspoons of olive oil and brush over fruits and vegetables before grilling. The mayonnaise burns off over the flames and does a great job protecting vegetables and fruits alike while cooking.

Grill produce for 4 to 5 minutes until crisp yet tender. Turn veggies and brush again with the mayo mix as you go. Grill fruits & vegetables directly on the grate to get the grill marks.

If you do not have an outdoor grill, vegetables can be roasted in a hot oven. Wash, trim and dress as directed above, then place in a jelly roll pan in 425 degree oven for 5 to 15 minutes (depending on vegetable), turning 1 to 2 times.

Garlic Chips

These slivers of crispy garlic take just a minute to prepare and can elevate grilled asparagus to the next level.

3 to 4 cloves garlic
1 Tablespoon olive oil, cold

Slice garlic cloves very thin lengthwise, like a chip. Then place in a skillet with 1 Tablespoon of olive oil; cook over medium heat until just brown, stirring frequently.

Sprinkle chips onto grilled asparagus and serve.

Fleurs de Courgettes

Lightly battered and fried zucchini flowers are delicate and remarkably flavorful.

PRONOUNCED: FLUR DA CORE-GAY

SERVES: EIGHT TO TWELVE

24 fresh zucchini blossoms

1 quart oil (peanut or sunflower)

3 large egg whites, beaten

12 ounces light beer

1 teaspoon each, kosher salt and freshly ground pepper

¾ cup all-purpose flour

½ cup cornstarch

Fleur de sel

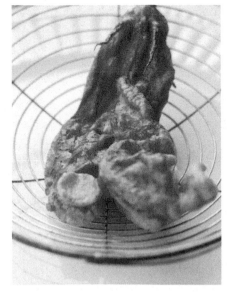

Fried Zucchini Flowers can either be scrumptious and light, or not worth eating.

The secret is to use very fresh flowers and very hot oil.

If desired, place a thin strip of mozzarella cheese into each blossoms before dipping in the batter.

Choose fresh blossoms, not droopy, and do not wash flowers. If blossoms are moist, pat dry or allow to *thoroughly* dry naturally.

In a large pot, heat oil to 350 degrees - hot but not smoking.

Use a candy thermometer to test oil temperature.

In a medium-sized bowl, whisk together the egg **whites** and beer.

Add salt and pepper.

Whisk together the flour and cornstarch, then whisk into egg mixture until a smooth batter is formed.

Dip flowers in the batter, gently shaking off any excess batter before carefully dropping flowers into the hot oil. Fry for just 2 to 3 minutes *total*, flipping once during this time, or until blossoms are golden brown and crispy.

Fry flowers in batches to avoid overcrowding. Drain on a plate lined with salted paper toweling, and immediately season flowers with sea salt.

Fleurs de Courgettes are especially good served immediately, while hot.

French Fruit Tart with Butter Pastry & Vanilla Cream

This incredibly flaky pastry is filled with a sweet vanilla cream filling and topped with seasonal fruits. With every bite you will think you are in Paris! To help ensure your success, see Baking Secrets, Rolling & Baking Pies, p. 358.

SERVES: EIGHT TO TEN

BUTTER PASTRY

A buttery pastry can be hard to work with, but its taste makes mastering this delicate pastry worth the practice.

YIELD: ONE-HALF PIE SHELL

½ cup unsalted butter, cold
1¼ cups all-purpose flour
¼ cup granulated sugar
½ teaspoon kosher salt
1 egg yolk
2 Tablespoons Half and Half cream

Cut cold butter into small cubes and keep in the refrigerator until ready to use. Then, measure all other ingredients and have ready next to the food processor so that you can work seamlessly. Also, combine egg **yolk** and cream before beginning.

In a food processor, place flour, sugar and salt; pulse once or twice to combine. Then add cold butter cubes. Pulse 10 to 15 times.

Then add yolk and cream mixture to flour mixture.

Continue to pulse *just* until butter pieces are the size of peas and the mixture looks like a coarse meal and is beginning to come together.

Do not allow mixture to form into a ball in the machine or it will be tough.

Turn moist meal mixture out onto a clean and dry counter top and knead the dough away from you 3 to 6 times, or just enough to bind the dough together and form it into a ball.

Then gather the dough into a 6-inch ball and pat together well and seal in plastic wrap. Refrigerate **15 to 20 minutes** or until the butter has hardened slightly.

Have a 9-inch tart pan and dough scraper ready; dust counter top and rolling pin lightly with flour.

Flatten the dough into a patty with your hands, then roll from the center out to form an 11-inch circle. Flip the dough every few rolls to prevent it from sticking to the counter (use the dough scraper to loosen pastry from the counter top as necessary), and repair any cracks in the dough by pressing it back together with your fingertips.

Use the rolling pin to help pick up the dough and transfer it to the pan by loosely rolling dough over the pin and raising it up and in. Then center the dough over the tart pan, *being careful to not stretch dough or it will shrink as it cooks.*

Fit the pastry into the pan, pressing gently to fit and fill. Then roll the pin over the top edge of the tart pan. The weight of the rolling pin will trim off the excess dough in a perfectly straight line and alleviate the need to crimp the edges of pastry dough.

Using a fork, prick the dough on the bottom and sides of the pan to prevent air bubbles while baking. **Chill 30 minutes** before baking.

If using this pastry for other recipes, revert to that recipe at this point.

Preheat oven to 375 degrees.

To bake pie shell, cover with a piece of aluminum foil that has been buttered on the bottom side and then gently fitted into the pan. Cover the top side of the foil with *dry beans for the first half of baking time.

Bake 15 minutes, then carefully remove the foil and beans and bake another 5 minutes, or until the bottom of the shell is dry.

VANILLA PASTRY CREAM

2 cups whole milk
Seeds from 2 vanilla bean pods
6 large egg yolks
½ cup granulated sugar
⅓ cup cornstarch
3 ½ Tablespoons unsalted butter

Remove vanilla beans from pods; set aside. (See p. 388, *Vanilla.*)

In a small saucepan, bring milk, vanilla beans and pods to a boil. Then turn down the heat and let simmer 5 to 10 minutes.

Remove pods; discard.

In a medium saucepan, whisk egg **yolks** with sugar and cornstarch until thick and creamy, then place on the stove on medium heat.

Unbaked pastry can be frozen for one to two months.

Freeze the ball of dough by first wrapping in waxed paper and then sealing in a plastic baggie. Thaw dough in the refrigerator when ready to use.

Beans can be re-used to cook other pastry shells, but are no longer edible.

Egg yolks should always be "tempered" by mixing them with a small amount of hot liquid before incorporating them into a hot sauce. Unless the sauce is bound by flour, do not let it boil again after the yolks have been added or they will curdle.

Continue whisking while slowly adding ¾ cup vanilla milk to temper the eggs. Once incorporated, add remaining milk and whisk vigorously.

Continue cooking and whisking until the mixture boils, approximately 1 to 2 minutes.

Allow cream to sit 5 minutes, then whisk in the butter one Tablespoon at a time, and continue to whisk until cream is silky.

Remove cream to a bowl and cover with plastic wrap. Push the plastic wrap down until it is touching the surface of the cream to prevent a skin from forming. Refrigerate cream until cold.

Once well-chilled, whisk the cream into a baked and cooled pastry shell and gently top with rows of fresh fruits: From the outer rim to the center, place a row of blackberries; then place a row of blueberries; then a row of apricot halves; with a mound of cherries in the middle.

FRESH FRUIT TOPPING

These fruits were chosen because they are in season in June, but this tart can be made with any fresh fruits. Strawberries are especially delicious in the spring, and pears or apples are a good choice when made in the fall.

¼ cup blackberries
¼ cup blueberries
¼ cup apricots, halved
¼ cup bing cherries, pitted

APRICOT GLAZE

The glaze will keep your tart from drying out as well as provide an extra punch of sweetness.

⅓ cup apricot jam
1 teaspoon water

Gently boil jam with water while stirring just until dissolved. Allow to cool.

Glaze assembled tart, covering the pastry shell, berries and any exposed cream.

Classic French Macaroons –
Ooh la la!

These light confections of sugar, ground almond and egg whites can be colored and filled with a myriad of flavors and are quintessential French. There are many options for the filling, and I have provided my favorite three – lemon curd, raspberry, and classic vanilla. You will need a pastry bag fitted with a half-inch tip to make these cookies.

YIELD: TWENTY-FOUR MACAROONS, EIGHT IN EACH COLOR/FLAVOR

THE MERINGUES — LIGHT ALMOND COOKIES

1¾ cups, plus 2 Tablespoons powdered sugar
1¼ cup, plus 2 Tablespoons almond flour
4 large egg whites, at room temperature
¼ cup granulated sugar

SECRETS TO SUCCESSFUL MACAROONS

Line three cookie sheets with parchment paper; set aside.

Sift almond flour with the powdered sugar onto a sheet of waxed paper; set aside.

In a large bowl with an electric mixer, using a spotlessly clean bowl and beaters, whip egg **whites** until foamy and *soft* peaks form, approximately 1 to 2 minutes.

It is easiest to separate eggs while cold, but essential to whip egg whites at room temperature.

Slowly add 1 Tablespoon granulated sugar and continue to whip for 1 minute. Repeat this process three times, incorporating all remaining sugar and whipping between each addition.

Now, whip the whites for another 4 to 8 minutes, or until semi-stiff peaks form and whites are glossy.

Remove the bowl from the stand mixer, and with a large rubber spatula gently fold half of the powdered sugar mix into the whites by hand. Once this is incorporated, fold in the remaining sugar mixture until just combined, scraping the sides of the bowl as you go.

Your whites will deflate a bit during this process, but that is okay.

At this point, divide batter into thirds:

Macaroons are not difficult, but can be finicky. For greater success: Let the raw cookie rounds sit at room temperature for thirty minutes before you bake them; use care to not over mix the meringue or the batter; and use older eggs if possible. It is also best to avoid making meringues on a humid day.

Serve the same day cookies are made for best results.

Color ⅓ yellow, to use with the curd;

Color ⅓ pink, to use with raspberry buttercream;

Leave ⅓ without color to use with classic vanilla buttercream.

If you still end up with a peak on cookies, just dampen your index finger and swirl the batter gently until flattened. Also, gently pop the cookie sheet on the counter one to two times to flatten any small peaks and deflate any possible air bubbles.

Fill a pastry bag fitted with a ½-inch tip with one third of the cookie batter and pipe meringue onto the parchment paper in uniform rounds. Rounds should be small, 1½-inches in diameter and ¼ to ½-inch thick.

Hold the pastry bag directly above the baking sheet and pipe straight down, perpendicularly. With a flick of your wrist, cut off the piping when finished forming each cookie, to avoid having a peak.

Repeat with two remaining thirds of batter, cleaning bag and tip between each color. *You should have sixteen rounds in each color (eight cookies).*

Let meringue cookies rest for 20 to 30 minutes at room temperature, or until they no longer feel tacky before baking.

Preheat oven to 325 degrees and position two racks at the bottom third and top third of the oven.

Place two cookie sheets into the oven, then immediately turn temperature down to 300 degrees. Bake for 8 minutes, then rotate the sheets. Then continue to bake another 5 to 7 minutes or until the meringues are pale golden in color.

Cool the cookies completely on the baking sheets set over wire cooling racks.

To bake the third sheet of cookies, bring the oven temperature back up to 325 degrees. When the oven is at temperature, repeat the process.

Remove cooled meringues from the sheets and pair cookies by size and color.

Fill cookies by using a piping bag fitted with a 1-inch tip. Pipe approximately 1½ teaspoons of filling onto the bottom side of half of the cookies, then top with the matching cookies, bottom side down.

LEMON CURD FILLING

When making fillings for macaroons, remember that they should be thick enough to stand up well between the two cookie layers.

¼ cup unsalted butter

⅓ cup, plus 1 Tablespoon granulated sugar

¼ cup juice of fresh lemon

1½ Tablespoons zest of lemon

⅛ teaspoon salt

3 large egg yolks

8 fresh raspberries

Melt butter in a medium-sized saucepan over medium heat. Remove the pan from the heat and whisk in the sugar, lemon juice, zest and salt. Then whisk in the **yolks** until smooth.

Return the pan to medium heat and cook curd, whisking constantly, until the mixture becomes nice and thick, 5 to 6 minutes. *To check if curd is thick enough, dip a wooden spoon into it and draw your finger across the back of the spoon; your finger should leave a path.* Be sure to not allow the mixture to boil in the process. Refrigerate curd covered, until ready to use.

For an extra burst of flavor, place a fresh raspberry in the center of curd filling before topping with the second cookie.

BUTTERCREAM FILLING — RASPBERRY & VANILLA

1 cup unsalted butter
3 cups powdered sugar
Beans from 1 vanilla bean pod
⅛ teaspoon salt
½ cup raspberry jam

In a large bowl with an electric mixer, beat butter until creamy.

Add powdered sugar, extract and salt and continue to cream until well incorporated and fluffy.

Divide buttercream in half.

Mix ½ of the buttercream with ½ cup of raspberry jam to fill the pink cookies.

Mix the other half with the beans from a vanilla bean pod to fill the plain cookies.

THE COOL OASIS OF A
TRANQUIL GARDEN CAN BE
ONE OF THE NICEST PLACES
TO ENTERTAIN. WHEN THE
WEATHER IS BALMY, IT IS
FUN TO SET A TABLE THAT
COMPLEMENTS WHAT'S IN
BLOOM IN THE GARDEN AND
TREAT FRIENDS AND FAMILY
TO A MEAL OF SUMMERY
DELIGHTS OUT OF DOORS.

I LIKE TO KEEP THE MENU
LIGHT BUT FILLING WHEN
EATING OUTSIDE, WITH
SOMETHING COOL AND
SWEET FOR DESSERT.

A SUMMER NIGHT IN JUNE
Garden Party
FOR 8

Zucchini Corn Cakes with Crème Fraîche & Kelp Caviar

Grilled White Fish Tacos with Roasted Salsa
Roasted Beets in Puff Pastry with Mascarpone & Lemon Zest
Texas Caviar

Mama's Ice Cream Sandwiches

RECIPES

ZUCCHINI CORN CAKES WITH CRÈME FRAÎCHE & KELP CAVIAR

GRILLED WHITE FISH TACOS

ROASTED SALSA

ROASTED BEETS IN PUFF PASTRY WITH MASCARPONE & LEMON ZEST

TEXAS CAVIAR

MAMA'S ICE CREAM SANDWICHES

Serve a light, fruity, well-chilled Chenin Blanc or Riesling *with the grilled fish.*

TIME LINE
Alfresco!

A garden party is casual and served buffet style with a pretty dining table set outside. Be easy going and relaxed and your guests will be too.

For entertaining secrets see Kids Party Games, *p. 14.*

TWO DAYS BEFORE
Make Texas Caviar; refrigerate.

THE DAY BEFORE
Chill wines. Make ice cubes with flowers to have in an outside ice bucket   *See* Chilling with Style, *p. 50.*
Remove garlic clove from caviar mixture; discard clove and return caviar to refrigerator.
Make ice cream sandwiches; wrap individually in waxed paper and freeze.
Roast beets in muffin tins; cool, cover and refrigerate.
Make roasted salsa; refrigerate.

THE MORNING OF THE PARTY
Thaw puff pastry in refrigerator.
Prepare all toppings for tacos, place in serving bowls, cover and refrigerate.
Make batter for zucchini corn cakes; cover and set aside.
Set up a bar service for wine and appetizers that includes needed glasses, small plates and napkins.
Set the garden or patio table for dining.

FORTY-FIVE MINUTES BEFORE GUESTS ARRIVE
Bring beets to room temperature, then finish preparation of pastries, but wait to bake.
Fry corn cakes & top with cream and caviar, then plate to serve as a passed appetizer.

UPON ARRIVAL
Serve wine from a "stylish" bucket of floral ice cubes, with the cakes.
Put beet pastries in the oven to bake; *set a timer so you will not forget them!*

WHEN READY TO EAT
Grill fish and toast tortillas. Set out platters of fish, tortillas and the toppings, with a bowl of roasted salsa.
Plate and serve beet pasties hot.
Set out Texas Caviar. Pour wine.

FOR DESSERT
Serve Ice Cream Sandwiches straight from the freezer on a large tray with paper napkins.

Zucchini Corn Cakes with Crème Fraîche & Kelp Caviar

A tiny dollop of Kelp Caviar turns these zucchini and corn cakes into and elegant treat.

YIELD: TWELVE TINY CAKES

1 cup zucchini, grated
1 cup fresh corn kernels
1 cup all-purpose flour
1 teaspoon kosher salt
½ teaspoon baking powder
½ teaspoon baking soda
1 large egg
¼ cup milk
1½ Tablespoons unsalted butter
½ cup crème fraîche
½ 3.5 ounce jar kelp caviar

With a box grater, shred zucchini; set aside. Remove kernels from corn cob(s).

Onto a sheet of waxed paper, sift the flour, salt, powder and soda; set aside.

In a medium bowl, beat eggs with milk. Add zucchini and corn kernels and fold to combine. Then add flour mixture and fold by hand to incorporate.

In a large skillet over medium-high heat, melt half of the butter and fry pancakes in two batches of six for 2 minutes per side. Add remaining butter to skillet to fry the second batch. Cakes will be golden brown on the edges with a cooked center when done.

When ready to serve, top each warm cake with a dollop of approximately 1 teaspoon of crème fraîche and ½ teaspoon of Kelp Caviar.

Cakes can be held in a 200 degree oven to keep warm before adding the toppings and serving.

Kelp Caviar is a seaweed-based delicacy that tastes of the ocean but contains no fish roe. This product is great for Vegetarians!
See p. 376.

Grilled White Fish Tacos with Roasted Salsa

Light and spicy, these grilled white fish tacos served with a roasted carrots and a salsa of adobe sauce and chipotle peppers are served with peppery radishes and crunchy red cabbage. They are both light and filling, and just right for an alfresco meal.

SERVES: EIGHT

ROASTED SALSA

4 roma tomatoes, cut into wedges

1 yellow onion, cut into wedges

2 cloves garlic, peeled

2 to 3 carrots

½ cup olive oil

½ teaspoon kosher salt

1 cup cilantro leaves

4 teaspoons chipotle pepper in adobo sauce

Choose plump, firm heads of garlic that are free of sprouts and dark spots.

Garlic will stay fresh for months when stored in a cool, dark place - but not in the refrigerator.
See p. 373.

Preheat oven to 450 degrees.

Peel and slice carrots into quarters lengthwise, and then cut lengths in half.

Place tomatoes, onion, carrots and garlic on a jelly roll pan lined with foil. Drizzle with 1 Tablespoon olive oil; sprinkle with salt. Roast for 25 minutes, or until browned. Cool slightly.

In a food processor, place roasted tomatoes, onion, garlic with cilantro and chipotle pepper; process.

Gradually add the remaining olive oil while the processor is running and purée until smooth. Remove salsa from processor bowl to a serving bowl; cover and chill until ready to serve.

Place roasted carrots in serving dish and cover with foil to keep warm; set aside.

GRILLED WHITE FISH

2 pounds fresh or frozen white fish (Cod, Halibut or Sea Bass)

2 Tablespoons olive oil

2 teaspoons ground cumin

2 teaspoons chili powder

1 teaspoon kosher salt

½ teaspoon freshly ground black pepper

Preheat grill.

Cut fish into fillets ½-inch thick. Mix cumin, chili powder, salt and pepper. Brush fish with oil on both sides and rub with seasoning mix. Grill fillets uncovered over medium heat for 4 to 5 minutes per side. *Turn only once.* Fish should flake easily when done.

TACOS

16 6-inch corn tortillas
1 cup sour cream
4 to 6 radishes, sliced thin
4 cups red cabbage, shredded
4 scallions, chopped (including green parts)
2 cups black olives, roughly chopped
1½ to 2 cups cheddar cheese, grated
Juice of 2 limes
1 bunch cilantro leaves

Toast tortillas on the grill for just 30 seconds per side while fish is grilling. Remove from the grill and cover with foil to keep warm and soft.

Serve fish tacos by filling shells with cheese first, then fish and roasted carrot lengths, and then top with salsa and sour cream, radishes, red cabbage, green onions and olives. Squeeze fresh lime juice over the filled tacos and garnish with a few leaves of fresh cilantro.

Roasted Beets in Puff Pastry with Mascarpone & Lemon Zest

Beets are especially delicious roasted, which makes them as sweet as candy. Topped with creamed mascarpone cream cheese in a puff of buttery pastry, and each bite of these treats is both sweet and savory. Tarts do not keep well though, so plan to bake the pastry just before ready to serve.

PRONOUNCED: MAHS-CAR-POH-NAY

YIELD: TWELVE INDIVIDUAL TARTS

4 medium beets
6 Tablespoons olive oil
Zest of 2 lemons
2 teaspoon Himalayan pink salt
1 teaspoon freshly ground black pepper
1 17.3 ounce package frozen puff pastry, thawed
4 ounces mascarpone cheese
4 teaspoons fresh thyme leaves
3 teaspoons hazelnuts, toasted

You are actually forming a small cup or bowl with the pastry that will line the outer rim of the muffin cups while baking and hold the beets when inverted. Gently lift the center of pasty up just a bit as you work to help avoid bunching of the pastry edges when tucking them down. When the edges are in place, smooth and adjust the top of the pastry (and beets underneath) to be as flat and uniform as possible so that the cups will sit upright on your plate when inverted. It's a little tricky, but puff pastry is very easy to work with so keep gently adjusting (while trying not to stretch the dough), with the visual of a pastry "cup" in mind.

Preheat oven to 400 degrees.

Thaw pastry in refrigerator per package instructions. Peel beets; slice and cube into ½ inch pieces. Zest lemons; set aside. Toast hazelnuts and remove hull.

In a large bowl, combine oil, zest, salt and pepper. Add beets and toss to coat well.

Coat a 12-muffin tin well with cooking spray; add beet mixture, dividing evenly into the twelve cups. Cover tin tightly with foil to encourage steaming, and bake 25 minutes or until beets are tender.

On a lightly floured surface, roll pastry into two 12 x 10-inch (exact) rectangles. Using a 4-inch round pastry cutter (or glass/bowl) cut pastry into 12 circles. Place on a cookie sheet covered with parchment paper.

Re-roll any pastry scraps and cut into leaf shapes to garnish finished tarts. Chill all 12 rounds and leaf shapes until ready to bake.

Mix mascarpone and thyme; set aside at room temperature.

When beets have cooked through, remove from the oven and, while still in muffin tin, top each beet-filled cup with an unbaked pastry round. Tuck the sides of the pastry down into the cups (approximately ½-inch) to form a bowl shape when the cups are inverted. Use the blade of a knife to help tuck the pastry straight down the sides of each muffin cup.

Once the pastry is in place, bake for 15 to 20 minutes, or until puffy and golden brown.

Bake pastry "leaves" at the same time on a separate sheet of buttered foil.

Cool cups just 1 to 2 minutes, then invert onto serving platter by running the edge of a knife around the rim of each cup to loosen, then gently lifting pastry cups (and beets) out of the tin with the help of a fork. You will likely need to re-assemble the beets before adding the mascarpone as some may fall out when removing from the tin – that is fine.

Dollop 1 to 2 teaspoons of the cheese and thyme mixture to top of warm beets.

Garnish each tart with lemon curls and/or a pinch of chopped hazelnuts and serve warm.

When using puff pastry shop for the kind made with butter, and thaw pastry all day or overnight in the refrigerator to avoid dough that is sticky on one side.

See p. 383.

Texas Caviar

Make this caviar two days before serving. The longer it marinates, the better it gets.

SERVES: TEN TO TWELVE

1 15-ounce can black-eyed peas, rinsed
1 4-ounce can green chilies
1 teaspoon vegetable oil
¼ cup warm vinegar
1 teaspoon granulated sugar
1 clove garlic
¼ onion, sliced thin and chopped
½ teaspoon kosher salt
Freshly ground black pepper

Chop chilies, then combine with all other ingredients and mix thoroughly.

Store in a sealed container in the refrigerator for at least two days.

Remove the garlic clove after one day. Stir every 3 to 4 hours as the "caviar" marinates.

Mama's Ice Cream Sandwiches

These irresistible summer sandwiches are made from chocolate cookies that are crisp on the edges and chewy in the center - and filled to the brim with ice cream.

YIELD: TEN SANDWICHES

1¼ cups unsalted butter, softened
2 cups granulated sugar
2 large eggs
2 teaspoons pure vanilla extract
2 cups all-purpose flour
¾ cup good quality cocoa
1 teaspoon baking soda
½ teaspoon salt
½ gallon ice cream

Preheat oven to 350 degrees. Line two cookie sheets with parchment paper.

In a large bowl with an electric mixer, beat butter at medium speed until creamy. Gradually add sugar, beating well. Add eggs and vanilla, beating until well blended.

Sift flour with cocoa, soda and salt; gradually add to the butter mixture, beating at low speed just until blended after each addition.

Scoop dough into tablespoon-sized balls and drop onto cookie sheets. Use care to not over-crowd your cookie sheet, as these cookies spread and flatten quite a bit during baking.

Bake for 18 minutes, or until lightly browned and crisp around the edges.

Place sheets on wire cooling racks to cool completely.

Match cookies by size and shape in pairs, then fill with vanilla bean and/or coffee ice cream using a large ice cream scoop.

Gently place a second cookie on top of the ice cream scoop, press gently, then wrap sandwiches in waxed paper and return to the freezer for 3 to 4 hours to set.

THE SPIRIT OF THE GREAT UNITED STATE IS WHAT THE FOURTH IS ALL ABOUT. A RED, WHITE AND BLUE THEME WITH PLENTY OF AMERICAN FLAGS AND SPARKLERS WILL SET THE TONE FOR A HOT JULY DAY THAT SEEMS TO MELT INTO NIGHT. THIS HOME-SPUN MENU OF ALL-AMERICAN FOODS LIKE FRIED CHICKEN AND BAKED BEANS WILL BE JUST THE TICKET WHILE WAITING FOR THE SPARKLERS TO BE LIT AND THE FIREWORK SHOW TO BEGIN.

Independence Day Lawn Party

FOR 8

Front Porch Lemonade & **Blackberry Fizz**

Fried Chicken
Stuffed Lakeside Baguettes
The Bomb.com Baked Beans

Blackberry Rhubarb Chess Pie
Minty Sugar Cookies & **Old Fashioned Tea Cakes**
with **Lady Bug Pops** *for the Kids*

RECIPES

FRONT PORCH
LEMONADE

BLACKBERRY FIZZ

FRIED CHICKEN

STUFFED LAKESIDE
BAGUETTES

THE BOMB.COM
BAKED BEANS

BLACKBERRY
RHUBARB CHESS
PIE

MINTY SUGAR
COOKIES

OLD FASHIONED
TEA CAKES

LADY BUG POPS

Serve a buttery
Chardonnay
to emphasize the
succulent fried
chicken, and
Sauvignon Blanc
with the goat cheese
and veggie baguette.

163

TIME LINE
American the Beautiful

Serve this meal in three parts, buffet style, so guests can serve themselves and come back for more if they wish throughout the long afternoon. Arrange a separate area for drinks and have plenty of ice on hand. And don't forget to invite the kids indoors to choose a popsicle from the freezer while waiting for the meal to be served! *For entertaining secrets see* Entertaining with Children, *p. 14 and* The Meaning of Flowers & Symbolic Herbs, *p. 48-9.*

ONE WEEK BEFORE THE FOURTH

Make sugar cookies and/or tea cakes and freeze.

TWO DAYS BEFORE

Assess outdoor spaces and determine where food tables and seating should be located.

Check to make sure there is plenty of sunscreen and mosquito repellent on hand, along with a few sweaters and shawls for guests to borrow in case the night gets cool.

Make popsicles, wrap individually in wax paper, and freeze.

THE DAY BEFORE

Chill wines. Make Lemonade; refrigerate.

Save juiced lemon rinds (to use as vases for mini bouquets) by wrapping tightly in plastic wrap and refrigerating. See notes with Lemonade recipe for full instructions.

Make butter pastry; refrigerate. Assemble baked beans; refrigerate to bake the next day.

Soak chicken pieces in buttermilk for 8 hours or overnight.

THE MORNING OF THE PARTY

Assemble pie and bake. Fry chicken; cover and refrigerate. Then cool and store grease, and clean the stove top well before guests arrive.

Assemble baguettes; refrigerate as instructed at the end of the recipe.

Set up an assembly for the blackberry fizzes so that they can be made quickly and effortlessly.

Set the patio dining table in reds, whites and blues.

Make mini bouquets out of lemon rind shells. Remove cookies and/or tea cakes from freezer, plate and seal with plastic wrap until ready to serve.

TWO HOURS BEFORE THE FUN BEGINS

Bake the beans and cover with foil to keep warm and moist.

THIRTY MINUTES BEFORE

Bring chicken to room temperature. Have popsicles ready.

UPON ARRIVAL

Serve lemonade and fizzes over ice.

WHEN READY TO EAT

Set out chicken and beans. Slice baguettes and plate with a green garnish of fresh herbs. Serve wine.

FOR DESSERT

Serve cookies or tea cakes and pie.

Front Porch Lemonade

When I think of lemonade it is synonymous with sitting with my Grandma on her front porch after helping tend her garden on Findley Street all morning long. There is nothing quite so refreshing as a glass of sweet, tart and cold lemonade on a hot summer day when the shoes have been kicked off and the work of the day is behind you!

SERVES: SIX TO EIGHT

1½ cups fresh lemon juice
1¼ cups granulated sugar
½ cup boiling water
4½ cups ice-cold & filtered water
Lemon slices and fresh mint

Combine sugar and boiling water; stir to dissolve sugar, then let mixture cool completely.

In a large pitcher, add fresh lemon juice, cooled sugar water and ice-cold water. Mix well.

Chill for **2 to 4 hours.**

Serve over ice with fresh lemon slices and mint leaves to garnish glasses.

You will need 12 lemons to equal 1½ cups of lemon juice.

Crushed-Mint Lemonade

Add a small bunch of fresh mint to the sugar and boiling water mixture. Once cooled, run through a fine-mesh strainer before adding to lemon juice and cold water.

Honeyed Lemonade

Substitute 1¼ cups of sugar with ½ cup honey, ¼ cup fresh ginger (peeled and minced very fine) and ½ cups sugar.

Raspberry Lemonade

Purée 8 ounces of frozen raspberries (in syrup) and strain; add to mixture above.

WHAT TO DO WITH ALL THOSE LEMONS?

It would be a shame to throw away 12 lemon rinds when they make such cute flower vases for the table and outdoors nooks! Rather than slicing lemons in half to squeeze out the juice for lemonade , trim off just the top ¼ of the lemon rind and use a lemon juicer to gently remove the juice and pulp from the interior. Use care as you squeeze to not distort the shape of the fruit in the process. Fill these little gems with tiny fresh cut flowers and/or herbs and place at each place setting on your table, or cluster for a charming centerpiece. You may need to trim a tiny bit of peel from the bottom of the "vase" to ensure it sits upright on the table.

The lemons shown have been filled with red roses in the spirit of the Fourth of July. These tiny vase are also very pretty filled with yellow roses on a monochromatic table.

Blackberry Fizz

This refreshing cocktail of blackberries and ginger is a great way to celebrate life, liberty and the pursuit of happiness!

YIELD: TWO COCKTAILS

2 jiggers pear-infused vodka, frozen
1 jigger blackberry liqueur

Juice of 1 lime
Ginger ale
Crushed ice
Fresh mint

Combine vodka, liqueur and lime juice with crushed ice in a cocktail shaker and shake for **30 seconds**.

Pour cold vodka mixture into two highball glasses filled ¾ full with ice.

Top off glasses with ginger ale; garnish with a sprig of fresh mint and a skewer of fresh blackberries.

I use Leopold Brothers Rocky Mountain Blackberry Liqueur – which is also delicious over vanilla bean ice cream!

Fried Chicken

This fried chicken uses a time-honored cooking method that is just delicious! Start preparation at least 9 hours before planning to serve, because the chicken needs to soak in buttermilk to ensure those great southern-fried results. I also recommend frying the chicken an hour or two before the party so that it is ready when the guests arrive - and you've had plenty of time to clean up and remove the lingering smell of fried foods from the air. Keep chicken refrigerated until ready to serve, if holding for more than an hour.

SERVES: EIGHT

4 pounds organic chicken pieces (breasts, thighs and legs)

1½ cups buttermilk

1 12-ounce jar cherry peppers, partially drained

1 cup all-purpose flour

2 Tablespoons parmesan cheese, grated

1 teaspoon freshly ground black pepper

3 quarts vegetable oil

Chicken pieces should sit on the bottom of the pan, not float in the oil, to ensure extra crispness. See Fry, p. 373, for more tips of fried foods.

In a large bowl, pour the buttermilk over the chicken pieces and stir in the cherry peppers. Allow chicken to soak in this buttermilk mixture for **8 hours,** refrigerated.

On a large platter combine the flour, grated cheese and pepper.

In batches, dredge the soaked chicken pieces through the flour mixture to coat. Then set on a cooling rack for approximately **20 minutes** before frying.

In a large skillet, heat 1 to 1½-inches of oil to 365 degrees. When the oil is at temperature, fry the chicken in batches for approximately 10 minutes per side, or until golden brown.

Remove chicken to paper towels that have been lightly salted to drain; immediately season/salt chicken.

Serve while hot and crispy, or cold – both ways are good!

KEEP PICNIC FOODS CHILLED

When entertaining out of doors, the rule of thumb is to never consume foods that have been at room temperature (59 to 86 degrees) for more than four hours.

Keep picnic foods refrigerated until ready to serve, keep covered while out of doors, and return to the refrigerator as soon as possible after serving.

Your health will always be more important than throwing out foods that are no longer safe to consume.

Stuffed Lakeside Baguettes

Prepare this large vegetable sandwich early in the morning, because the flavors blend as the day wears on and the sandwich just keeps getting better and better. The secret to the delicious filling is in roasting the peppers and toasting the baguette. The crunchy edges of the toasted bread remain crisp even after several hours and provide a terrific contrast to the soft vegetable filling and creamy goat cheese.

SERVES: EIGHT

1 yellow pepper

1 red pepper

½ cup fresh parsley, coarsely chopped

1 15-ounce can large pitted black olives

½ pint cherry tomatoes, halved

½ bunch scallions, sliced thin (including green parts)

1 8-ounce jar capers, drained

Freshly ground black pepper & Kosher salt to taste

4 hard-boiled eggs

1 French baguette loaf

¼ cup vinaigrette dressing

8 ounces goat cheese, softened

Hard boil eggs, cool, peel and slice lengthwise per instructions on p. 372.

Make vinaigrette dressing per recipe(s) on p. 103.

Roast peppers by broiling them whole over an open flame, as close to the heat as possible, until skin is well browned/blackened. Then place in a brown paper bag with the top crumpled closed until they are cool enough to handle, approximately 20 minutes.

Peel peppers, leaving some of the charred skin intact; discard the rest of the skin, *but do not rinse.* Cut peppers in half and seed; then cut into long, thin strips and then into thirds, discarding any liquid. Place in a large bowl.

Drain and coarsely chop the olives; halve tomatoes and slice scallions; add. Coarsely chop the parsley and add with the capers; salt and pepper vegetables to taste.

Add *just enough* dressing to coat the vegetable mixture and stir to combine. Allow vegetables to marinate while you prepare the baguette loaf.

Preheat oven to 350 degrees.

Cut baguette in half lengthwise using a serrated knife. Leave a "hinge" on one side. Scoop out the middle of the loaf.

Save the removed bread and freeze it to use to make homemade bread crumbs on another day.

Leave a little bread in place along the edges of each loaf so the filling does not leak out.

Brush the insides of the bread shell gently with *just enough* dressing to cover, then lightly toast in the oven for 5 to 7 minutes. Remove bread from the oven, and allow loaf to cool.

Pack marinated vegetables into the toasted loaf. Place egg slices over the vegetables and sprinkle with a little more salt and pepper.

Close loaf and wrap tightly with plastic wrap; refrigerate, egg side down.

Just before serving, spread the goat cheese onto the inside of the top half of the baguette. Close loaf and slices on the diagonal into 8 pieces to serve.

The Bomb.com Baked Beans

The combination of beans with beer and brown sugar make each bite of these baked beans an unexpected wowser!

SERVES: EIGHT TO TEN

1 32-ounce can great northern beans, drained

1 16-ounce can cannellini beans, drained

1 16-ounce can pinto beans, drained

½ yellow onion, chopped

1 serrano chili pepper, seeded & minced

½ green pepper, chopped

3 to 4 cloves garlic, minced

¾ cup brown sugar, packed

4 Tablespoons ketchup

1 Tablespoon dijon-style mustard

6 ounces dark beer

1 teaspoon cholula hot sauce

3 strips applewood smoked bacon

When measuring brown sugar, always lightly pack the sugar into the measuring cup or spoon to deflate and ensure a more accurate measurement.

Preheat oven to 350 degrees. Butter a 9 x 11-inch baking dish

In a large bowl, add all ingredients except bacon and mix to combine well; pour into prepared dish.

Top beans with bacon slices that have been cut in half and bake approximately **1½ to 2 hours**, or until beans are bubbly and bacon is very crisp. Mixture should be thick and syrupy.

Blackberry Rhubarb Chess Pie

Big juicy blackberries are combined with tart rhubarb and baked into a sugary cream making a scrumptious pie.

SERVES: EIGHT

PASTRY

1 recipe Butter Pastry

(See p. 146.)

FILLING

2 cups rhubarb, sliced
1 cup blackberries, whole
1¼ cups granulated sugar
4 large eggs, lightly beaten
½ cup heavy cream
¼ cup unsalted butter, melted and cooled
Juice of 1 lemon
Juice of ½ lime
1 Tablespoon corn starch
1 Tablespoon finely ground corn meal
1 teaspoon pure vanilla extract
¼ teaspoon salt
Freshly ground nutmeg

Roll pastry and place in a pie plate, then prick with a fork; chill for 20 minutes.

Preheat oven to 375 degrees.

Bake chilled shell for 8 minutes with a smaller pie tin on top of it to prevent puffing. Then remove the smaller plate and continue baking shell for an additional 6 minutes.

Meanwhile, arrange the rhubarb slices on a baking sheet, and bake alongside the pastry shell for 10 minutes.

Remove rhubarb from the oven and combine with the blackberries; sprinkle with ¼ cup sugar; toss. Set aside to cool.

In a food processor, pulse eggs. Then add the remaining cup of sugar with the cream, butter, juices, corn starch, corn meal, extract and salt. Pulse to combine well.

Place fruits into the partially baked pie shell and evenly distribute. Then pour the egg mixture over the fruit pieces, and dust the top of the filling lightly with nutmeg along with a sprinkling of granulated sugar.

Bake 25 minutes, using a pie shield to protect the crust from over-browning.

Then remove the pie shield and bake pie an additional 5 to 10 minutes, or until the center is set and the crust is lightly browned.

Cool completely before serving.

This pie is best with fresh in-season fruits, but if not available use frozen.

Minty Sugar Cookies

What could be better than a soft cookie studded with fresh summery mint and sprinkled with sugar?

YIELD: THIRTY-SIX FLOWER SHAPED COOKIES

1 cup unsalted butter, softened
1¼ cups granulated sugar
1 large egg
½ cup crème fraîche
¼ teaspoon mint extract
¼ cup fresh mint leaves, minced
4 cups all-purpose flour
1 teaspoon baking powder
½ teaspoon baking soda
¼ teaspoon salt
Additional granulated sugar
Un-blanched almond slices

In a large bowl with an electric mixer, beat butter, sugar and egg at medium speed until light and fluffy, approximately 3 minutes.

At low speed, mix in the crème fraîche and mint extract until smooth. Fold in the mint leaves by hand.

Also by hand, gradually fold in 2 cups of flour that has been whisked with baking powder, soda and salt to combine. Fold in just enough of the remaining flour to form a stiff dough, being careful to not over mix.

Divide the dough into four equal parts; wrap each part in waxed paper and refrigerate for **1 hour.**

Preheat oven to 375 degrees. Lightly butter three cookie sheets.

On a clean, lightly floured surface, roll dough (one section at a time) until ¼-inch thick. With a 2 to 3-inch flower-shaped cookie cutter, cut out cookies and place them on a baking sheet.

Reroll trimmings and cut more cookies, using care to avoid over-handling cookie dough as much as possible. *Be sure to roll dough to a consistent thickness each time to ensure cookies bake evenly.*

Lightly sprinkle each cookie with granulated sugar, and gently press an almond slice in the center of each cookie before baking.

Bake 8 to 10 minutes, or until golden brown around the edges. Remove to wire rack to cool.

Blanched almonds have had the skin removed from the nut; un-blanched almonds have not.

Use un-blanched almonds to top these cookies for the added colors of the brown skin and white nut.

Fresh mint is a must in these cookies!

Old Fashioned Tea Cakes

These cake-like sugar cookies are meant to be served on the front porch with friends and lemonade.

YIELD: TWENTY-FOUR LARGE ROUNDS

1 cup crisco shortening
1½ cups granulated sugar
3 large eggs
4 cups all-purpose flour
2 teaspoons baking powder
1 teaspoon baking soda
½ teaspoon salt
¼ cup buttermilk
1¼ teaspoons almond extract

In a large bowl with an electric mixer, cream shortening and sugar until light and fluffy, approximately 3 minutes. Add eggs and continue to cream.

Whisk dry ingredients (flour, powder, soda and salt) together. Mix dry ingredients with butter mixture alternately with buttermilk.

Fold in extract and incorporate by hand until combined.

Divide dough into 3 to 4 sections, wrap each in waxed paper and chill for approximately **1 hour**.

Preheat oven to 350 degrees.

Roll out cookies and cut with a large (2½-inch round) cookie cutter with a decorative crimped edge. Place cookies on a buttered cookie sheet. Sprinkle each cookie generously with granulated sugar, and bake for 15 minutes, or until lightly browned at the edges and puffy.

Lady Bug Pops

These naturally sweet popsicles look just like tiny lady bugs and are a delightful treat for children. I like to have these on hand as a pre-meal snack (that won't spoil an appetite) for the kids, who often have a hard time waiting until the grown-ups are ready to eat.

YIELD: FIFTEEN TINY POPS

2 cups fresh strawberries
Juice of 1 orange
Juice of ½ lime
2 Tablespoons lavender honey
½ to 1 cup fresh blueberries
Ice cube tray
15 Popsicle sticks

Wash and hull strawberries then chop into uniform quarters.

In a food processor, add strawberries, juices and honey, and purée until smooth.

Add fruit mixture to ice cube trays, filling each compartment approximately ¾ full. Drop 3 to 4 blueberries into each compartment.

Freeze pops for **1 to 2 hours** until partially set.

Then insert popsicle sticks into each compartment.

Freeze an additional **4 to 5 hours**, or until well set.

Neighbors, Cameron and E.B. *love Lady Bug Pops!*

Lady Bug Pops are made with fresh berries, honey and the sunny flavor of orange – the leading lady of citrus.

THERE IS NOTHING MORE FUN THAN HOSTING A ROOM FULL OF LOVELY YOUNG WOMEN WHO HAVE COME FROM FAR AND WIDE TO CELEBRATE A MUTUAL FRIEND.

A BRIDE'S MAIDS LUNCHEON ALSO PROVIDES A TIME FOR THE BRIDE TO THANK HER FRIENDS FOR STANDING UP WITH HER AND TREAT THEM TO A MEMORABLE MEAL THAT INCLUDES MOTHERS, GRANDMOTHERS AND AUNTS AS WELL.

I'LL NEVER FORGET MY OWN LUNCHEON, WHERE ONLY ONE OF MY MAIDS WAS ALREADY MARRIED. FOR THOSE REMAINING MAIDENS THE TREAT OF FINDING AN ALMOND IN THEIR CAKE, WITH THE PROMISE OF BEING THE NEXT IN LINE FOR THE NUPTIALS, WAS A LAUGH RIOT TO WATCH. I DON'T THINK A BITE OF THE CAKE WAS ACTUALLY EATEN UNTIL THAT ILLUSIVE ALMOND WAS FOUND!

WEDDINGS ARE THE PERFECT TIME TO INCORPORATE AGE-OLD TRADITIONS, PULL OUT ALL THE STOPS WHEN ENTERTAINING, AND HEART-ILY CELEBRATE THE PROMISE OF PARTNERSHIP FOR LIFE.

A WEEKEND IN JULY

Bride's Maids Luncheon
FOR 12

Chèvre & Cherry Crostini

Grilled Salmon & Basil Cream
Fresh Corn Salsa
Lemon Nut Bread

**Grandma's Shortcakes with Lemon Curd,
Fresh Berries & Almond Cream**

RECIPES
CHÈVRE & CHERRY CROSTINI

GRILLED SALMON

BASIL CREAM

FRESH CORN SALSA

LEMON NUT BREAD

GRANDMA'S SHORTCAKES WITH LEMON CURD, FRESH BERRIES & ALMOND CREAM

A well-balanced chardonnay will be especially good with the sweet corn and rich salmon.

TIME LINE
Honoring the Wedding Party

This formal luncheon for twelve is designed to be served. Ask a friend to help or hire an assistant to be sure the focus is on fun *For entertaining secrets see Hostess Gifts & Party Favors, p. 62-3.*

TWO DAYS BEFORE THE LUNCHEON

Set a pretty table, less a floral centerpiece. Make lemon curd; refrigerate. Make nut bread; wrap tightly and freeze.

THE DAY BEFORE

Make *a double batch of corn salsa;* refrigerate.

Chill wines. Make and bake shortcakes, including one with an almond, wrap tightly and refrigerate.

Be sure to mark the cake with the almond by sticking a toothpick into the batter. You want to be sure to serve this cake to one of the bride's maids – who will be anxiously awaiting their fate!

LUNCHEON MORNING

Add a floral centerpiece to table. Remove nut bread from freezer. Prepare *a double recipe of grilled salmon;* cover and refrigerate until time to grill.

Wash and hull strawberries for cakes and add sugar to get the juices running; refrigerate.

ONE HOUR BEFORE ARRIVAL

Prepare *a double recipe of basil cream;* hold at room temperature.

THIRTY MINUTES BEFORE THE BRIDE AND HER MAIDS ARRIVE

Assemble crostini. Set up a serving area for the wine and appetizers with pretty napkins.

Grill salmon; tent with foil to keep warm.

Place shortcakes in a 350 degree oven for approximately 5 to 7 minutes - just to crisp. Set aside. Whip almond cream; refrigerate.

UPON ARRIVAL

Serve crostini with wine.

FOR THE LUNCHEON

Plate salmon, salsa and basil cream.

Slice and place nut bread on individual bread plates with a pat of butter and an edible flower or two. Pour wine and water.

FOR THE DESSERT

Plate shortcakes with curd and berries and serve.

Place almond cream in a serving bowl to pass. Invite the girls to take as much or little as desired.

Encourage the bride to present her gifts to each maid – after the almond has been found!

Chèvre & Cherry Crostini

Sourwood honey and Bing cherries are a match made in heaven to goat cheese on crispy French bread.

PRONOUNCED: CROW-STEEN-E

SERVES: EIGHT TO TWELVE

16 slices French baguette
2 Tablespoons butter, softened
Himalayan pink salt
4 ounces chèvre
16 to 24 fresh bing cherries, pitted and halved
3 Tablespoons sourwood honey
1 Tablespoon fresh thyme leaves

Preheat a large griddle over medium heat. Cut baguette diagonally into ¼ to ½ -inch thick slices.

Brush each bread slice on one side with softened butter; sprinkle each slice with a pinch of salt. Toast bread butter side down, on the hot griddle for 3 to 5 minutes, or until it is golden brown with crispy browned edges.

Transfer toasted bread to a serving platter.

Spread each slice of toast with chèvre, dividing evenly.

Top cheese with 2 to 4 cherry halves, a drizzle of honey, and a sprinkle of thyme.

Serve crostini room temperature.

If fresh cherries are not available, use frozen.

The honey from the Sourwood tree is extra-light and extremely aromatic with a distinctive, rich honey flavor. No other honey can match this Appalachian wonder. See p. 387.

Grilled Salmon & Basil Cream with Fresh Corn Salsa

This light summery dish needs nothing more than a well-balanced chardonnay wine. Roasted salsa can be made ahead, but the basil cream does not keep well. It is best to make it while the salmon marinates.

SERVES: SIX

Salmon can be either farm raised or wild. See p. 384.

GRILLED SALMON

6 3 to 4-ounce salmon fillets, cut ½-inch thick

⅓ cup good olive oil

Zest of ½ fresh lemon

1 teaspoon kosher salt

¼ teaspoon freshly ground black pepper

Basil Cream
Fresh Corn Salsa
Fresh parsley

In a mixing bowl, whisk together the olive oil, lemon zest, salt, and pepper. Rub the salmon with this mixture and marinate in refrigerator for **1 hour.**

Grill the marinated salmon on a medium hot grill for 15 to 20 minutes.

Leave the skin on the salmon while grilling, as it will help the fillet hold together and not flake and fall through the cracks while grilling.

Peel skin from fillet before serving.

BASIL CREAM

1 Tablespoon olive oil
1 medium shallot, chopped
4 large cloves garlic, minced
½ cup sauvignon blanc wine
2 cups chicken broth
1/4 teaspoon star anise, ground
1 cup Half and Half cream
2 cups basil leaves, packed
1 Tablespoon parsley, chopped
Kosher salt &
Freshly ground black pepper
Juice of 1 fresh lemon
1 plum tomato, dice

Crush star anise in a mortar and pestle to release the flavor.

In a medium saucepan, heat the olive oil and sauté shallots and garlic until soft and brown. Add the wine, broth and ground anise; bring to a boil. Then lower the heat and reduce by half. Add the cream and reduce to a light sauce consistency.

Blanch the basil leaves for just 30 seconds in lightly salted boiling water. Drain and run cold water over them immediately to stop the cooking. Pat dry. Chop the bright green basil leaves and the parsley and add to the cream mixture.

With an immersion blender, process until smooth. Season with salt, pepper, and a few drops of lemon juice.

At serving time, stir in the diced tomatoes and serve warm.

FRESH CORN SALSA

4 large ears fresh corn kernels
¼ cup olive oil

Basil is especially good with fish and shellfish. Added at the end of a dish, basil can totally change the composition and infuse a minty freshness that was not there before.

For me, basil says "summer" and is equally delicious used with strawberries, citrus fruits and sweet sauces or syrups as well.

See Salts, p. 385.

The corn flavor is kept pure in this salsa, as it should be.

Basil, bell peppers and salmon are natural flavor affinities to corn and complement its sweet intense flavor.

1½ teaspoons kosher salt

½ teaspoon freshly ground black pepper

½ red bell pepper, diced

¼ red onion, diced

¼ cup fresh basil, chopped

½ serrano chili, seeded & minced

1 Tablespoon rice wine vinegar

2 Tablespoons sherry

2 teaspoons juice of fresh lemon

1½ teaspoons lavender honey

Preheat oven to 425 degrees. Remove corn kernels from cobs.

Toss kernels with olive oil and lightly season with salt and pepper. Spread out the kernels in a single layer on a baking sheet and roast until very lightly browned, approximately 10 minutes. Set aside.

In a separate bowl, combine the remaining ingredients.

Stir in the roasted corn. Season to taste with additional salt and pepper, lemon juice and honey. Cover and refrigerate.

To serve, plate the salmon, then top with corn salsa. Spoon the basil cream over both the salmon and salsa and garnish with a sprig or two of fresh parsley.

When purchasing fresh corn, check for natural moisture. The husks should not appear dry or show signs of wilting, and when pulled back, the kernels should be plump, tight, and vivid yellow in color. Squeeze the ears to check for freshness and ensure the kernels are full and juicy. See p. 370.

Lemon Nut Bread

Right out of the oven, a tart lemon syrup is glazed over this sweet nut bread.

SERVES: TWELVE

NUT BREAD

1½ cups all-purpose flour

½ teaspoon salt

1 teaspoon baking powder

½ cup unsalted butter, softened

1 cup granulated sugar

2 large eggs, slightly beaten

½ cup milk

½ cup pecans, chopped

Zest of 1 lemon

Preheat oven to 350 degrees.

Whisk flour, salt and baking powder together; set aside.

In a large bowl with an electric mixer, cream butter and sugar until light and fluffy, approximately 3 minutes. Beat in the eggs.

Add the dry ingredients to the butter mixture alternately with the milk. Mix until smooth. Fold in the pecans and lemon zest by hand.

Pour the batter into a buttered loaf pan. Bake for 45 to 50 minutes or until a toothpick inserted into the center of the loaf comes out clean.

LEMON GLAZE

¼ cup granulated sugar

Juice of 1 fresh lemon

Combine sugar and lemon juice.

Prick hot loaf with a toothpick across the entire top surface, inserting the full length of the toothpick into the bread. Slowly pour on the glaze, letting the syrup seep into the bread. Then let the loaf stand for 15 to 20 minutes before removing the glazed bread from the pan.

Remove from the pan and allow to cool completely before slicing.

Blueberries & lemon are great together. An option for this bread is to fold 1 cup fresh blueberries, coated with 1 Tablespoon flour, into the batter after incorporating the nuts and zest. Bake this blueberry-infused version in a Bundt pan for 45 to 55 minutes. Glaze as directed, using a long skewer rather than a toothpick to pierce the entire cake before glazing.

Grandma's Shortcake with Lemon Curd, Fresh Berries & Almond Cream

This biscuit-like shortcake is filled with fresh berries, lemon curd and whipped cream — turning familiar shortcake into a sophisticated finale!

SERVES: EIGHT TO TWELVE

LEMON CURD

½ cup unsalted butter
¾ cup granulated sugar
Juice of 3½ fresh lemons
Zest of 3½ lemons
⅛ teaspoon kosher salt
6 large egg yolks

Melt butter in a medium-sized saucepan over medium heat. Then remove the pan from the heat and whisk in the sugar, lemon juice, zest and salt. Whisk in the **yolks** until smooth.

Return pan to medium heat and cook the curd, whisking constantly, until the mixture thickens, approximately 5 to 6 minutes. *To check if curd is thick enough, dip a wooden spoon into it and draw your finger across the back of the spoon; your finger should leave a path.* Be sure to not allow the mixture to boil. Refrigerate covered, until ready to use.

SHORT CAKES

2 cups all-purpose flour
1 teaspoon salt
4 teaspoons baking powder
5⅓ Tablespoons unsalted butter
5 Tablespoons granulated sugar, divided
⅔ cup buttermilk, plus 2 to 3 Tablespoons
2 pints ripe berries in season, sliced & sweetened with sugar

Preheat oven to 425 degrees. Butter a jelly roll pan.

Sift the flour, **4 Tablespoons sugar,** baking powder and salt to combine. Cube butter into ¼-inch pieces.

With a pastry blender, cut butter into the flour mixture until it resembles a coarse

If you do not have buttermilk on hand, you can make it. Simply add 1 Tablespoon of white vinegar or lemon juice to 1 cup of sweet milk. Allow this mixture to stand at room temperature for 10 to 15 minutes then add "soured milk" to recipe.

meal and the butter is reduced to the size of small peas.

Using a fork, fold in ⅔ cup of the buttermilk until just blended, then fold in up to 3 Tablespoons additional buttermilk as needed until dough sticks together and forms a ball, but is not wet. *Use care to not overwork the dough.*

With two forks, divide dough into 8 to 12 equal-sized balls, then shape into uniform rounds and flatten rounds slightly to approximately 1-inch thick. *The dough will be sticky, but the forks will make it easier to handle and help avoid overworking.*

Space biscuits 1-inch apart to allow for expansion while baking.

Liberally sprinkle the remaining Tablespoon of sugar on top of the biscuit rounds.

Tuck an almond into one of the rounds to bring good fortune to a young maid. Mark it with a toothpick to ensure it is served to a maiden.

Bake for 10 to 15 minutes, or until golden brown and crunchy on the outside.

While biscuits bake, wash and hull the berries. Then slice and sweeten with sugar to get the juices running. Cover and refrigerate until ready to use.

WHIPPED CREAM

½ pint heavy cream, chilled

¼ cup powdered sugar

1 teaspoon almond extract

Whip cream until soft peaks form, then beat in the sugar and extract. Refrigerate until ready to serve.

ASSEMBLY

Using a serrated knife, carefully cut biscuits in two horizontally.

Place approximately 1 heaping Tablespoon of curd on the bottom half of each biscuit, and spoon on approximately 1 heaping Tablespoon of fresh berries.

Top with a dollop of whipped cream (approximately 1 heaping Tablespoon) and a strawberry fan and/or sprig of fresh mint on top as a garnish.

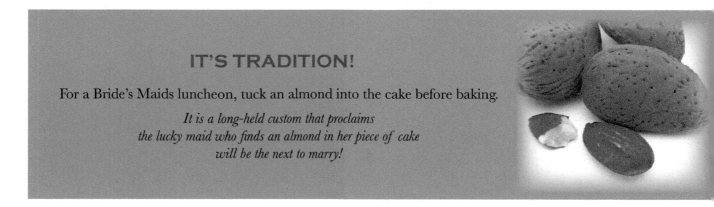

IT'S TRADITION!

For a Bride's Maids luncheon, tuck an almond into the cake before baking.

*It is a long-held custom that proclaims
the lucky maid who finds an almond in her piece of cake
will be the next to marry!*

THE WEDDING REHEARSAL DINNER PROVIDES AN OPPORTUNITY FOR THE GROOM'S FAMILY, WHO TYPICALLY HOST THIS EVENT, TO SHARE THEIR TRADITIONS AND CULTURE. BE IT A BACKYARD BARBECUE, A MEXICAN FIESTA WITH MARIACHIS AND MARGARITAS, OR A NO-HOLDS-BARRED AFFAIR ATOP A SKYSCRAPER DOWNTOWN, THE REHEARSAL DINNER IS AN EXTENSION OF THE WEDDING CELEBRATION AND A FEAST TO BE SAVORED. FROM THE MUSIC AND FOOD TO THE LOCATION, THIS EVENING IS ALL ABOUT BEING WITH FRIENDS AND FAMILY AS TOASTS ARE MADE IN GREAT FANFARE.

THE WEDDING PARTY, FAMILY AND OUT-OF-TOWN GUESTS ARE OFTEN INCLUDED IN THIS UNHURRIED EVENING.

THE NIGHT BEFORE THE NUPTIALS

Wedding Rehearsal Dinner

FOR 30

French 75 Cocktails
Seasonal Crudité
Assorted Cheeses, Breads & Saucisson

Roasted Salmon & Carved Roast Beef
Tuscan Lasagna with Sausage & Three Cheeses
Scallop of Sweetened Gold
Tomatoes & Pineapple Gratin

Tart & Tangy Lemon Squares with Berry Glaze
Carrot & Coconut Torte
Caramelized Pears

RECIPES

FRENCH 75
COCKTAILS

SEASONAL
CRUDITÉ

ROASTED SALMON

TUSCAN LASAGNA
WITH SAUSAGE &
THREE CHEESES

SCALLOP OF
SWEETENED GOLD

TOMATOES &
PINEAPPLE GRATIN

TART & TANGY
LEMON SQUARES

BERRY GLAZE

CARROT &
COCONUT TORTE

CARAMELIZED
PEARS

A soft red like a Pinot Noir *or* Merlot *will be a good match for the salmon & beef. Serve a bright, acidic* Italian Chianti *or a* Sangiovese *wine with the lasagna and tomato sauce.*

TIME LINE
Uniting Two Families

This very large party for thirty can be served two ways, served two ways. As a buffet with guests being seated for dinner, or with full dinner service provided by a staff of experienced personnel.

For a buffet, be sure to expedite service by placing plates at both ends or sides of the table and include a separate area for drink service and desserts.

If you choose to have this meal served pre-plated be sure to hire the staff necessary for seamless service, and ask guests to choose one entrée (either fish, beef or pasta) when they reply to your invitation. Serve the potato scallops and gratin with the salmon and beef. Serve the lasagna with a simple green salad.

For either choice, appetizers can be passed, with an easily accessible station designated for guests to pick-up cocktails. Desserts can be served (again, by the guest's pre-designated choice), or set at a station for self-service. *For entertaining secrets see* The Guest List: Crafting the Right Mix, *p. 2 and* Wines: Choosing, Opening, Pouring, Serving & Calculating, *p. 19-27.*

SIX MONTHS BEFORE THE DINNER
Determine location for dinner and reserve (or prepare) space as necessary. Rent tables, chairs, linens and serving pieces as necessary. Draft guest list.

TWO MONTHS BEFORE THE DINNER
Hire a minimum of four experienced wait and kitchen staffers to help with the event set-up, service and break down/clean-up.

ONE MONTH BEFORE
Finalize guest list, issue invitations. Order flowers; arrange delivery. Make lemon squares and freeze (without cutting into bars). Make carrot torte, wrap tightly in plastic wrap and foil; freeze (without frosting).

ONE WEEK BEFORE
Secure a final count for dinner and make adjustments as needed. Buy all ingredients for meal.
Buy wines for (30) guests and cocktail ingredients.

TWO DAYS BEFORE
Assemble wait staff and kitchen help to assist and train.
Lay the buffet table (if this is the route you choose) and review layout for balance (See page 10-12, The Buffet Service).
Decorate location/venue. Set dinner tables with flowers, linens and silver and ensure one table is showcased for the bride, groom and their parents. Assemble plates, silver, and napkins for the dessert buffet.
Assemble glasses & napkins for bar set up. Prepare cocktail glasses and chill.

TIME LINE Continued

Purchase assorted cheeses, breads, Saucisson and a roast beef for 30 guests. Chill white wines. Prepare *a double recipe of berry glaze;* refrigerate. Make frosting for carrot torte; refrigerate.

THE DAY BEFORE

Prepare *a triple recipe of crudité;* seal and refrigerate on serving platter.
Prepare *a triple recipe of vinaigrette dressing* to serve with crudité; refrigerate. *See recipe, p. 103.*
Prepare *a triple recipe of lasagna;* seal and refrigerate.
Caramelize *a triple recipe of pears;* refrigerate (sealed in plastic wrap) in individual glasses or bowls from which they will be served.
Assemble *triple recipes of both the potato scallops and tomato gratin.*

REHEARSAL MORNING

Thaw and assemble the carrot torte; hold covered in the refrigerator.
Remove lasagnas from freezer and let thaw in refrigerator. Add flower arrangements to tables.

ONE AND A HALF HOURS BEFORE GUEST ARRIVAL

Wait staff and kitchen help to arrive and begin work.
Assemble platter for cheeses; seal and keep cool.
Assemble all ingredients for 30 cocktails with an easy system for measuring and mixing drinks as guests arrive – *assign at least one person to this task.*

Bake lasagnas; hold at room temperature when finished baking. Have basil ready to top lasagna with just before serving. Bring lemon squares to room temperature, then cut and arrange on a pretty serving platter with garnishes of fresh lemon slices and flowers; wrap in plastic until ready to serve.

THIRTY MINUTES BEFORE ARRIVAL

Carve beef and cover to serve at room temperature.
Prepare triple recipe of salmon; hold at room temperature.
Bake potato scallops; hold at room temperature. Bake tomato gratin; hold at room temperature.

UPON ARRIVAL

Make and serve cocktails. Serve crudité and cheeses.
Quickly heat salmon, lasagnas, scallops and tomato dishes while guests mingle.
Pour wines & fill all water glasses at tables.

FOR THE DINNER

Set out buffet of salmon, roast beef, lasagna, potatoes and tomato gratin, or,
Serve dinner pre-plated via wait staff as described above.
Invite guests to the self-serve buffet, or into the dining room for the meal service.
While guests are having dinner, set out desserts and pre-slice the cake.

FOLLOWING THE MEAL WHILE TOASTING

Serve desserts and wines as requested.
Encourage the father of the groom to give the first toast.

RECOMMENDED FOR A PARTY THIS SIZE:

Access to a second refrigerator to hold quantities of foods and to chill cocktail glasses, etc.

French 75 Cocktails

This James Bond-like cocktail is a chic choice for a wedding jubilee. Be sure to assign at least one person to make these drinks as guests arrive because they are best made just two at a time.

Shaken, not stirred!

SERVES: TWO

2 Tablespoons juice of fresh lemon

2 Tablespoons powdered sugar

2 jiggers citrus infused vodka, frozen

2 jiggers champagne, chilled

Lemon curls

Lemon juice

Granulated sugar

Freshly ground nutmeg

Be sure to not add the champagne to the cocktail shaker with the vodka and sugar, or you will take the bubbly out of the bubbly!

Approximately two hours before guests arrive, prepare cocktail (martini) glasses by lightly dipping rims first in fresh lemon juice, and then into a plate of granulated sugar mixed with a pinch of nutmeg. Allow rims to dry on the counter for an hour, then place in the freezer to chill the glasses before time to serve.

To make drinks, fill a cocktail shaker with ice; add fresh lemon juice, powdered sugar and frozen vodka.

Shake for **30 seconds** to ensure drinks are well infused and chilled.

Pour mixture into two prepared glasses; splash a jigger of champagne into each glass.

Garnish cocktails with lemon rind curls.

Seasonal Crudité

Crudité comes from the French, and simply means a selection of seasonal vegetables, typically served with plenty of vinaigrette or dipping sauce.

PRONOUNCED: CREW-DI-TAY

SERVES: TEN

4 heirloom carrots, peeled and sliced lengthwise

4 celery stalks, sliced into thin strips

1 pint grape tomatoes

2 medium beets, sliced and halved

4 artichokes, quartered

1 bunch fresh green beans, blanched

1 cup snow peas, blanched

1 cup radishes

Green olives

Cold roasted peppers, sliced

Gherkins

Mushroom caps

& Other vegetables in season

Clean and slice all vegetables into manageable pieces, then artfully arrange in groupings on a serving tray lined with a bed of lettuce and/or herbs.

Use the tender middle stalks of celery and leave a few of the tender leaves intact. Leave some radishes whole and half the rest.

Garnish the serving platter with edible flowers and/or lemon and lime slices.

Roasted Salmon

Ever wonder how restaurant chefs cook salmon so perfectly? Here's their secret. Once I learned to cook salmon correctly, it became a favorite fish. Salmon is rich and fatty and pairs well with tomatoes. It is especially good with the Tomatoes Pineapple Gratin in this menu.

SERVES: TEN

Parsley is a natural with fish, and added at the last moment, brings a "marine" flavor that is wonderful.

10 3 to 4-ounce salmon fillets

Olive oil

Kosher salt

Freshly ground black pepper

Fresh parsley

Preheat oven to 400 degrees.

In a skillet, heat olive oil until searing hot.

Meanwhile, leave the skin on the salmon and pat dry, then brush all over with olive oil and generously season with salt and pepper on both sides.

Place fillets, skin side up, in searing oil and brown for 3 minutes. Do not disturb fillets while searing.

With a metal spatula, carefully flip fillets and brown second side for 3 more minutes.

Transfer the skillet to a hot oven and cook for an additional 3 minutes.

Remove salmon from hot oven and cover *tightly* with aluminum foil. Allow to rest for 10 minutes.

To serve, remove skin from fillets and garnish with fresh parsley.

Tuscan Lasagna with
Sausage & Three Cheeses

This pasta dish is reminiscent of Tuscany, with its medieval hill towns and rolling countryside. Simple yet flavorful, the rustic lasagna is distinguished by an excellence of ingredients, including fresh pasta. Dried lasagna noodles will work fine, but fresh homemade lasagna noodles make this dish exceptional. (See p. 222, Handmade Pasta, *and make pasta for four servings.*)

SERVES: EIGHT TO TEN

6 large sheets fresh lasagna noodles, or
9 sheets dried

3 Tablespoons olive oil, plus more for
tossing

¾ pound sweet Italian sausage

1 cup water

5 large cloves garlic, sliced thin

1 35-ounce can Italian peeled tomatoes

Kosher salt &

Freshly ground black pepper

4 to 5 ounces fresh parmesan cheese

8 ounces fresh mozzarella cheese

8½ ounces Italian fontina cheese

¼ cup fresh basil leaves, julienned

Make fresh pasta per recipe on p. 222; wrap and allow dough to rest for 30 minutes before rolling. Then divide dough into 3 rounds and roll 3 long sheets of pasta from each round. Cut sheets in half lengthwise to get the six sheets of pasta needed. Homemade pasta sheets will be slightly longer than the baking dish. That is fine, just fold them over and layer on sauce and cheeses as directed below.

Preheat oven to 425 degrees.

In a large pot of boiling salted water, cook the lasagna noodles al dente, or approximately 1 minute for fresh pasta and 5 minutes for dried.

Noodles will cook through in the poaching liquid.

Drain and then run the noodles under very cold water to stop the cooking, and let stand for 2 to 3 minutes. Then toss with olive oil to prevent sticking, and set aside.

In a medium skillet, heat **1 Tablespoon** of the olive oil. Add the sausage, cover and cook over medium heat, turning/stirring until browned well. Crumble sausage as it cooks. Add the water once sausage is browned, cover and simmer until the sausage is just cooked through, approximately 4 to 5 minutes.

In a large skillet, heat the remaining olive oil. Add the garlic and cook over low heat until golden - just 2 to 3 minutes. Add the tomatoes, their juices and cook over medium heat for 10 minutes, stirring occasionally and breaking tomatoes apart slightly as you stir.

Meanwhile, slice mozzarella and fontina cheese into thin pieces; grate parmesan.

Transfer the sausage to a plate; set aside.

Add the sausage poaching liquid to the tomatoes and simmer over medium heat until thickened, approximately 10 to 15 minutes. Taste sauce, and then season with salt and pepper as needed.

In a well-buttered, 9 x 13-inch baking dish, arrange two fresh (or three dried) lasagna noodles. (Fresh noodles may not fit pan exactly, so just fold them over at edges as needed.) Then spoon about ⅓ cup of the tomato sauce over lasagna noodles and sprinkle with grated parmesan cheese. Then place pieces of the mozzarella and fontina on noodles and add a heaping spoonful of browned sausage. Repeat the process two more times with the remaining lasagna noodles, tomato sauce and parmesan, mozzarella and fontina, and sausage, sprinkling with a little more parmesan to end.

Bake the lasagna on the top rack of the oven for 20 minutes, until the sauce starts to bubble. Then raise the oven temperature to 450 degrees, move lasagna to middle rack in the oven and bake for 5 to 7 minutes longer, until the top is bubbly and brown.

Allow the lasagna to rest for approximately 10 minutes, then scatter the sliced basil on top, cut into squares and serve.

Scallop of Sweetened Gold

This delightful scallop mixes sweet with gold potatoes, and the soft potato combination is especially good with the creamy white sauce and the crispy baked topping.

SERVES: EIGHT TO TEN

4 yukon gold potatoes
2 medium sweet potatoes
1 clove garlic
1 Tablespoon unsalted butter, softened
1 large onion, sliced very thin
2 Tablespoons olive oil
2½ teaspoons fresh thyme leaves
2½ cups milk
3 Tablespoons additional butter
3 Tablespoons all-purpose flour
1 cup fontina cheese, sliced
¼ cup fresh parmesan cheese, grated
Freshly ground nutmeg

Fontina cheese has a mild nutty flavor and excellent melting qualities, making it a very good choice for this scallop.

Preheat oven to 350 degrees.

Peel all potatoes. Using a food processor, slice potatoes very thin; reserve to a separate bowl. Then in the processor, slice onion very thin.

Slice a garlic clove in two and vigorously rub onto the inside of a 9 x 11-inch baking dish. Then coat dish with 1 Tablespoon of butter.

In a large skillet over medium heat, cook onions in olive oil until translucent. Season with salt and pepper. Remove from heat; stir in thyme leaves and set aside.

In a small saucepan, heat milk until simmering.

Melt the butter in another medium saucepan, and whisk in the flour to make a rue. Remove this pan from the heat and slowly drizzle in the warmed milk, whisking constantly, until a smooth sauce develops.

Then return the pan to the heat and bring to a boil; cooking for 3 minutes, or until thick.

Slice fontina cheese and grate parmesan cheese.

Layer ⅓ of the gold and sweet potatoes, mixed, in the prepared baking dish and season with salt, pepper. Then scatter ⅓ of the onions over the seasoned potatoes. Spoon ⅓ of the cream sauce over the potatoes and onions. Sprinkle ⅓ of cheese, mixed, over the top.

Repeat this process two times, ending with the cheese, and then adding the freshly ground nutmeg over the top of the casserole. Bake uncovered for 45 minutes in the middle rack of the oven.

After 45 minutes, increase the oven temperature to 425 degrees and bake 10 to 15 minutes more. Scallop should be brown and bubbly and potatoes tender when ready. Let stand 5 to 10 minutes to allow time to set up before serving.

Tomatoes & Pineapple Gratin

Tomatoes and pineapple pair really well together. The tomatoes get fruitier when cooked with pineapple, and the end result is a new flavor that is not entirely tomato or pineapple. This dish can be prepared ahead to the topping, then held in the refrigerator until party time. When ready, just bring the dish to room temperature and roast as directed in the final step.

SERVES: EIGHT TO TEN

2 large tomatoes
1 cup fresh pineapple
1 teaspoon kosher salt
½ teaspoon freshly ground black pepper
1 clove garlic, minced
3 scallions, chopped fine (including green parts)
¼ cup fresh parsley, minced
1½ teaspoons fresh thyme leaves
¼ cup olive oil
Dash of sauvignon blanc wine
1 cup cornbread crumbs

Preheat oven to 400 degrees. Butter a 9 x 9-inch (square or round) casserole dish.

Roughly chop tomatoes and pineapple and place into prepared casserole dish; season with salt and pepper.

In a large bowl, mix all remaining ingredients, except the cornbread. Once incorporated, fold the cornbread into the mix and sprinkle on the tomato pineapple mixture as a topping.

Roast for 20 to 25 minutes on the center rack of the oven, or until tomatoes and pineapples are bubbling, tender and browned at the edges, with the topping nicely browned.

Tart & Tangy Lemon Squares

Tart lemon bites in a sweet shortbread crust. Mmm!

YIELD: THIRTY BITE-SIZED SQUARES

SWEET SHORTBREAD CRUST

1 ¾ cups all-purpose flour

⅔ cup powdered sugar, plus more for sifting on top

¼ cup cornstarch

¾ teaspoon kosher salt

12 Tablespoons unsalted butter, cold

Line a 9 x 11-inch baking pan with parchment paper and butter both the pan and parchment.

Cut butter into 12 pieces; set aside.

Combine the flour, powdered sugar, cornstarch and salt in a food processor. Piece by piece, add the cold butter, working quickly to ensure the butter does not melt. Pulse 8 to 10 times or until the mixture resembles a coarse meal but has not formed into a ball.

Transfer the crust mixture into the prepared pan and press (with your hands) until the dough covers the pan in an even layer with approximately a ½- inch rim up the sides of the pan.

Refrigerate for **20 to 30 minutes.**

Preheat oven to 350 degrees and place oven rack in middle position.

Bake crust for 15 to 20 minutes, or until golden brown.

While crust is baking, prepare the filling.

TART & TANGY LEMON FILLING

4 large eggs

1 ⅓ cups granulated sugar

3 Tablespoons all-purpose flour

Zest of 2 lemons

Juice of 3 lemons

⅓ cup milk

⅛ teaspoon kosher salt

Reduce oven temperature to 325 degrees.

Whisk together the eggs, sugar and flour in a medium bowl. Stir in the lemon zest, juice and milk. Pour the filling onto the warm baked crust

Be sure the crust is still warm so the filling can incorporate into the top layers of the shortbread crust.

Bake for 18 to 20 minutes, or until the lemon filling sets and feels slightly firm to the touch. Cool to room temperature, then lightly sift powdered sugar over top using a fine mesh sieve.

Using a large spatula, remove to a cutting board and cut into squares with a pizza cutter.

To serve, drizzle with raspberry glaze and top with lemon curls.

If Lemon Squares are your only dessert, cut into larger bars as desired.

Berry Glaze

This glaze is delicious over lemon bars and other desserts — and equally good on grilled chicken.

YIELD: ONE CUP

½ **pint fresh or frozen raspberries**
½ **pint fresh or frozen strawberries**
¼ **cup lavender honey**
Juice of ½ fresh lemon
½ **teaspoon pure vanilla extract**

Rinse raspberries and drain. Rinse, hull and quarter strawberries.

In a large saucepan, combine all ingredients and cook over low heat, mashing fruits as they soften.

When the mixture begins to boil, remove from heat and let it cool slightly.

Press glaze through a fine-mesh sieve to remove any seeds from the fruit.

Cover and leave at room temperature until ready to drizzle; best served warm.

Store glaze in refrigerator for up to one week and bring back to room temperature before using.

Always cook strawberries on a very low heat to preserve their fresh flavor.

When raspberries and other berries are not in season, it is better to choose frozen berries. They will have better flavor than berries that have been shipped across the country in the off season.

Carrot & Coconut Torte

This dense carrot and spice creation includes coconut, the intense flavor of walnuts, and a frosting of lemony cream cheese.

To help ensure your success, see Baking Secrets, Light & Airy Cakes, *p. 361.*

SERVES: TWELVE TO EIGHTEEN

CARROT & COCONUT TORTE

3 cups carrots, grated
¾ cup angle flake coconut
½ cup walnuts, chopped
2 cups all-purpose flour
2 teaspoons baking soda
1 teaspoon kosher salt
1 teaspoons cinnamon
½ teaspoon allspice
½ teaspoon cloves
¼ teaspoon cumin
1½ cups vegetable oil
2 cups granulated sugar
½ teaspoon pure vanilla extract
1 teaspoon rum
4 large eggs, beaten lightly

Preheat oven to 350 degrees. Butter two 8-inch cake rounds; set aside.

Using a box grater, grate carrots. Toast walnuts for 5 to 8 minutes in a 350 degree oven; chop.

Sift together the flour, soda, salt, cinnamon and other spices onto a sheet of waxed paper; set aside.

In a large bowl with an electric mixer, mix oil, sugar, vanilla and eggs. Gradually add the flour mixture and blend to incorporate.

Stir in the carrots, coconut and walnuts. Fold to incorporate.

Pour batter evenly into prepared pans.

Bake for 50 to 60 minutes, or until toothpick inserted into center of round comes out clean. Cool 5 to 10 minutes in pans, then transfer to a wire rack to cool completely before frosting.

CREAM CHEESE FROSTING

8 ounces cream cheese, softened

¼ cup unsalted butter, softened

½ teaspoon pure vanilla extract

1 teaspoon rum

1 teaspoon zest of fresh lemon

2¼ cups powdered sugar

In a large bowl with an electric mixer, cream together the cheese and butter until light and fluffy. Mix in vanilla, rum and zest.

Gradually add powdered sugar, blending well as you add, until frosting is thick and creamy.

Frost cake between layers only, leaving sides bare.

Keep cake refrigerated until party time, then allow to come to room temperature before slicing. Store leftover cake in refrigerator.

Caramelized Pears

These sweet pears are a light alternative to pastry, and can be stored in the refrigerator for up to one week.

SERVES: TEN

5 bartlett pears, peeled, cored and quartered
5 Tablespoons unsalted butter
2 Tablespoons granulated sugar
3 Tablespoons light brown sugar, packed
8 Tablespoons bourbon

In a large span, sauté pears in butter and sugars until they begin to soften slightly.

Add bourbon and continue slowly cooking until the sugars have caramelized and become a dark, rich sauce.

Hold at room temperature until ready to serve.

.

AUGUST 14TH
Anniversary Candlelight Dinner
FOR 2

**Lobster & Scallops in Corn Husks
& Vanilla Butter
with Tomato Roses**

**Marinated Flank Steak
Katy Fries
Roasted Seasonal Vegetables
Grilled Peaches**

Brandied Alexanders

RECIPES
LOBSTER &
SCALLOPS IN CORN
HUSKS & VANILLA
BUTTER

TOMATO ROSES

MARINATED FLANK
STEAK

KATY FRIES

GRILLED PEACHES

BRANDIED
ALEXANDERS

Serve a Cabernet
Sauvignon, *or
full-bodied dark red
with a strong oak
influence, with the
grilled beef.*

HOW TO
CHIFFONADE
FORMING TAMALES

203

TIME LINE

Eros, Agape, Philia, Storge - that's Amore!

This romantic meal for two is designed to be prepared and served together, with the preparation being as much a part of the celebration as the meal itself.

For entertaining secrets see Traditional Wedding Anniversary Gifts, *p. 64.*

THE DAY BEFORE THE ANNIVERSARY

Marinate flank steak.

ANNIVERSARY MORNING

Set a pretty table in a favorite room with plenty of candles.

Make tomato roses.

ONE HOUR BEFORE THE DINNER

Prepare fries and vegetables for cooking; cover and hold.

Assemble lobster scallops.

THIRTY MINUTES BEFORE

Bake fries, roast vegetables.

TEN MINUTES BEFORE

Broil scallops and enjoy.

Grill steak; allow to rest before slicing.

Grill peaches; cover to keep warm.

FOR THE MEAL

Slice steak, and plate with fries, peaches and vegetables. Garnish platters with tomato roses.

Serve wine.

FOLLOWING THE MEAL

Make brandied Alexanders together and enjoy.

EACH AND EVERY WEDDING ANNIVERSARY SHOULD BE CELEBRATED!

THE MEAL DOES NOT HAVE TO BE FANCY, BUT RATHER SHOULD BE A COMPILATION OF FOODS THE COUPLE ENJOYS.

CANDLES WILL CREATE AN INTIMATE MOOD SO THE EVENING CAN BECOME A TIME TO RELAX AND REMINISCE O'ER THE SHARED LOVE THAT BINDS TWO SOULS OVER TIME.

Lobster & Scallops in Corn Husks & Vanilla Butter

Vanilla is delicious with shellfish, and brings out the natural sweetness in succulent meats from the sea.

YIELD: EIGHT PACKAGES (SERVES FOUR)

1 pound fresh lobster meat

8 fresh scallops

½ cup unsalted butter

Seeds from ½ vanilla bean pod

1 teaspoon pure vanilla extract

4 cups lightly salted water

Kernels from 1 ear corn, cooked

Kosher salt

8 large corn husks

8 to 10 basil leaves, cut into chiffonade

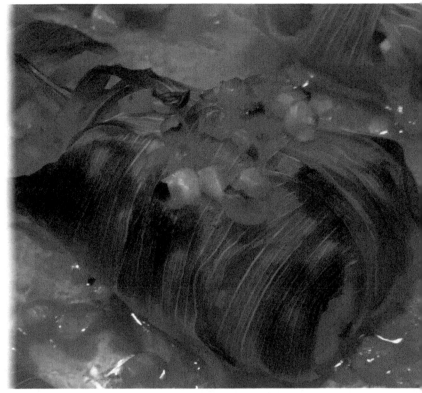

Soak corn husks in hot water until pliable, approximately 15 minutes. Preheat broiler.

Cream together the butter, vanilla bean and extract; refrigerate until ready to use.

Parboil the lobster in water until three-quarters cooked (15 to 18 minutes). Cool and shred/slice.

Remove the hard nub from the scallops with a small knife. Then divide scallops, lobster and corn evenly between the eight corn husks. Top shell fish and corn with 1 Tablespoon of creamed vanilla butter and a pinch of salt.

Roll and tie the corn husks, securing with strings of the corn husks and/or kitchen string at both ends per instructions that follow. Top each "package" with a tiny dollop of the remaining butter and sprinkle of remaining corn to form a "bow" on the top of a package!

Broil packages until the scallops are cooked, approximately 6 to 8 minutes. Broil on low setting for the first 6 minutes, then turn to high setting for remaining 2 to 3 minutes to brown. *Some of the butter will leak out while broiling. The more securely the tamales are wrapped the less butter will be lost.*

Serve tamales hot, garnished with fresh basil leaves.

HOW TO CHIFFONADE BASIL & OTHER HERBS

Begin by stacking leaves so you can cut through many layers at once. Once you have a stack of approximately ten leaves, roll the leaves in to a tight cylinder.

Then slice as thinly as possible with a very sharp knife to create herb ribbons.

FORMING TAMALES

Tamales are like little presents, formed much like wrapping & tying a package.

Start by soaking husks in hot water until soft and pliable, approximately 15 minutes.

Then separate corn husks into two piles, large and small.

Large pieces should be approximately ½ of the husk of one ear of corn, or large enough to hold 2 to 3 Tablespoons of filling.

Tear the smaller pieces into strips approximately 6 x ¼-inches.

You can also use kitchen string as needed to tightly secure the filling, as some strips of husks may not be long enough to tie securely.

Lay out one (larger) husk with the narrow part pointed away.

Place filling in the center area of the square.

Fold one side of the tamale over the other to cover the filling.

Then roll the folded husk up (lengthwise) completely.

Fold the top over and tie it with a bow with one of the thin strips created from smaller husks and/or string.

Secure the bottom end with a second strip and bow.

Tomato Roses

Add a little romance to your serving platter by garnishing with tomato roses.

YIELD: TWO ROSES

1 ripe red tomato

Using a sharp paring knife, peel tomatoes. Start at the top and carefully remove peel in a ½-inch wide strip, trying to peel one continuous ribbon, unbroken.

Then cut the long strip of ribbon in half to form two roses. Roll each piece gently but tightly from end to end to form/resemble a red rose.

Secure roses in place by laying the end piece down on a platter so its weight can help hold the rings.

Nestle roses in a bed of herbs or Bibb lettuce to help hold the blooms in place.

Marinated Flank Steak

The flavorful marinade for this steak acts as a tenderizer and the honey caramelizes as the meat grills, creating a slightly crispy exterior with a juicy and tender interior.

SERVES: FOUR

2 pounds flank steak
¼ cup soy sauce
2 Tablespoons honey
½ cup vegetable oil
2 Tablespoons apple cider vinegar
1½ teaspoons garlic powder
1½ teaspoons ground ginger
2 scallions, chopped (including green parts)

Combine soy sauce, honey, oil, vinegar, garlic powder, ginger and scallions.

The soy sauce is a wonderful tenderizer and the oil will help prevent the meat from sticking to the grill.

Flank steak is very flavorful but tough. It must be tenderized. Marinate for a minimum of twelve hours; overnight is preferable.

Place steak in a 9 x 11-inch casserole dish.

Pour sauce over steak; cover and **marinate overnight.**

Preheat grill. Place steak on a *hot* grill and carefully pour half of the remaining marinade on top to encourage flaming and charring. Pour the second half of the marinade over steak after flipping. *Flames will rise quickly when you pour on the marinade – use caution!*

Cook to desired doneness, flipping only once, approximately 4 to 6 minutes on each side for medium rare.

At five minutes per side you will have a steak that is medium rare in the middle and medium on the edges – something for every preference.

Allow steak to rest, tented with foil, for approximately 10 minutes before slicing.

Slice ¼ to ½-inch thick, pulling knife down across the grain on the diagonal.

Katy Fries

Crisp, buttery roasted potatoes that are always easy and always good!

SERVES: FOUR

4 potatoes, scrubbed and sliced thin
4 Tablespoons unsalted butter
Kosher salt &
Freshly ground black pepper

Preheat oven to 350 degrees.

Place potato slices (with skin on) onto a buttered cookie sheet.

Cut butter into small cubes and dot potatoes with butter. Season with salt and pepper.

Roast for 45 minutes, turning and stirring once or twice during the cooking process. When finished cooking, the edges of the potatoes will be golden brown and crispy while the centers remain soft. Serve hot.

These potatoes are also good with a little fresh rosemary sprinkled on top before baking.

This method also works well with sweet potatoes cut into matchsticks.

Grilled Peaches

From asparagus to peaches, seasonal fruits & vegetables roasted on the grill have a delicious smoky flavor with a crisp and slightly charred exterior.

Fragrant grilled peaches are cooked just long enough to become infused with the rich flavors of honey and vanilla, and are an unexpected delight.

SERVES: FOUR

2 large peaches, pitted and halved
Hazelnut oil
4 teaspoons honey
½ teaspoon pure vanilla extract
Freshly ground nutmeg

Preheat grill to moderately high heat; lightly oil the grate. Mix honey and vanilla.

Lightly brush peaches with hazelnut oil to keep them from drying out or sticking to the grate, and grill until lightly browned and tender, approximately 2 minutes per side, or just long enough to get the dark grill marks.

After turning, fill the peach centers with 1 teaspoon of vanilla honey for the second 2 minutes of grilling time.

Remove to a serving platter and lightly dust with nutmeg.

Good served either warm or cold.

Brandied Alexanders

These Brandied Alexanders are made with gelato and chocolate liqueur - very decadent!

YIELD: FOUR DRINKS

2 jiggers brandy
1 jigger godiva chocolate liqueur
½ cup milk
1 pint vanilla bean gelato (Italian ice cream)
Nutmeg, freshly ground

One hour before serving, place snifters in the freezer to chill. Cut straws to fit glasses.

Put all ingredients (except nutmeg) into a blender and pulse until smooth and incorporated but still thick in consistency.

Pour mixture into chilled brandy snifters and grate a touch of nutmeg on top.

Add a straw and serve immediately.

Occasions

Indian Summer Tailgate Picnic

Autumn

Seasonal Fruits & Vegetables

FRUITS & NUTS

Almonds
Apples
Coconut
Cranberries
Dates
Figs
Grapes
Pears
Pistachios
Quince
Walnuts

VEGETABLES & HERBS

Artichokes
Basil
Beans
Beets
Broccoli
Brussels Sprouts
Butternut Squash
Celery Root
Chard
Fennel
Kale

Leeks
Peppers, Bell
Peppers, Chili
Pumpkin
Sweet Potato

ON OUR FIRST
TRIP TO ROME WE
STROLLED THROUGH
THE BEAUTIFUL
BORGHESE GARDENS,
STOPPING FOR LUNCH
AT AN ALFRESCO
RESTAURANT. HERE
IN THE MIDDLE OF THE
PARK, A SIMPLE TENT
HAD BEEN ERECTED
AND THE DINING AREA
WAS FILLED WITH
TABLES LAID WITH
LINEN CLOTHS, CHINA
AND CRYSTAL. I WILL
NEVER FORGET THAT
CULTURAL IMMERSION
AND GLIMPSE INTO HOW
ITALIANS SAVOR THE
DINING EXPERIENCE.
ITALIAN NIGHT IN YOUR
HOME SHOULD BE SLOW
AND DELIBERATE — NO
RUSH. PLAY CLASSICAL
GUITAR MUSIC, AND
SERVE DELICIOUS FOODS
IN MULTIPLE COURSES
WITH HANDMADE PASTA
AND GOOD WINES.
USE CLASSY LINENS,
RUSTIC POTTERY
AND GLASSWARE,
AND CREATE YOUR
OWN "LITTLE ITALY"
TRATTORIA.

Italian Night

FOR 6

Grilled Shrimp Wrapped in Bacon & Basil with Green Olives & Potato Chips

Spinach & Ricotta Ravioli with Toasted Prosciutto
Brown Butter Sage Sauce with Balsamic Vinegar Glaze

Lemon Lavender Shortbread

RECIPES

GRILLED SHRIMP WRAPPED IN BACON & BASIL

SPINACH & RICOTTA RAVIOLI WITH TOASTED PROSCIUTTO

HANDMADE PASTA

BROWN BUTTER SAGE SAUCE

BALSAMIC VINEGAR GLAZE

LEMON LAVENDER SHORTBREAD

Serve an Italian Vernaccia *with the Antipasti. Serve a* Red Sangiovese *with notes of black currant with the Secondi Piatti. Serve* Vino Santo *with the Frutta.*

MAKING LAMINATED PARSLEY PASTA

TIME LINE

Ciao!

I recommend serving this meal Family Style one course at a time so that foods can be passed and the evening is relaxed and long.

For entertaining secrets see Setting a Formal Table: Menu Cards, *p. 34 and* Glossary of Wines, *p. 25-7.*

TWO DAYS BEFORE ITALIAN NIGHT

Determine the perfect spot for an alfresco meal that has a view to be savored along with the meal. **Purchase** large green olives and good, kettle-cooked potato chips.

THE DAY BEFORE

Prepare ricotta filling for raviolis; seal in plastic and refrigerate.

Bake shortbread and cool; seal tightly and refrigerate. Chill Vernaccia wine.

ITALIAN NIGHT MORNING

Lay the outside dining table with beautiful yet simple linens and rustic dishes; add fresh flowers. Clean shrimp and wrap in basil and bacon; refrigerate until time to grill.

Ready a wine and appetizer station that includes glasses for each course on the menu, cocktail napkins and small plates for the antipasti.

Set out dessert plates and coffee service that includes cups, saucers, spoons, a creamer and sugar bowl. Ready the coffee pot to brew with the touch of a button after dinner.

Grate cheese and divide into two bowls, one for the plating of the ravioli, and one in a pretty bowl to place on the table for topping the ravioli during the meal.

JUST AFTER LUNCH — MID DAY

Make the pasta dough for the raviolis; allow to rest 30 minutes. Bring ravioli filling to room temperature. Then construct and fill the raviolis, tossing in polenta corn flour once completed, and covering with a clean and dry kitchen towel until time to cook. Make brown butter sauce; hold at room temperature.

Make balsamic glaze; hold at room temperature. *Be sure to watch balsamic vinegar closely to ensure it does not get too thick.*

Bring shortbread to room temperature and plate with fresh lavender blossoms on the serving platter with one or two whole lemons or other garnishes; cover until ready to serve.

Toast prosciutto in the oven then drain on a plate lined with paper toweling.

UPON ARRIVAL & FOR THE ANTIPASTI

Invite guests to the alfresco dining area and serve chilled Vernaccia with small bowls of big green olives and potato chips. Grill shrimp while guests settle in and then serve the shrimp with more wine, taking time to visit and enjoy an evening with friends.

When guests are ready for the next course, get the water boiling for the pasta.

FOR THE SECONDI PIATTI

Quickly cook raviolis and plate. While raviolis are cooking warm the prosciutto by popping into a hot oven for just a few minutes; and quickly heat brown butter sauce. Top pasta with butter sauce, balsamic glaze, a dash of good olive oil, freshly grated parmesan cheese and then the toasted prosciutto. Set out more cheese for guests, as might be desired during the meal.

Serve Red Sangiovese and cold sparkling water.

FOR THE FRUTTA

Serve shortbread and Vino Santo and linger over coffee and conversation.

Grilled Shrimp Wrapped in Bacon & Basil

These shrimp bites are marinated in basil and champagne and then grilled so the shrimp becomes infused with the lip-smacking smoky flavor of the bacon!

YIELD: FIFTEEN HORS D'OEUVRES

1 pound large shrimp
5 slices lean bacon
¾ cup olive oil
¾ cup champagne
4 Tablespoons fresh basil, minced
2 cloves garlic, minced
1 teaspoon kosher salt
½ teaspoon freshly ground black pepper

One pound yields approximately fifteen shrimp.

Always shop for the freshest shrimp you can find and buy shrimp that has been peeled and deveined by machine, if you can. See p. 386.

Peel and devein shrimp.

Combine oil, champagne, basil, garlic, salt and pepper. Add shrimp and **marinate overnight.**

Preheat grill.

Cut each slice of bacon into thirds and wrap around each shrimp.

Secure bacon with a toothpick once wrapped.

Grill shrimp over medium-high heat until the bacon is crisp and the shrimp is cooked through, approximately 7 to 8 minutes in total, turning just once during the cooking process.

Something as simple as chips and olives can be terrific with a glass of wine and Shrimp in Bacon and Basil on an autumn evening.

Spinach & Ricotta Ravioli with Toasted Prosciutto

This authentic ravioli incorporates the five "must have" ingredients for any Italian cook — fresh pasta, extra-virgin olive oil, prosciutto, balsamic vinegar and Parmigiana-Reggiana cheese! Homemade ravioli is surprisingly easy to make, especially with this formula. The trick to making this ravioli is to be sure the spinach is very dry before adding to the rest of the filling ingredients. If the filling is too wet, it will disintegrate the pasta while cooking and the raviolis will break open in the water.

SERVES: SIX TO EIGHT

SPINACH & RICOTTA FILLING

2 bunches fresh spinach leaves

7.5 ounces mascarpone cheese

7.5 ounces ricotta cheese

2½ cups fresh parmigiano-reggiana cheese, grated

1 large egg

1 teaspoon nutmeg, freshly ground

1 teaspoon kosher salt

½ teaspoon freshly ground black pepper

Fresh handmade pasta made into sheets for ravioli

Extra-virgin olive oil

Freshly grated parmigiano-reggiana cheese (additional)

Prepare enough pasta dough for six to eight servings (see recipe that follows), and set aside to rest while making the filling.

Wash and steam the spinach in a large saucepan covered with 1 cup of water. Once briefly steamed, remove the spinach from the heat and run under very cold water to stop the cooking process and cool the leaves.

When spinach leaves are cool enough to handle, place them in paper toweling and squeeze all of the water out by wringing with your hands, ensuring the spinach is as dry as possible.

As an added precaution, place dried spinach in a colander to slowly drip and strain out any remaining moisture while preparing the rest of the filling.

In a large mixing bowl, combine the mascarpone, ricotta, parmesan, lightly beaten egg and seasonings. Taste and adjust seasoning as necessary.

Then add the dried spinach and mix all of the ingredients until well combined; set aside.

Using a pasta machine, prepare sheets of pasta for the ravioli. Then place a sheet of fresh pasta on a lightly floured surface and spoon the filling onto the sheet, *one teaspoon* at a time. *Do not use more than a teaspoon of filling for each ravioli, or they will be too big to seal.*

Leave a ½-inch space around all four edges of each dollop. Then lightly wet your finger tip and trace around each dollop to moisten the pasta. *This added moisture will help the second sheet adhere to the first and seal the ravioli for cooking.*

Place a second sheet of fresh pasta on top of the bottom sheet with the filling. Using your fingers, gently press the top sheet around each dollop of filling to remove any air bubbles and tap around the dollop to seal both sheets together.

Using a pasta cutter, cut the pasta into raviolis by cutting strips that are approximately ¼-inch from each of the four sides of filling. *This will also allow approximately ¼ to ½-inch area of dough around the ball of filling.*

Place finished ravioli on a cookie sheet dusted with polenta flour and toss to coat; check periodically and toss again while making additional ravioli. Continue until all of the filling has been used.

In a large pot of gently boiling salted water place raviolis, stirring gently to ensure they do not touch. Cook 4 to 5 minutes at a gentle boil or until raviolis are floating on top of the water and begin to take on a yellow color and looked cooked.

Once you have made ravioli a time or two, these steps will become second nature and you will know what to look for. Remember three things: Do not add too much filling to the raviolis; keep water at a gentle boil; and watch the ravioli as it cooks as you learn to discern subtle changes in color.

TOASTED PROSCIUTTO

9 to 12 slices prosciutto

While ravioli is cooking, place prosciutto slices onto a wire rack set in a jelly roll pan lined with foil. Toast in a 350 degree oven for approximately 7 minutes, or until the prosciutto has begun to crisp and the fat has rendered.

Serve ravioli topped with Brown Butter Sage Sauce and grated Parmigiano-Reggiana cheese. Then drizzled with olive oil and Balsamic Vinegar Glaze and the toasted prosciutto slices.

Finely ground polenta corn flour will drop to the bottom of the cooking pot while the water is boiling and not become gummy like flour can.

If the pasta water is boiling too vigorously, ravioli is more likely to split open while cooking.

Brown Butter Sage Sauce

One of my favorite flavors is brown butter, which pairs well with this ravioli as well as anything nutty. You are not adding anything to the taste of the butter in the browning process, but transforming it so that is becomes even more intense. The process is simple, but it is important to remember that the butter continues to brown even after being removed from the heat. When using brown butter for baking, stop the cooking by plunging the hot pan into a bowl of ice water. When using brown butter in cooking and for this recipe, whisk the butter approximately halfway through the cooking process, and remove from the heat completely when it caramelizes and suddenly turns amber in color. Whisking will intensify the butter flavor and also keeps it from overcooking.

Fresh sage is also good cooked as a sauce with olive oil and bacon fat.

NUMBER SERVED	UNSALTED BUTTER	FRESH SAGE LEAVES
2	½ cup	½ cup
4	1 cup	1 cup
6	1½ cups	1½ cups

Place butter with clean and dry sage leaves into saucepan on very low heat (setting 2 of 10) and gently simmer for approximately 10 to 15 minutes, or until butter browns and the sage leaves are crispy at the edges yet still somewhat supple. *Watch the sauce carefully as it simmers to ensure it does not burn.*

Pour the sauce over plated pasta and top with toasted prosciutto.

When using sage, always cook this herb. Fresh sage makes a lovely garnish for savory dishes and roasts, but it just does not taste as good eaten raw.

BALSAMIC VINEGAR GLAZE

In a small saucepan, slowly cook high quality balsamic vinegar until it transforms from a liquid to a sauce consistency. Cook the vinegar very slowly and watch carefully to ensure it does not become too thick – which can happen in an instant.

Handmade Pasta

Fresh pasta only takes approximately fifteen minutes to make (plus thirty minutes resting time). Here's my simple formula for great pasta that is also easy to work with.

NUMBER SERVED	AMOUNT OO FLOUR	NUMBER EGGS	FINE SALT
1	¾ cup	1	⅛ teaspoon
2	1½ cups	2	¼ teaspoon
3	2¼ cups	3	½ teaspoon
4	3 cups	4	1 teaspoon
6	4½ cups	6	1½ teaspoons

Hold back ¼ to ½ cup of the flour until the level of humidity can be determined.

Mound remaining flour on a clean counter top or board and gently mix in the salt. Make a well in the center of the flour-salt mixture, then crack the egg(s) into the well one at a time. Using a fork, gently begin incorporating each of the eggs by whisking with one hand, and using your other hand to keep the well walls intact.

As you add each egg and gradually incorporate it with the flour, keep the outer walls of flour intact with all of the moisture in the center.

Do not worry if the initial dough is lumpy. Just keep gradually incorporating more and more flour into the eggs with your fork until you have wet dough that can then be manipulated with just your hands.

Now, set the fork aside and finish incorporating the remaining flour with your hands a little at a time. If your dough is too dry (crumbly) then add a teaspoon of olive oil.

If your dough sticks to your hands, it is too wet and needs more flour.

When the flour has been added to your satisfaction, knead the dough with the heel of your hand for approximately 10 to 15 minutes, or until you have an elastic and silky smooth ball of dough.

Wrap dough in plastic wrap and allow to rest at room temperature for **30 minutes.**

After resting, remove a tennis ball-sized amount of dough from the plastic wrap and re-wrap the remaining dough. Using your fingers, flatten the ball of dough to approximately ½-inch thick. Using a pasta machine, insert the disc of dough through the machine rollers at the widest setting. Then fold the rolled dough into thirds and roll it through again, folded, at same setting. *Dough will go through the machine twice on the first setting, and then just once on each of the remaining settings.*

Now increase the settings one by one and roll the dough through each setting until it goes through a final time on the highest setting and is a long, very thin soft sheet of dough.

If your dough sticks to the machine, swish it through a bit of flour on the counter top. But avoid using more flour than needed to ensure a light and chewy pasta when cooked.

Place finished pasta on a cookie sheet covered in polenta flour and swish to coat and keep the pasta from sticking while you roll the remaining dough.

To cook pasta, add to a large pot of boiling water with a handful of salt and just 1 to 2 teaspoons of olive oil. Stir gently to ensure no pieces stick together while cooking. Gently boil for 4 to 5 minutes. Drain and serve.

Stretch the ball of dough as you knead to check for stickiness. If the stretched open section of dough is wet, add more flour. Your dough should feel like play dough when ready to rest, and have neither a sticky center nor feel dry and crumbly.

Laminated Parsley Pasta

Making Parsley Pasta is a great way to use fresh herbs and creates something different for dinner. In this pasta, fresh parsley (or other flat leaf herb) is "laminated" between two sheets of fresh pasta dough. It is easy and quick to make, and delicious served simply with Brown Butter Sage Sauce.

Four servings of pasta will require 1 cup of fresh parsley.

Wash parsley (or other flat leaf herb of choice, like basil) and pick individual leaves from the stems. Allow to air dry on paper toweling. *Leaves should be slightly damp during the assembly process to ensure that they stick to the dough and do not move while being laminated.*

Roll four equal-sized sheets of pasta. Swish one side of each sheet in flour, and place on the counter, flour side down.

Place parsley leaves on these two lengths of the dough and press them gently into the dough to ensure they do not slip when they are run through the machine.

Then lay the remaining two pieces of dough, flour side up, atop leaves and gently press to hold the two sheets of dough together.

With a pasta machine set on the second to last setting, insert the laminated pasta through once, then again on the highest setting to securely laminate. Repeat with second sheet.

On a lightly floured surface, cut sheets crosswise into one-inch strips of dough and then into bite-sized triangles or squares. Remove to cookie sheet(s) lined with polenta flour to prevent sticking. Allow to dry 5 to 10 minutes while the water boils.

Lemon Lavender Shortbread

Lavender is delicious in buttery desserts, and the savory aroma of this floral herb pairs beautifully with lemon. Cookies can be kept in airtight container for a few days or frozen. To help ensure your success, see Baking Secrets, Cookies, p. 356.

YIELD: THIRTY SQUARE COOKIES

2 cups all-purpose flour
¼ teaspoon salt
Zest of 1 lemon
2 teaspoons fresh lavender petals
1 cup unsalted butter, softened
¾ cup powdered sugar
1 teaspoon pure vanilla extract
1 teaspoon juice of fresh lemon
Granulated sugar

In a small bowl, whisk the flour with salt, lemon zest and lavender; set aside.

In a large bowl with an electric mixer, beat butter with powdered sugar until light and fluffy; approximately 3 minutes.

Add vanilla and lemon juice and beat to combine.

Slowly incorporate the flour mixture then fold by hand until just combined.

Divide dough into four parts, wrap in plastic and form into discs.

Chill dough for **1 hour,** or until firm.

Preheat oven to 325 degrees. Line a baking sheet with parchment paper.

On a clean, lightly floured surface, roll discs into ¼-inch thick **squares.** Using a crimped pasta cutter, cut dough into 1½ x 1½ -inch squares. Gather scraps and re-roll until all the dough has been made into squares.

Place cookies on baking sheet and lightly sprinkle each cookie with granulated sugar.

Bake 10 to 12 minutes, or until lightly browned at the edges.

Remove to wire rack and cool completely.

A good shortbread should have an interior composed of multiple flakes of buttery pastry, so be sure to handle dough as little as possible.

Shortbread does not rise while baking so be sure to roll dough only to ¼-inch thick or it will be too crispy.

A TAILGATE PICNIC IS THE PERFECT OPPORTUNITY TO PULL OUT YOUR
TARTAN PLAIDS, PICNIC HAMPERS AND OUTSIDE TABLEWARE. TUCK
A MASON JAR INTO THE MIX AND FILL IT WITH PRETTY WILDFLOWERS
WHEN YOU ARRIVE AT THE PICNIC SPOT.
IT IS FUN TO ALSO PACK THINGS LIKE A FOOTBALL, LAWN GAMES OR
BOULES BALLS, AND A PAIR OF BINOCULARS FOR BIRDWATCHING.
ALL FOR A RELAXED DAY OUT OF DOORS WITH GOOD FOOD
AND GOOD FRIENDS.

A SEPTEMBER AFTERNOON

Indian Summer Tailgate Picnic

FOR 8

Soul Food Chili
Kale Caesar!
Lemon Poppy Seed Zucchini Bread

Oatmeal Cookies with Warm Coffee Glaze
and/or
Concord Grape Cobbler

RECIPES

SOUL FOOD CHILI

KALE CAESAR!

LEMON POPPY
SEED ZUCCHINI
BREAD

OATMEAL COOKIES
WITH WARM
COFFEE GLAZE

CONCORD GRAPE
COBBLER

Serve a fruity and spicy Zinfandel *with the chili.*

TIME LINE

When the days are warm enough for swimming and the nights cool enough for fires.

This easy picnic is casual. Make it simple by setting dishes on a blanket and inviting everyone to help themselves. Store foods in the car or cooler and forget about clean-up until you get back home!

For entertaining secrets see Getting Organized, *p. 37.*

TWO DAYS BEFORE THE PICNIC

Bake cookies; seal and freeze. *Be sure to freeze glazed cookies on a cookie sheet first to harden before stacking.* Then, place in a plastic container to store once the glaze is solid.

Bake breads; seal and freeze.

THE DAY BEFORE

Pack the picnic hamper, including plenty of napkins, extra plates and utensils.

Get out the ice chest and lawn games and check to be sure all is clean and ready to use. Chill wine and water.

Make chili. Make croutons for the salad.

Wash and trim the kale, wrap in a damp paper towel and refrigerate.

THE NIGHT BEFORE

Bake cobbler; cool and seal at room temperature.

PICNIC MORNING

Buy twice as much ice as you think you'll need.

Assemble everything needed for the salad, seal in plastic ware and pack in the cooler.

Pack the car with the hamper, ice chest (and ice), games and all the food. *Make a check list to be sure to not forgotten anything!* And don't forget the mason jar!

Pack breads, cookies and cobbler in pretty Tupperware containers (or dishes that are un-breakable and can easily be sealed) and ensure these dishes are nice looking enough to also serve from at the picnic.

Pack wine in ice chest, along with lots of water to drink.

Pack the chili in an insulated wrap to keep it warm.

Coddle the egg for the salad and pack in the cooler/ice chest.

UPON ARRIVAL AT THE PICNIC SPOT

Lay blankets in a sunny spot and hold them in place with rocks – *be sure to watch out for ant hills!*

Set out the picnic hamper and pick some wild flowers to add to the mix, creating a relaxed and inviting outdoor setting.

WHEN EVERYONE IS READY TO EAT

Set out the chili and slice breads.

Make the salad in a showy fashion while friends enjoy the production!

Lay out cookies and cobbler for self-service throughout the afternoon.

Soul Food Chili

This soul satisfying chili is made with ground bison, mixed beans and dark beer. Top it with grated cheese, more chopped chilies and sour cream… Now you're talkin'!

SERVES: EIGHT

1 pound ground bison
1 Tablespoon olive oil
1½ cups onion, chopped
5 garlic cloves, minced
1 Tablespoon chili powder, divided
1 Tablespoon fresh oregano
1 teaspoon ground cumin
1 teaspoon freshly grated nutmeg
2 teaspoons kosher salt
½ teaspoon freshly ground black pepper
1 8-ounce can hatch chilies
1 35-ounce can whole tomatoes
1 cup cherry tomatoes
12 ounces dark beer
16 ounces beef broth
1 15-ounce can black beans, drained
1 15-ounce can cannellini beans, drained
1 Tablespoon granulated sugar
Cheddar cheese, grated
Sour Cream
Additional chilies

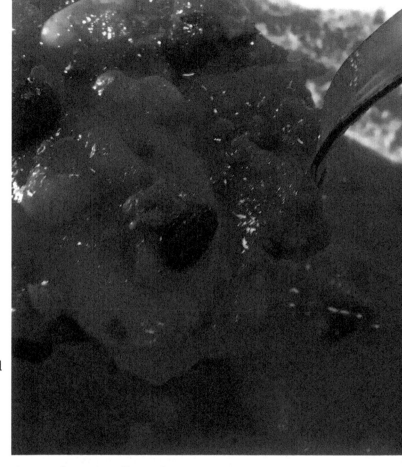

Heat oil in a stock pot over medium heat. Add onions and sauté until translucent.

Add garlic and cook just until soft, approximately 1 minute. Stir in **half** of the chili powder and all remaining spices.

Add the bison and cook until lightly browned, stirring as it cooks to crumble the meat.

Add chilies, tomatoes, beer, broth and remaining chili powder; bring to gentle boil. Then reduce heat and simmer uncovered for 1½ hours, stirring occasionally.

Stir in both kinds of beans and the sugar, and simmer another ½ hour.

To serve, top bowls of chili with grated cheddar, chopped chilies and a dollop of sour cream.

The first step to enjoying kale is to remove the stems, which can be tough and stringy even when cooked. Start by removing the stem from the center of the leaf by folding each leaf in half. With the back of the leaf on the outside, cut away the center vein from the bottom to top in a V-shape. Wash greens in cool water and pat dry. Unlike lettuce, which should be gently torn to avoid bruising, kale leaves can be cut/chopped with a knife. See p. 376.

Kale Caesar!

Have fun preparing this regal salad – and be theatrical, like a waiter in an old fashioned supper club! Assemble the salad just before ready to eat, and prepare it in front of guests or at a picnic table.

SERVES: FOUR

CROUTONS

1 clove garlic, crushed and minced
2 Tablespoons olive oil
1 cup stale baguette bread, cubed

Crush and mince garlic and heat gently in a skillet over low heat with 2 Tablespoons olive oil.

Add bread cubes and sauté over medium heat, stirring constantly to coat bread cubes well, until cubes are crisp and golden brown on all sides.

Remove to paper toweling to drain.

SALAD

1 bunch fresh kale

Wash and trim kale, then chop into bite-sized pieces and refrigerate (or place in the cooler) wrapped in damp paper toweling until ready to assemble the salad.

CAESAR DRESSING – THE STAR OF THE SHOW!

1 large egg, organically grown
1 clove garlic
½ cup, *less* 2 Tablespoons olive oil
½ teaspoon worcestershire sauce
½ teaspoon kosher salt
¼ teaspoon freshly ground black pepper
Juice of ½ lemon
4 anchovy fillets, quartered lengthwise
¼ cup fresh parmesan cheese, grated

Begin the dressing – which is the star of the show, by coddling the egg. Coddling is done by partially cooking an egg in its shell for 1 minute in boiling water. *This can be done before leaving home on picnic day.*

Then gather all remaining salad and dressing ingredients on a tray or in the area where assembly will take place.

Begin assembly by peeling garlic clove and cutting it in half. Crush the two halves in the bottom of the salad bowl.

Add chopped kale and olive oil, and toss to coat each leaf with the garlic flavor and oil. Add Worcestershire sauce, salt and pepper.

While guests are enthralled with the production, break the coddled egg over the salad and toss until the kale leaves glisten!

Then stick a fork into the half lemon and, holding the fork in one hand and the lemon in the other, squeeze lemon juice over the kale and other ingredients. Toss again until the dressing begins to look creamy.

Add the anchovies and mix. Taste for seasoning.

To finish, toss in the grated cheese and toasted croutons.

Take a bow and serve immediately!

Consuming raw or undercooked eggs is not advisable for young children, pregnant women or those with certain medical conditions. Use flash pasteurized raw eggs to avoid salmonella concerns.

Lemon-Poppy Seed Zucchini Bread

This sweet bread is made moist with zucchini and tart with lemon and sour cream. These small loaves also make terrific gifts.

YIELD: THREE FIVE-INCH LOAVES

½ cup unsalted butter, softened

1⅓ cups granulated sugar

3 large eggs

1½ cups all-purpose flour

½ teaspoon salt

¼ teaspoon baking soda

½ cup sour cream

1 cup zucchini, grated

Zest of 1 lemon

2 teaspoons poppy seeds

Use a box grater to grate the zucchini. A food processor will create too much moisture which will then cause the batter to fall in the oven from this extra weight. When adding ingredients like zucchini and carrots to baked goods, use this hand-held tool for grating to avoid excess moisture.

Preheat oven to 325 degrees. Butter three 5 x 3-inch loaf pans well.

Sift together the flour, salt and soda onto a sheet of waxed paper; set aside.

In a large bowl with an electric mixer, beat butter until creamy.

Gradually add sugar and continue beating until light and fluffy, approximately 3 minutes.

Add eggs, one at a time, blending well after each addition.

In a separate bowl, mix zucchini, lemon zest and poppy seeds; set aside.

Alternately add the flour mixture to the butter mixture with sour cream. Fold in zucchini mixture by hand.

Spoon batter into prepared pans to ¾ full - only. Bake 35 to 40 minutes, or until toothpick inserted into center of each loaf comes out clean. *These loaves rise quite a bit during baking. If you have extra batter after filling the three pans, don't be tempted to top off the loaves, but make a cupcake with the extra batter instead. If pans are too full, the batter will spill over the top while baking.*

Cool loaves in pans for 5 to 10 minutes then, remove to a wire rack to cool completely.

Oatmeal Cookies with Warm Coffee Glaze

These oatmeal cookies are drizzled with a sweet coffee glaze while still warm!

YIELD: THIRTY-SIX GLAZED COOKIES

COOKIES

½ cup butter, softened

½ cup shortening

1 cup brown sugar, packed

1 cup granulated sugar

2 large eggs

1½ teaspoons pure vanilla extract

1¾ cups all-purpose flour

1 teaspoon baking soda

1 teaspoon salt

3 cups old fashioned rolled oats

½ cup raisins, plumped

Be sure to use old fashioned rolled oats, not instant for this recipe.

Plump raisins in one cup of strong hot coffee for 20 to 30 minutes, or until soft and supple.

Preheat oven to 375 degrees.

In a large bowl with an electric mixer, cream butter and shortening with sugars until light and fluffy, approximately 3 minutes. Add eggs and continue to cream until well incorporated. Add vanilla; mix.

Whisk dry ingredients (flour, soda and salt) together, then stir in the oats. Mix dry ingredients with the butter mixture. Then remove batter from mixer and fold in the raisins by hand.

Scoop dough in uniform rounds, using a medium-sized ice cream scoop, and place on cookie sheets lined with parchment paper.

Bake 10 to 12 minutes, or until golden brown with crisp edges.

Set cookie sheets over a cooling rack and immediately spoon the warm glaze over the hot cookies (while still on the parchment), one teaspoonful at a time.

WARM COFFEE GLAZE

2 Tablespoons butter

4 Tablespoons strong brewed coffee

1 teaspoon pure vanilla extract

1 teaspoon cinnamon

1 cup powdered sugar

Brew one cup of strong coffee.

Melt butter. Whisk in coffee, vanilla and cinnamon.

Sift powdered sugar into the butter-coffee mixture and whisk to combine.

Drizzle glaze over the cookies right out of the oven, using approximately one teaspoon of glaze for each cookie.

Allow cookies to cool.

Occasions   Oatmeal Cookies with Warm Coffee Glaze

Concord Grape Cobbler

Concord grapes are in season in September and October and have a wonderful sugary sweet taste. This cobbler takes me back to my childhood in Indiana where my grandmother grew grapes and made unusual and delicious baked treats.

SERVES: TWELVE

COBBLER

1⅓ cups all-purpose flour

½ cup granulated sugar

2 teaspoons baking powder

½ teaspoon salt

7 Tablespoons unsalted butter, cold

1 large egg

½ cup Half and Half cream

Preheat oven to 375 degrees. Butter an 8-inch square baking dish.

In a medium sized bowl, whisk the flour, sugar, powder and salt.

Cut 6 Tablespoons of the butter into cubes. Add butter cubes to flour mixture and using a pastry cutter, cut in until the mixture resembles a coarse meal and the butter pieces are about the size of a pea.

Beat the egg and add to the cream. Then add this mixture to the flour mixture and stir until a sticky dough forms.

Drop dough into 12 heaping Tablespoons over grape filling, leaving an approximately ½-inch space between each dollop.

Sprinkle cobbler with 1 to 2 teaspoons of granulated sugar and dot with 1 teaspoon of butter cut into small cubes. Bake 40 to 45 minutes, or until the cobbler is golden brown and the filling is bubbly.

Serve warm topped with a splash of Half and Half cream.

CONCORD GRAPE FILLING

6 cups concord grapes, seeded and halved

2½ Tablespoons all-purpose flour

½ cup granulated sugar, with 2 Tablespoons reserved for topping

1 teaspoon pure vanilla extract

Juice of ½ fresh lemon

¼ teaspoon kosher salt

In a large bowl, combine all ingredients and toss to coat grapes. Spread filling into prepare baking dish, top with cobbler and bake as directed above.

GERMANY IS RECOGNIZED FOR ITS VERY REGIONAL AND DIVERSE CUISINE.

THE TINY VILLAGE OF WALDECK (NEAR CASSEL) FOR EXAMPLE, IS KNOWN FOR DISHES LIKE SAUERBRATEN (ROAST BEEF MARINATED IN VINEGAR) AND DELICIOUS PASTRIES. HERE AN ANCIENT CASTLE STANDS GUARD OVER BOTH THE PRINCIPALITY AND THE WALDECK SEE, A LOVELY FRESH WATER LAKE ADJACENT TO A QUAINT VILLAGE OF HALF-TIMBERED BUILDINGS AND MEDIEVAL CHURCHES. A PATCHWORK QUILT OF SOFT YELLOWS AND GREENS BECKONS ONE TO THE ROLLING COUNTRYSIDE OF TREE-LINED ROADS AND MANICURED FARMS BEYOND.

I RECOMMEND A VISIT TO THIS UNASSUMING CORNER OF THE WORLD. IN THE MEANTIME, ENJOY GERMAN CUISINE AT HOME VIA THIS AUTHENTIC MENU.

OKTOBERFEST WEEKEND

German Oktoberfest

FOR 6

Figs, Almonds & Brie – *Oh My!*

Sauerbraten with Ginger Sauce
Wilted Swiss Chard Salad
Grau-oder Mischbrot

Just Peachy Yellow Roses in German Pie Pastry

Serve a German Shiraz *with a fruity or chocolatey influence with a heavy meat like* Sauerbraten.

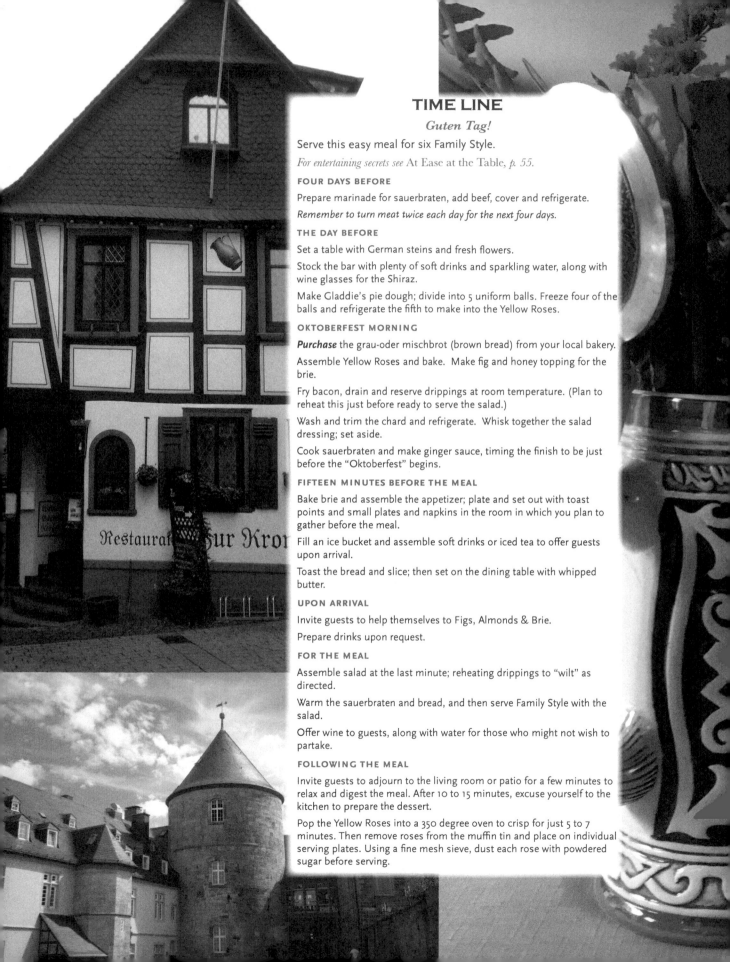

TIME LINE

Guten Tag!

Serve this easy meal for six Family Style.

For entertaining secrets see At Ease at the Table, *p. 55.*

FOUR DAYS BEFORE

Prepare marinade for sauerbraten, add beef, cover and refrigerate.

Remember to turn meat twice each day for the next four days.

THE DAY BEFORE

Set a table with German steins and fresh flowers.

Stock the bar with plenty of soft drinks and sparkling water, along with wine glasses for the Shiraz.

Make Gladdie's pie dough; divide into 5 uniform balls. Freeze four of the balls and refrigerate the fifth to make into the Yellow Roses.

OKTOBERFEST MORNING

Purchase the grau-oder mischbrot (brown bread) from your local bakery.

Assemble Yellow Roses and bake. Make fig and honey topping for the brie.

Fry bacon, drain and reserve drippings at room temperature. (Plan to reheat this just before ready to serve the salad.)

Wash and trim the chard and refrigerate. Whisk together the salad dressing; set aside.

Cook sauerbraten and make ginger sauce, timing the finish to be just before the "Oktoberfest" begins.

FIFTEEN MINUTES BEFORE THE MEAL

Bake brie and assemble the appetizer; plate and set out with toast points and small plates and napkins in the room in which you plan to gather before the meal.

Fill an ice bucket and assemble soft drinks or iced tea to offer guests upon arrival.

Toast the bread and slice; then set on the dining table with whipped butter.

UPON ARRIVAL

Invite guests to help themselves to Figs, Almonds & Brie.

Prepare drinks upon request.

FOR THE MEAL

Assemble salad at the last minute; reheating drippings to "wilt" as directed.

Warm the sauerbraten and bread, and then serve Family Style with the salad.

Offer wine to guests, along with water for those who might not wish to partake.

FOLLOWING THE MEAL

Invite guests to adjourn to the living room or patio for a few minutes to relax and digest the meal. After 10 to 15 minutes, excuse yourself to the kitchen to prepare the dessert.

Pop the Yellow Roses into a 350 degree oven to crisp for just 5 to 7 minutes. Then remove roses from the muffin tin and place on individual serving plates. Using a fine mesh sieve, dust each rose with powdered sugar before serving.

Figs, Almonds & Brie - *Oh My!*

Figs are great in the fall, especially when paired with the savory flavor of brie.

SERVES: SIX TO EIGHT

1 8-ounce round brie cheese
¼ cup sourwood honey
1 Tablespoon water
4 fresh figs, stemmed and quartered
½ teaspoon pure vanilla extract
⅓ cup almonds

Toast almonds in a 350 degree oven for approximately 8 minutes; cool and chop.

Reduce oven to 325 degrees.

In a small saucepan, heat water with honey until dissolved.

Add figs and vanilla and continue cooking until the figs are soft, approximately 10 minutes.

Stir in toasted and chopped almonds.

Place Brie on a jelly roll pan covered with parchment paper and drizzle fig and nut mixture over the top. Bake for 5 to 10 minutes, or until the brie starts to ooze and is soft and buttery, but not melted.

Serve immediately with toast points or crackers.

Fresh figs are in season summer to autumn, but can be hard to find. If you are unable to find fresh, use black Mission dried figs and re-hydrate in very hot water with a squeeze of fresh lemon. See p. 372.

Brie is a French cheese originally made in the Seine-et-Marne area of France, and is delicious served warm as an easy appetizer.

Baking makes Brie buttery soft and this creamy ripe cheese pairs beautifully with Sourwood honey and fresh figs.

Sauerbraten with Ginger Sauce

This "sour" beef roast is fork-tender with a sweet and tart sauce that is quintessential German. The roast must marinate for three to four days, so be sure to plan accordingly.

PRONOUNCED: SOW-ER-BRA-TIN

SERVES: SIX

2 pounds chuck roast
1 Tablespoon kosher salt
1 yellow onion, chopped
10 whole black peppercorns
2 to 3 whole allspice berries
2 dried bay leaves
3 to 5 whole cloves
½ cup apple cider vinegar
¾ cup red wine
⅛ cup all-purpose flour, divided
⅛ cup vegetable oil
1 Tablespoon brown sugar, packed
¼ cup gingersnap cookies, crushed

Bay leaves are warmly associated with hearty dishes like sauerbraten and pot roasts with big flavors. Temper any fondness you may have for this herb however, because it only takes one or two leaves to alter the flavor of a dish. Fresh bay leaves are especially pungent, much more so than dried. See p. 367.

Place beef in a large Dutch oven or covered cast-iron cooking pot.

In a medium bowl, mix salt, onion, peppercorns, allspice, bay leaves, cloves, vinegar and wine. Pour over the meat.

Cover pot and refrigerate for **3 to 4 days**, turning meat twice each day.

Preheat oven to 300 degrees.

Remove meat from marinade; set aside. Reserve marinade in separate bowl; set aside.

Dry meat with paper toweling, then roll in ⅛ cup flour *less 1 Tablespoon.*

Heat vegetable oil in the Dutch oven and brown meat over medium-high heat on all sides. Return marinade to Dutch oven and bring to a boil.

Cover pot and cook in the oven for **2½ hours.**

Remove meat from cooking liquid and set aside.

Skim any fat from the remaining liquid and strain through a sieve into a 4-cup measuring bowl. Discard solids, then add water to make 3½ cups of liquid.

Mix brown sugar with remaining Tablespoon of flour, then whisk in ¼ cup of water.

In small increments, add the brown sugar mixture to the cooking liquid, whisking with each addition, until all is incorporated.

Turn heat to low and add the gingersnaps; stir gently just to incorporate. Add the beef back into the pot, and simmer 15 minutes, watching the heat to ensure the sauce remains fluid and does not become too thick.

Slice meat and serve with sauce.

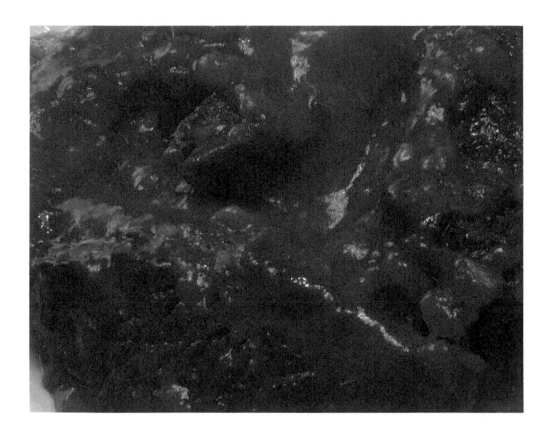

Wilted Swiss Chard Salad

I learned to make this sweet and sour wilted salad as a girl from our beloved Mrs. Grimes, a family friend and utterly German lady who greatly impacted our younger years. Wilted Salad is a classic German dish that incorporates the drippings of bacon in a warm dressing that "wilts" the salad leaves while adding enormous flavor.

SERVES: SIX TO EIGHT

1 bunch Swiss chard
3 slices smoked bacon and drippings
1 shallot
3 Tablespoons sourwood honey
1 teaspoon stone ground mustard
1 teaspoon kosher salt
½ teaspoon freshly ground black pepper
2 Tablespoons olive oil
2 Tablespoons sherry wine vinegar

Wash, remove stems, trim and spin dry Swiss Chard; chop or tear onto a serving platter and set aside. Dice bacon and shallot.

In a small saucepan over medium heat, sauté the bacon pieces with the shallot until bacon is crispy and shallot is translucent.

Whisk in the honey, mustard, salt and pepper. Whisk in olive oil until well incorporated and light.

Then remove the pan from the heat and carefully add the vinegar (watch for splattering). Stir well.

Pour hot dressing over chard salad and serve immediately.

It would not be a German meal without Grau-oder Mischbrot!

Just Peachy Yellow Roses

Sweet and buttery, these pretty little tarts look just like a yellow rose in bloom and make one just-the-right-size serving of yummy fruit pastry for each guest. To help ensure your success, see Baking Secrets, Rolling & Baking Pies, p. 358.

YIELD: SIX ROSES, OR INDIVIDUAL SERVINGS

PIE CRUST

¹/₅ recipe Gladdie's Pie Dough

(See recipe that follows)

YELLOW ROSES

3 to 4 ripe peaches
Juice of ½ fresh lemon
½ cup granulated sugar
2 Tablespoons all-purpose flour
¼ teaspoon cinnamon
3 Tablespoons butter, divided
Powdered sugar

Preheat oven to 375 degrees. Butter a muffin tin well with cooking spray.

Wash, peel, seed and slice peaches very thin. Place in a large microwave-safe bowl with the juice of ½ lemon. Microwave peaches for 1 minute to ensure slices are supple enough to roll.

Melt 2 Tablespoons of butter. In the meantime, mix sugar with flour and cinnamon. Then add melted butter and stir to make a paste.

Choose ripe yet firm peaches for this recipe. If fruit is too ripe it will not hold up to the assembly.

Roll pie dough into a large 12 x 12-inch **square.** Using a pastry cutter with a crinkled edge, slice dough into six 2-inch wide strips.

Lift and lightly swish each strip through a small mound of flour on the counter top, to and fro, to coat lightly and prevent the dough from softening and sticking to the counter while the roses are being assembled.

One at a time, spread sugar and butter paste down the middle of each 2-inch strip.

Lay peach slices across the top half of the pastry strip with the arch of the peach slices up. Slices should cover only half of the pastry strip. Overlap peach slices from the center of each preceding slice until the entire strip of dough is covered in a ripple of yellow.

Now, fold the bottom half of the pastry strip over the bottom ½-inch of the peach slices, to secure them between the top and bottom parts of the pastry.

Then gently roll each filled pastry strip from one long end to the other to form a "rose." Use your hands to keep/hold strips intact as you place each "blossom" into an individual muffin cup. Adjust peaches as necessary once they are in the tin to ensure uniform "petals" and rose shapes.

Once all six roses are assembled and placed in the tin, cut the remaining Tablespoon of butter into six uniform cubes.

After sprinkling granulated sugar over each rose, dot with a tiny cube of butter before putting into the oven to bake.

Lay a loose sheet of foil on top of the filled muffin tin to prevent peaches from browning and losing their bright color during the first 25 minutes of baking time, then remove and discard foil.

Bake roses for 35 to 45 minutes *in total*, or until pastry is cooked through.

While still warm, remove roses from the muffin tin by running a knife around the outer rim of each muffin cup and lifting roses out gently with the help of a spatula or fork. *If making roses ahead, briefly re-heat them before removing from tins to prevent sticking.*

Using a fine mesh sieve, lightly dust each rose with powdered sugar before serving. *If you are unable to find fresh peaches, use frozen and slice thin.*

This is a work of art, so use your imagination and visualize the flower! Do not try to make a tight roll, but gently work with peaches and dough to roll into what will really and truly look like a yellow rose and fit perfectly into the muffin cups.

Shown here:
TOP - Peach slices laid on the top half of the pastry strip.
MIDDLE - The bottom half of pastry folded over the edge of the peach slices.
BOTTOM - Gently rolling the long strip into a yellow rose.

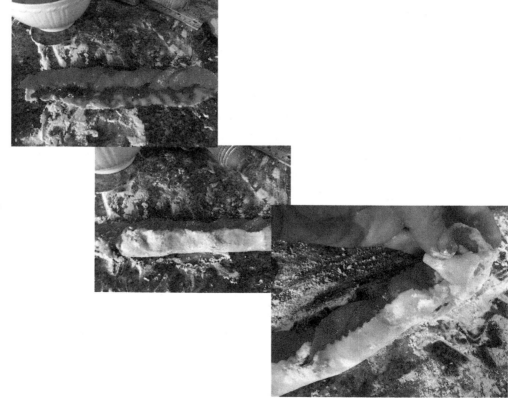

Gladdie's Pie Dough

This is my mother's recipe for pie dough that is both scrumptious and easy to work with. When mother was young lady working as a book keeper, she rented a room from a woman from Germany who taught her how to bake pies and breads in the tradition of her homeland. The pastries mother learned to bake from Mrs. Creig are authentically German and truly delicious.

YIELD: TWO DOUBLE-CRUST PIES, PLUS ONE SINGLE-CRUST PIE

4 cups all-purpose flour, sifted once with

1 teaspoon kosher salt

1½ cups crisco shortening, chilled

½ cup cold water

1 Tablespoon white vinegar

1 large egg

Beat egg lightly with a fork. Combine the chilled water, egg and vinegar in separate bowl.

In a large bowl using an electric mixer set with a dough hook; add the sifted flour and salt.

Working quickly, mix in the cold shortening that has been cut into small cubes, and combine just until crumbly.

Gradually add the "wet" ingredients to the flour mixture while mixer is running and mix just until dough forms into a ball. *Be careful to not over-mix the dough or it will become tough and not be the flaky pastry desired.*

Separate out enough dough for the recipe and store the rest. Pie dough can be made ahead and refrigerated for up to 3 days or frozen for later use. Thaw frozen dough in the refrigerator.

When rolling pastry, avoid stretching the dough. When stretched, dough will fall in the oven.

Purchase shortening in bars for easy measuring, and store shortening in the refrigerator so that it is always cold when you are ready to bake.

Always check liquid measurements at eye level for accuracy.

Use liquid measuring cups for wet ingredients and dry measuring cups for dry ingredients.

WHAT COULD BE MORE MEANINGFUL THAN WELCOMING A LITTLE BABY
AND NEW LIFE INTO THE WORLD? WHETHER IT IS ON CHRISTENING
SUNDAY OR A SATURDAY AFTERNOON, BABY'S WELCOMING BRUNCH
IS ONE OF FAMILY AND MEMORIES IN-THE-MAKING. THIS BRUNCH
MENU INCLUDES SOMETHING FOR EVERYONE TO ENJOY WHILE
TAKING TURNS HOLDING AND LOVING THE NEW BUNDLE OF JOY!

AN OCTOBER WEEKEND MORNING

Baby's Welcoming Brunch

FOR 12

Grapefruit Grenadine Mocktails

Chili Infused Eggs & Bacon Roses in Puff
Pastry
Orange & Pomegranate Toss

Pistachio Snowballs
Pot de Crème au Chocolat with Caramel
Sauce & Fleur de Sel

Serve a
Johannisberg
Riesling *with a
hint of sweetness to
balance the bacon
and eggs. Serve*
Madeira *wine with
the desserts.*

THE WATER BATH

TIME LINE
Celebrating Precious Cargo

This brunch is designed to be served buffet style with seating in the dining room.

For entertaining secrets see When Accidents Happen, *p. 57.*

TWO DAYS BEFORE THE BRUNCH

Lay a pretty buffet table from which to serve brunch.

Set the dining room table with pastel plates, linens and baby items from generations past.

Use place cards for pre-planned seating so Great Grandma and the new mother can get to and from the table with ease.

Purchase good quality caramel sauce for the Pot de Crème.

Chill Riesling wine and grapefruit juice. Chill mocktail glasses and make grenadine.

THE DAY BEFORE

Prepare *a double recipe of Pot De Crème;* refrigerate in individual cups or ramekins without baking.

Bake snowballs; cool, seal on serving platter and refrigerate.

Prepare the orange & pomegranate toss; seal and refrigerate.

Thaw puff pastry in refrigerator overnight.

EARLY MORNING ON THE DAY OF BRUNCH

Assemble *a double recipe of chili infused eggs;* hold in sealed container until ready to add to puff pastry and bake.

Fry *a double recipe of bacon* and assemble bacon roses. Hold at room temperature until ready to add to egg casserole.

Bring snowballs to room temperature.

FORTY-FIVE MINUTES BEFORE GUESTS ARRIVE

Roll puff pastry and fit into casserole dish; roll second sheet to top, and make cutouts. Assemble and bake egg casseroles – *be sure to set a timer so you don't forget they are in the oven in the excitement of the day!*

Assemble all ingredients for mocktails and fill an ice bucket with ice. Bring pot de crème to room temperature.

UPON ARRIVAL

Make and serve mocktails and/or Riesling wine.

Have a table designated for gifts and decorate it with Baby's pictures and keepsakes.

FOR THE BRUNCH

Fill wine and water glasses. Put pot de crème in oven to bake – *be sure to set a timer!* Add bacon roses to egg casserole and bake for final 5 to 8 minutes. Set fruit toss on buffet.

When eggs are hot out of the oven, invite guests to serve themselves from the buffet after a moment of thanks. *As the host/hostess, keep an eye on the young parents and help them serve the young children and little siblings, if needed.*

AFTER BRUNCH

Gather everyone for a group picture with Baby to commemorate the day. Then serve snowball cookies and pot de crème (with caramel and sea salt) along with Madeira wine, if guests desire.

Grapefruit Grenadine Mocktails

It is always nice to offer guests a non-alcoholic "mocktail," and this one is especially good for brunch. Be sure to make these drinks one at a time.

See p. 383, *How to Make Pomegranate Juice.*

YIELD: EIGHT MOCKTAILS

¼ cup grenadine syrup
1½ quarts fresh grapefruit juice, chilled
8 sprigs fresh rosemary
1 grapefruit

Chill eight highball glasses for 1 to 2 hours in the freezer.

When ready to serve, pour 1½ teaspoons of grenadine into each glass that has been filled half-way with ice.

Holding the teaspoon down in the glass, right side up, *slowly* pour ¼ cup grapefruit juice into the bowl of the spoon so that it trickles over the surface but does not mix directly with the grenadine.

Do not shake or stir!

Cut grapefruit into 8 wedges. Garnish mocktails with a sprig of fresh rosemary and wedge of grapefruit.

GRENADINE

Grenadine syrup is easy to make and much better fresh!

1 cup pure pomegranate juice
1 cup granulated sugar
Juice of 1 fresh lemon
¼ teaspoon zest of lemon

In a saucepan, combine pomegranate juice with sugar and bring to a boil. Reduce heat and simmer for 10 to 15 minutes.

Add lemon juice and zest and stir to mix thoroughly.

Then cool completely before using in non-alcoholic drinks.

Chili Infused Eggs &
Bacon Roses in Puff Pastry

These buttery eggs with a chili kick are baked in puff pastry and topped with bacon roses. Serve with a toss of orange slices and pomegranate seeds for a perfectly balanced meal.

SERVES: SIX

CHILI INFUSED EGGS

5 large eggs
¼ cup all-purpose flour
½ teaspoon baking powder
1 teaspoon kosher salt
1 cup cottage cheese
8 ounces cheddar cheese, grated
¼ cup unsalted butter, melted
1 4-ounce can hatch green chilies, drained and diced

Preheat oven to 375 degrees.

In a large bowl, beat eggs.

Whisk flour, baking powder and salt together; then add to beaten eggs.

Fold in the cheeses, melted butter and chilies; mix to incorporate.

Pour egg mixture into prepared puff pastry; assemble and bake as directed below.

PUFF PASTRY

1 17.3-ounce package puff pastry (two sheets)
All-purpose flour
1 egg white

Thaw puff pastry as directed in the refrigerator overnight.

Lightly butter a 9 x 9-inch square casserole dish; set aside. Place pastry on a lightly floured surface and roll out pastry sheets one at a time.

Roll the first sheet into a twelve inch square; fit into the baking dish, lining both the bottom of the dish and all four sides.

Roll the second sheet into a 9-inch square. With a sharp knife, cut an 8-inch square from the center of this piece, leaving a one-inch-wide frame; set aside.

Now, fill the pastry shell with the egg mixture. Score the top rim of the pastry in the dish. With a pastry brush, cover the entire rim of scored pastry with egg white.

Top the scored and brushed pastry with the pastry frame, aligning the outer edges and pressing gently to adhere together. Now brush the top of the frame with egg white.

Using a leaf-shaped cutter, or pastry wheel freehand, cut twenty 2-inch leaves or flower shapes from remaining pastry. Score lines in the dough to resemble the veins in a natural petal or leaf. Place the "leaves/petals" atop the pastry frame around the circumference of the dish, pressing to stick these to the sheet of pastry very gently - trying to not deform the shapes.

Bake for 35 to 40 minutes, or until eggs are set, browned and bubbly and the pastry is puffy and golden.

Bacon Roses

8 slices bacon

Toothpicks

While eggs are baking, prepare bacon roses. Separate bacon slices and arrange on a griddle. Cook slowly until bacon begins to brown, but is still pliable (not crisp).

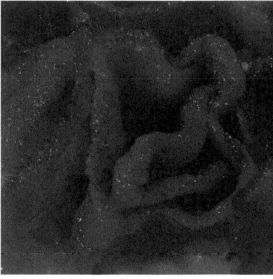

Remove to a plate lined with paper toweling to drain *just a minute or two*. When the bacon is just cool enough to touch, loosely roll each slice lengthwise to form a rose shape, and secure with a toothpick (if necessary) on the lower edge of one side.

It is important to move quickly to rolling the bacon before it dries, or it will not roll, but crumble.

When the Chili Infused Eggs and pastry are within 5 to 8 minutes of being fully cooked, remove from the oven and arrange bacon roses in the center of the dish by clustering them on top of the eggs.

Return casserole to the oven for final baking time and to crisp the bacon a bit more. Serve immediately.

Orange & Pomegranate Toss

Orange and pomegranate are a natural fruit pairing in the fall, and this quick and easy salad balances beautifully with rich eggs and bacon.

SERVES: TWELVE

6 navel oranges, peeled
Seeds of 2 pomegranates
Juice of 1 orange

Peel oranges, separate pieces and cut each piece in two.

Toss orange pieces with pomegranate seeds to combine. Then toss once or twice more after adding the orange juice to coat the fruits.

Cover and chill until ready to serve.

To seed a pomegranate, cut the fruit in half and hold the open end over a bowl. Using a wooden spoon, pop the back of the fruit to release the ruby red jewels inside. Seeds will spill out into the bowl with each rap of the spoon. Be sure to use care when separating the seeds from the inner white membrane and to not burst the individual juice sacs. Once the seeds are removed, pick any bitter membrane from the seeds. Seeds will keep for up to one week refrigerated.
Pomegranate juice stains, so protect your clothing!

Pistachio Snowballs

These nutty cookies are coated with sweet powdered sugar, and made with salted pistachios to add a savory twist. Cookies can be kept in an airtight container for a few days or frozen.

YIELD: TWENTY-FOUR COOKIES

¼ **cup granulated sugar**

¾ **cup unsalted butter, softened**

1 **teaspoon pure vanilla extract**

1½ **cups all-purpose flour**

1½ **cups lightly salted pistachios, chopped fine**

¼ **teaspoon kosher salt**

1 **to** 1½ **cups powdered sugar**

Preheat oven to 325 degrees. Line two baking sheets with parchment paper.

In a large bowl with an electric mixer, beat butter with sugar until creamy and pale yellow in color; approximately 4 to 5 minutes.

Add vanilla and combine.

Sift flour with salt and add to creamed mixture; mix until just combined.

Fold in the pistachios by hand.

Pinch off small sections of dough and roll into 1-inch diameter balls between the palms of your two hands; place on baking sheets.

Bake 15 minutes, or until outside edges begin to turn golden brown.

As soon as cookies are cool enough to touch (just 1 to 2 minutes), place four at a time into a medium-sized bowl filled with powdered sugar. Lift the bowl and swirl the sugar around the cookies to coat them well.

Let cookies cool, and then toss in the powdered sugar *again* to coat heavily.

Pot De Crème Au Chocolat with Caramel Sauce & Fleur de Sel

These rich, creamy chocolatey cups of "heaven" are traditionally served in tiny china cups with lids, but if you do not have cups specifically for Pot De Crème, coffee cups or ramekins can be called into service.

PRONOUNCED: PO-DU-CREM

YIELD: SIX CUPS OF HEAVEN

2 cups Half and Half cream
⅓ cup granulated sugar
Seeds from 1 vanilla bean pod
4 ounces semi-sweet chocolate
1 teaspoon cocoa powder
5 large egg yolks
Caramel sauce
Fleur de sel

In a double boiler, combine the cream with sugar; stir to dissolve. Split vanilla bean pod in two and scrape out the seeds; add seeds to the cream mixture.

Bring sweet vanilla cream to a boil, then remove from the heat and allow to infuse, covered, for 30 minutes.

Preheat oven to 325 degrees. Place a jelly roll pan in the middle of the oven and fill half-way with water.

Return cream mixture to medium heat and add chocolate and cocoa powder; stir to melt and blend. Remove from the heat and allow to cool.

In a large bowl with an electric mixture, whip egg **yolks** for 1 minute.

Reduce speed and add ¼ of the cream/chocolate mixture to temper the eggs. Then add the remaining cream and chocolate, and mix well on medium-high speed.

Fill Pot De Crème cups (or ramekins) to ⅔ full. Place in the Water Bath already in the center of the oven.

Bake 20 to 25 minutes, or until custards are firm with the center being still a bit jiggly. Allow to cool.

Once cooled, cover each cup with plastic wrap and press it gently down until it touches the custard to prevent a skin from forming. Chill covered pots for **2 hours.**

When ready to serve, top Pot De Crème with a slight drizzle of caramel sauce and a sprinkle of sea salt before serving.

The Water Bath method ensures even, slow cooking and guards against curdled custards or cracked cheese cakes.

Start by placing a jelly roll pan in a cold oven and filling it with enough water to reach the half-way point. Now, preheat oven as per recipe and allow the water to heat while the oven heats. When custard or cakes are ready to bake, set the smaller cups or ramekins directly into the hot water for a constant heat source while baking. When finished baking, allow the water to cool in the jelly roll pan before removing from the oven.

Thanksgiving ushers in the holiday season with the rich fall colors of Bittersweet, eggplant and cranberry and is a time to celebrate family. I like to gather colorful leaves and berries and set a table that is pretty yet relaxed.

A long standing tradition for my family is to take a long run together and work up an appetite before settling in to prepare the feast. After dinner we walk through the neighborhood and watch the lights come on as Christmas begins - and our meal digests!

The traditional Thanksgiving meal is one of those menus with loads of things to do at the very last minute. We often have a houseful of family that like to help in the kitchen though, so I happily enlist them. My mother-in-law is charged with making the gravy, my son Robby is in charge of the turkey, Todd or his Dad will carve the bird and Michael usually keeps everyone supplied with Black-Eyed Susans and good humor!

The "occasion" of Thanksgiving is all about being thankful for one another and blessings, so it seems apropos to have lots of hands preparing the meal.

THANKSGIVING DAY

Thanksgiving

FOR 12

Black-Eyed Susans

Roast Turkey
Mashed Idaho Potatoes & Pan Gravy
Southern Cornbread Dressing
Oven Roasted Root Vegetables
Steamed Green Beans with Toasted Almonds

Holiday Pie with a Braided Crust
Ginger Ginger Ginger Cookies

RECIPES
BLACK-EYED
SUSANS

ROAST TURKEY

PAN GRAVY

SOUTHERN
CORNBREAD
DRESSING

HOLIDAY PIE WITH
A BRAIDED CRUST

GINGER GINGER
GINGER COOKIES

Serve a barrel-aged Chardonnay *with the Black Eyed Susans. Serve a refreshing* Pinot Grigio, *or a light red like a* Pinot Noir *or* Merlot *with the turkey.*

BRINING,
CHOOSING AND
CARVING A BIRD

BRAIDING PIE
DOUGH

GINGER IN A SNAP

TIME LINE

Thank you for the food before us, the family around us
& the love amongst us.

I like to keep Thanksgiving elegant, but also make it easy. This dinner for twelve is designed to be served with the foods set on a buffet so guests can fill their plates and then return to the table. This is my favorite way of serving a formal dinner because it permits more room on the dining table for decorations and also allows for more elbow room. This means of service also keeps the foods in a separate area where they can be covered and kept warm (in case anyone wants seconds), yet still allows everything to be easily accessible. *For entertaining secrets see* The Formal Seated Dinner, *p. 8.*

ONE MONTH BEFORE THANKSGIVING

Assemble the Black-Eyed Susans and freeze without baking. Make and bake the ginger cookies and freeze.

ONE WEEK BEFORE THANKSGIVING

Assemble dressing and freeze (unbaked). Do final grocery shopping and purchase or reserve a turkey. Choose and purchase the wines.

TWO DAYS BEFORE

Set the table; arrange centerpiece, but hold perishable flowers in refrigerator to add on Thanksgiving day. Make/print place cards and coordinate other table decorations for the occasion. Make pie dough; refrigerate in 5 separate balls of dough, wrapped. Chill wine.

ONE DAY BEFORE

Mix up the brine, add the turkey; refrigerate covered overnight.

Prepare pan gravy through first steps to straining of fat; cool and refrigerate.

Toast almonds; store in an air tight container. Wash and snap green beans; then refrigerate wrapped in damp paper toweling in a sealed container or large baggie.

Prep root vegetables for roasting with the turkey; wrap in damp toweling and refrigerate to avoid discoloring.

EARLY THANKSGIVING MORNING

Get out early for some exercise in the fresh fall air; then dress for the day and begin!

Assemble Holiday Pie and bake before the kitchen gets busy.

Assemble turkey for roasting with root vegetables; roast as directed – timing the finish to within ½ hour of stated meal time. Remove cornbread, cookies and Susans from the freezer. Add fresh flowers to the centerpiece and place.

ONE HOUR BEFORE SERVING

Peel potatoes and refrigerate wrapped in damp paper toweling and sealed. Bake dressing. Bake and serve Black-Eyed Susans with beverage of choice.

ONE HALF HOUR BEFORE SERVING

Steam beans. Mash potatoes and hold, covered, to keep warm. Finish gravy.

Tent turkey and allow to rest before carving.

JUST BEFORE SERVING

Call in the troops! Assign everyone with a task or two so that the meal can come together all at once. Here's what is left to do:

Fill water and wine glasses. Carve turkey and arrange on a platter with root vegetables, herbs and fresh grapes. Add almonds to beans and season; set on buffet.

Place potatoes in a large serving bowl and add a dot of butter to the top; set on buffet. Fill gravy boat with pan gravy. Place dressing on buffet.

AT THE DESSERT STATION

Have pie, cookies, plates, forks and napkins ready; plan to allow guests to serve themselves. Offer coffee and refill water glasses after the entrée.

Black-Eyed Susans

These savory cheese cookies with sweet dates and crunchy toasted almonds are a pleasing combination. The cookies are easy to make, but stuffing the dates takes a bit of time, so make ahead and chill or freeze (before baking on Thanksgiving day). Then just thaw in the refrigerator and bake as directed when ready to serve.

YIELD: THIRTY-TWO SUSANS

4 ounces sharp cheddar cheese, grated
½ cup unsalted butter, chilled
1 cup all-purpose flour
2 Tablespoons parmesan cheese, ground
¼ teaspoon kosher salt
⅛ teaspoon ground red pepper
16 whole dates, pitted & halved lengthwise
32 whole blanched almonds
Freshly ground black pepper

Preheat oven to 350 degrees.

In a food processor, grate the cheddar cheese, remove and set aside. Then also in the food processor, grind the parmesan cheese into tiny pieces by processing; remove and set aside.

Add cheddar cheese back into processor and pulse with butter and parmesan until combined. Gradually add the flour, processing until combined. Mix the flour, salt, and **red** pepper. Add to cheese mixture in the food processor and pulse until combined and dough just begins to form into a ball.

Divide the mixture into two logs, approximately 1-inch in diameter and 8-inches long. Wrap in plastic wrap and refrigerate approximately **1 hour** or until firm.

While dough is chilling, stuff each date half with a whole almond and set aside.

Slice chilled logs into ¼-inch rounds. Shape each round into an oblong boat-shape with your fingers, while wrapping around the bottom and up to the open edge of each almond-stuffed date. Place cookies on a baking sheet lined with parchment paper, and dust lightly with freshly ground black pepper.

Bake 10 minutes or until cookies are golden brown.

Remove and cool slightly, 5 to 8 minutes, on a wire rack.

Serve warm.

Roast Turkey

This is a no-fail formula for a perfectly moist turkey that's seasoned to the bone.

The secret is in the brining. Two good things happen in this process. Salt draws out the blood, cleansing the bird, and is absorbed in the meat - which becomes juicy and seasoned right down to the bone. Second, the sugar rounds out the salty flavor and helps the turkey brown. If you have purchased a frozen turkey, brining will greatly improve the flavor. The turkey can be prepared through removal from the brine and refrigerated for up to eight hours before roasting.

This method can also be used to roast a chicken - but don't brine automatically.

If you have a bird that is fresh and you know will cook naturally juicy it doesn't need the help of a brine. But if you know your bird will likely be dry or that it has been frozen, then brine it first.

SERVES: TWELVE

BRINING & ROASTING THE BIRD

Brine turkey for 10 to 12 hours before roasting it. Don't worry if a small portion of the turkey is not completely submerged in the brine during this process.

In a large stockpot, mix 1½ gallons of water with 1½ cups of kosher salt and one cup of sugar; stir to dissolve. Add the turkey to the brine, breast side down, and **refrigerate for 10 to 12 hours, covered.**

Remove the turkey from the brine and rinse in cold water; pat dry with paper towels. Discard the brine.

1 12 to 14-pound turkey

1½ cups kosher salt

1 cup granulated sugar

2 medium onions, coarsely chopped

2 carrots, coarsely chopped

2 celery ribs, coarsely chopped

Fresh sage, rosemary & thyme

3 Tablespoons unsalted butter, melted

Preheat the oven to 400 degrees.

Remove neck, wing tips, giblets and cavity fat from the bird.

Tie herbs into a small bundle with kitchen string. Prepare vegetables; set aside.

Place approximately ¼ of the onions, carrots, celery, along with the bundle of herbs into the turkey cavity.

Using kitchen string tie the turkey legs together. Then bring the string around the turkey and tie the wings at the breast.

Scatter the remaining onions, carrots and celery, along with root vegetables, in a large roasting pan. Oil a V-shaped rack and set it in the pan. Transfer the turkey to the rack, breast side up. Brush the turkey with melted butter.

Pour 1 cup of water into the pan and roast the turkey for **45 MINUTES.**

Baste the turkey with the pan juices and add 1 more cup of water to the pan. Roast the turkey for approximately 1 hour and 45 minutes longer, basting it with the pan juices every 30 minutes or so, and adding another ½ cup of water to the roasting pan whenever the vegetables begin to brown. *The turkey is done when an instant-read thermometer inserted into an inner thigh registers 170 degrees.*

Now - *Let it rest!*

Transfer the turkey to a carving board, tent (cover loosely with foil) and let the turkey rest for 20 to 30 minutes to ensure juices are retained in the meat before carving.

Reserve the juices in the roasting pan for making the gravy.

To ensure juicy breast meat, rotate the turkey a quarter turn each time you baste it.

CHOOSE A SMALL, FRESH TURKEY IN THE 14-POUND & UNDER CATEGORY

Large turkeys take longer to cook, making the outer meat likely to overcook and dry out before the interior meat is cooked. If you are feeding more than 12 people, buy two small turkeys rather than one big one.

When serving two small turkeys, cook the first one early in the day. Carve it just before serving time, arrange it on an oven proof platter and cover it with foil. Meanwhile, roast the second turkey. Just before serving, set the platter in a 350 degree oven to warm the meat. Use the whole bird for show and pass the carved turkey.

Carve the second turkey once everyone has had a first serving.

THE DRESSING

Cook the dressing in an oven proof dish, not inside the turkey. A stuffed bird takes longer to cook through than an unstuffed one. The longer the turkey sits in a hot oven, the more it overcooks and dries out.

Steps for carving a bird:

Remove both wings first.

Separate each wing from the body at the joint.

Remove each leg and set aside.

Remove each breast half from the bone in one piece, then thinly slice each half crosswise while on the cutting board.

Cut each leg at the joint, and then carve the meat from the thigh and drumstick.

Use clusters of grapes, fresh parsley and roasted vegetables to garnish the serving platter.

As shown below, root vegetables include beets, carrots, celery root, parsnips, radishes, rutabaga and turnips.

Pan Gravy

2 teaspoons vegetable oil
1 medium yellow onion, chopped
4½ cups water
Reserved pan juices from turkey
1 cup sauvignon blanc wine
3 Tablespoons cornstarch
Freshly ground black pepper

In a large saucepan, heat oil. Add onion and cook over medium high heat until lightly browned, approximately 5 minutes. Cover and continue to cook over low heat for approximately 20 minutes. Add 4 cups of the water and bring to a boil. Cover partially and simmer over low heat until the broth is reduced to 3 cups, approximately **1 hour.** Strain broth into a medium saucepan and skim off the fat.

Gravy can be made ahead to this point and held until the turkey has finished roasting.

Pour the reserved turkey pan juices into a glass measuring cup and skim off the fat that rises to the top. Set the roasting pan over two stove burners on medium high heat.

Add the wine and boil for 2 minutes, scraping up the flavorful brown bits from the bottom of the pan. Scape the contents of the pan into a strainer set over the turkey broth and press on the roasted vegetables to remove juices, then discard. Bring the broth to a boil.

Whisk the cornstarch with the remaining ½ cup of water until smooth, and then whisk this mixture into the boiling broth. Reduce the heat to low and simmer until lightly thickened, approximately 2 minutes.

Season with pepper, pour into a gravy boat and serve immediately.

Roast the root vegetables on a cookie sheet alongside the turkey. Sprinkle lightly with olive oil, salt and pepper before roasting.

Southern Cornbread Dressing

No Thanksgiving dinner seems complete without cornbread dressing, a time-honored Southern classic. Dressing can be prepared and cooked for forty-five minutes, then kept warm and held. To then serve, all you will need to do is bake dressing the final fifteen to twenty minutes of cooking time.

SERVES: TWELVE

1 loaf corn bread
6 slices multi-grain bread
8 Tablespoons unsalted butter, melted
1 large yellow onion, chopped
2 cups celery, chopped
6 cups chicken broth
1 teaspoon kosher salt
½ teaspoon freshly ground black pepper
1 Tablespoon fresh sage, minced
2 teaspoons poultry seasoning
5 large eggs, beaten lightly

Prepare cornbread; cool, cube and set aside on a cookie sheet to dry in the open air. Dry multi-grain bread in a 300 degree oven for 30 minutes; cool and cut into cubes.

Preheat oven to 350 degrees. Butter a 9 x 11-inch casserole dish; set aside.

In a very large bowl, crumble the cornbread and add multi-grain bread. Set aside uncovered so that it can continue to air dry.

In a large skillet, melt butter over medium heat. Add onion and celery; cook until translucent, approximately 8 to 10 minutes.

Pour vegetables over breads. Add broth and mix well. Season with salt, pepper, sage and poultry seasoning and mix to incorporate.

Add beaten eggs to mixture and fold into other ingredients.

Pour mixture into prepared casserole dish and bake for 50 to 60 minutes, or until dressing is cooked through and top is well-browned.

Holiday Pie with a Braided Crust

What could be better than a pie that combines the perfect pecan pie with the perfect pumpkin pie? The tang of fresh lemon provides definitive pizazz to the filling, and a braided crust using my mother's pie dough recipe makes Holiday Pie irresistible any time of year.

SERVES: EIGHT TO TWELVE

PIE CRUST

½ recipe Gladdie's Pie Dough

(See p. 245.)

This amount allows for one pie shell, a braided crust and decorative cuts-outs.
See Baking Secrets, Using Pie Shields, *p. 259.*

Roll half of the pie dough to ⅛-inch thick and fit into 9-inch pie plate.

Braid remaining crust and adhere to the rim of the dough in the plate per instructions that follow. Chill the shell while making the pie fillings.

PUMPKIN LAYER

¾ cup canned pure pumpkin purée
2 Tablespoons light brown sugar, packed
1 large egg, beaten lightly
2 Tablespoons sour cream
⅛ teaspoon cinnamon
⅛ teaspoon freshly ground nutmeg

In a small bowl whisk together ingredients for pumpkin layer until mixture is smooth.

PECAN LAYER

¾ cup light corn syrup
½ cup light brown sugar, packed
3 large eggs, beaten lightly
3 Tablespoons unsalted butter
2 teaspoons pure vanilla extract
¼ teaspoon zest of lemon
1½ teaspoons juice of fresh lemon
¼ teaspoon kosher salt
1½ cups pecans, chopped

Melt butter and cool. Zest lemon. Chop nuts.

Pie can be baked one day ahead and chilled, loosely covered with plastic wrap. When ready to serve, reheat in a 350-degree oven until the crust is crisp and the center is puffy, approximately fifteen minutes.

In a medium-size bowl, combine all ingredients for pecan layer, except pecans. Once incorporated, fold in the pecans.

ASSEMBLY

Preheat oven to 425 degrees.

Spread pumpkin mixture evenly in to the chilled pie shell and spoon pecan mixture over the pumpkin. Go slowly and spoon the pecan mixture over the top to ensure it remains a separate layer from the pumpkin.

Top unbaked pie with holly-shaped cut outs of dough (at Christmas time) or maple leaves for Thanksgiving.

Cover the braided crust with a pie crust shield or aluminum foil. Bake pie in upper third of oven for 20 minutes.

Reduce heat to 350 degrees, remove foil/shield, and bake for 20 to 30 minutes more, until the filling is puffed slightly and crust is browned.

The center will not appear to be quite set, and that is okay.

Cool on a wire rack.

Roll dough to ⅛–inch thick and cut into sets of three 8-inch lengths.

Braid three lengths at a time by flipping and lapping the sides over the middle length.

Place lengths on the rim of pie shell after scoring both the bottom of the braid and the rim.

Gently press lengths down onto the rim of the pie shell to ensure they are adhered to pie, as well as the individual braids to each other, for a seamless braid all around.

One pie typically needs four pieces of braid to cover the circumference of the pie plate. Use 1-inch lengths of dough crosswise to cover areas where two braids have been pinched together.

A braided crust takes roughly the same amount of dough as needed for a single crust pie.

Ginger Ginger Ginger Cookies

When my sons were little we would frequent a local bakery for ginger cookies after school. I could never match the recipe for those cookies at home, until now . . .
To help ensure your success, see Baking Secrets, Cookies, p. 356.

YIELD: TWENTY-FOUR COOKIES

When possible buy spices whole and grind or crush the seeds yourself just before using to release the full impact of their warm heady flavors.

2¼ cups all-purpose flour
1 teaspoon baking soda
2 teaspoons ground cinnamon
2 teaspoons ground ginger
1 teaspoon ground cloves
½ teaspoon freshly ground nutmeg
¼ teaspoon cardamom
½ teaspoon salt
¼ teaspoon white pepper
1 cup golden brown sugar, packed
⅓ cup unsalted butter, melted and cooled
⅓ cup molasses
1 large egg
1 Tablespoon fresh ginger, peeled and minced fine
½ cup crystallized ginger (2.7 ounces), chopped
½ cup demerara sugar crystals

Preheat oven to 350 degrees. Melt butter and allow to cool.

Sift the first nine ingredients (flour to white pepper) onto a sheet of waxed paper; set aside.

Measure all other ingredients and have ready to incorporate near the mixer.

In a large bowl with an electric mixer, beat the sugar, butter and molasses on high for 3 minutes. Scrape the sides of bowl and continue beating another 3 minutes.

With mixer on low, add egg and incorporate.

Add fresh and crystallized ginger and incorporate.

Continuing on low speed, mix the flour and other dry ingredients, adding gradually and mixing for 2 to 3 minute until a stiff dough forms.

Pinch out 24 uniform pieces of dough, then roll dough into 1-inch balls, by swirling gently between your two palms approximately 5 times.

Lightly roll each ball in Demerara sugar crystals to coat the outside of the balls. *Go easy on the Demerara sugar. Even though it is yummy, a little goes a long way.*

Place sugar-coated balls on a cookie sheet covered with parchment paper.

Bake 10 to 12 minutes. *Cookies will be cracked on top yet soft inside and lightly browned on the bottom when finished baking.*

Let cool 1 to 2 minutes then slide cookies, while still on the parchment paper, off the cookie sheet and onto a wire rack to cool completely.

Should you make these cookies at Christmas time, try rolling in crushed peppermint candies rather than Demerara sugar crystals.

The distinct flavor of ginger is refreshing, sweet and spicy-hot at once, and can be used fresh, ground into powder form or crystallized. See p. 374.

THERE IS NOTHING MORE FUN THAN LISTENING TO AND RECOUNTING EXPERIENCES FROM TRAVELS. HOSTING A TRAVELER'S NIGHT FOR FRIENDS THAT SHARE A PASSION FOR EXPLORATION IS A GREAT WAY TO NOT ONLY COMPARE NOTES OF WHAT'S BEEN SEEN AND LEARNED ALONG THE WAY, BUT ALSO A GREAT TIME TO BEGIN DREAMING OF YOUR NEXT ADVENTURE.

MAKE THE MOST OF YOUR TABLE SETTING ON NIGHTS LIKE THIS TO SHOWCASE THINGS YOU'VE COLLECTED FROM ACROSS THE GLOBE. USE MAPS FROM FAR-AWAY PLACES AND FASCINATING METROPOLISES AS YOUR TABLE "CLOTH,"

AND THEN LINGER OVER LEMON MERINGUE PIE AND COFFEE WHILE YOU SWAP AND SHARE STORIES INTO THE NIGHT.

A SUNDAY NIGHT IN NOVEMBER

Travelers' Night

FOR 4

Cold Avocado & Cucumber Soup

**Casablanca Chops with
Apple & Bell Pepper Coulis
Sweet Potato Purée**

Lemon Meringue Pie

RECIPES

COLD AVOCADO &
CUCUMBER SOUP

CASABLANCA
CHOPS

APPLE & BELL
PEPPER COULIS

SWEET POTATO
PURÉE

LEMON MERINGUE
PIE

Serve **Johannisberg Riesling** *with an apricot or peach influence with the pork.*

SECRETS TO A
GOOD MERINGUE

TIME LINE

Oh, What a Wonderful World!

Serve Traveler's Night plated, in three courses. *For entertaining secrets see* Accepting an Invitation: RSVP, *p. 6.*

THE DAY BEFORE TRAVELERS' NIGHT

Set a table chocked full of memorabilia, maps and travel guides and dishes from across the globe.

Reserve a place in or near the dining room to set up for dessert, and include coffee cups and coffee service with dessert plates, forks and serving utensils.

Make pie dough; refrigerate. Make soup; refrigerate. Chill wine.

THE AFTERNOON OF THE PARTY

Assemble and bake Lemon Meringue pie.

Ready coffee machine for instant brewing later that night.

FORTY-FIVE MINUTES TO ONE HOUR BEFORE FELLOW TRAVELERS ARRIVE

Make sweet potato purée. Prepare chops and coulis.

Cover and hold all three dishes to keep warm.

Tidy up the kitchen and wash all dirty dishes and utensils before guests arrive.

FOR THE FIRST COURSE

Serve soup cold in individual bowls with pretty garnishes.

Pour wines and also offer cold water on ice, or iced tea.

Remove soup bowls and serve entrée.

FOR THE MAIN COURSE

Plate chops and coulis with potatoes for each guest; serve.

Re-fill glasses as requested.

Remove dinner plates and serve dessert.

WHEN TIME FOR DESSERT

Serve the pie at the table with coffee, and talk the night away!

THESE BEAUTIFUL ROSE MEDALLION DISHES BELONG TO MY MOTHER-IN-LAW, BETTY. SHE COLLECTED THE DISHES AND THE OTHER ASIAN ITEMS ON THE TABLE DURING HER TRAVELS THROUGH THE ORIENT.

Cold Avocado & Cucumber Soup

Balance a hearty November meal with this creamy yet vibrant cold soup.

SERVES: SIX

Avocados add a mild, nutty flavor and buttery texture to your dishes. For an easy preparation method, see p. 367.

2 cucumbers, peeled and chopped

2 avocados, peeled and seeded

½ bunch scallions, chopped (including green parts)

1 clove garlic

1 teaspoon juice of fresh lemon

1 teaspoon juice of fresh lime

2 Tablespoons chicken broth

2 cups ice water

1 cup Half and Half cream

1 cup crème fraîche

1 teaspoon worcestershire sauce

1 teaspoon kosher salt

½ teaspoon freshly ground black pepper

2 to 3 dashes sriracha sauce

½ jalapeno pepper, diced

Fresh herbs and edible blossoms

In a food processor, place first seven ingredients (through chicken broth) and process until smooth. Remove from processor to a large bowl; set aside.

Then, in the food processor, purée water, cream and crème fraîche until smooth.

Add cream mixture to cucumber purée.

Season with Worcestershire, salt, pepper, Sriracha and jalapeno. Chill **2 to 3 hours** until cold.

Garnish individual serving bowls with dill sprigs and fresh edible flowers (in a contrasting color like chive blossoms).

Serve cold.

Casablanca Chops with Apple & Bell Pepper Coulis

Amp up pork chops with the fragrant spices of Casablanca smothered in a fruit and pepper coulis for an evening with fellow travelers.

SERVES: FOUR

CASABLANCA CHOPS

4 6-ounce bone-in pork loin chops

1 Tablespoon olive oil

1 teaspoon sourwood honey

½ teaspoon kosher salt

¼ teaspoon freshly ground black pepper

Heat oil in a large skillet over medium-high heat.

Rub salt and pepper into chops, then rub on the honey.

Add chops to hot oil and cook 4 to 6 minutes on each side, or to desired degree of doneness.

APPLE & BELL PEPPER COULIS

This sauce is also terrific on sandwiches!

½ red bell pepper, roasted

½ red apple, cooked

2 Tablespoons olive oil

1 heaping tablespoon almonds, toasted

1 clove garlic

½ teaspoon kosher salt

¼ teaspoon cinnamon

¼ teaspoon cumin

Juice of ½ fresh lemon

1 Tablespoon sourwood honey

Roast pepper over an open flame until well charred; cool and seed. Toast almonds at 375 degrees for 5 to 8 minutes, then once cool, roughly chop. Cook apple in microwave for 4 to 5 minutes; reserve juices.

Then, in a food processor, combine roasted bell pepper, cooked apple, olive oil, toasted almonds, garlic clove, salt, cinnamon and cumin; process until smooth. Remove mixture to microwave-safe bowl and heat for 2 minutes. Then stir in lemon juice and honey.

To serve, pour a generous portion of coulis sauce over cooked chops.

Sweet Potato Purée

Fresh orange brightens the flavor of these mashed sweet potatoes and a pinch of cayenne pepper, added at the very last minute, gives them a super charge!

SERVES: FOUR

2 medium sweet potatoes, peeled and cubed
¼ cup milk
1 teaspoon zest of orange
¼ cup fresh orange juice
1 teaspoon kosher salt
½ teaspoon freshly ground black pepper
2 Tablespoons unsalted butter, softened
¼ to ½ teaspoon cayenne pepper

In a large pot, cover potato cubes with salted water and boil until fork-tender. Drain potatoes but leave in the pot.

With an electric mixer, mix sweet potatoes to crush. Then add milk, zest, juice, salt, pepper and whip until well incorporated and creamy.

Add one Tablespoon of butter, then whip to combine.

Add cayenne (to taste) just before serving, and fold to incorporate.

Top hot potatoes with remaining butter and serve.

Lemon Meringue Pie

A tart lemon custard and sugary meringue combine to make a scrumptious pie!

SERVES: EIGHT

PIE CRUST

⅓ recipe Gladdie's Pie Dough

(See p. 245.)

Bake a 9-inch pie shell at 375 degrees for 12 to 15 minutes, or until browned. Let cool before filling.

LEMON FILLING

1½ cups granulated sugar

1½ cups water

½ teaspoon kosher salt

½ cup cornstarch

⅓ cup water

4 large egg yolks, **slightly beaten**

½ cup juice of fresh lemon

3 Tablespoons unsalted butter

1 teaspoon zest of lemon

Combine sugar, 1½ cups water and salt in a large saucepan. Heat to boiling.

Mix cornstarch and an additional ⅓ cup of water to make a smooth paste. Add paste to the boiling mixture gradually, stirring constantly. Cook until thick and clear. Remove from the heat and set aside.

Combine egg **yolks** and lemon juice; stir into the thickened mixture. Return to heat and cook, stirring constantly until mixture bubbles again. Remove from heat. Stir in the butter and lemon zest.

Cover and cool until lukewarm.

MERINGUE

4 large egg whites

¼ teaspoon salt

½ cup granulated sugar

Preheat oven to 325 degrees.

Bring eggs **whites t**o room temperature. Add salt to egg whites. Beat until frothy. Slowly add ½ cup sugar, and continue beating until stiff, glossy peaks are formed.

Stir two rounded Tablespoons of meringue into lukewarm filling. Pour filling into cool pie shell. Pile remaining meringue on top and spread lightly over the custard filling, spreading to seal the edges to the crust and mounding in the center. Then sprinkle meringue lightly with granulated sugar.

Bake for approximately 15 minutes, or until meringue is lightly browned and sugar on top begins to caramelize.

Cool on a rack for at least one hour before cutting.

Secrets to a Good Meringue: *Use room temperature eggs for meringues, and add the sugar very slowly so as not to defeat the meringue. Also, be sure to always use spotlessly clean and dry beaters.* See p. 377.

Winter
Occasions

Christmas Eve Dinner

New Year's Eve Buffet

De-LIGHT-ful Dinner

Powder Day

Alpine Feast

Formal Birthday Dinner Party

Winter
Seasonal Fruits & Vegetables

FRUITS & NUTS

Bananas
Citrus
Grapefruit
Kumquats
Oranges, Blood
Oranges, Clementine
Persimmon
Pomegranate

VEGETABLES & HERBS

Broccoli
Brussels Spouts
Cabbage
Greens, Winter
Jicama
Kale
Potatoes
Parsnips
Squash, Butternut
Squash, Winter

THE MAGIC OF CHRISTMAS LIES IN THE BUILD UP TO DECEMBER 25TH. IT IS A SPECIAL TIME BECAUSE EVERYONE GETS INTO THE SPIRIT AND THE ANTICIPATION MOUNTS DAILY. WE ALL SEEM TO FIND OURSELVES KEEPING SECRETS CLOSE TO THE VEST WHILE WE CONTRIBUTE OUR OWN UNIQUE ELEMENT OF CHEER IN A MYRIAD OF WAYS.

CHRISTMAS EVE HAS ALWAYS BEEN A FAVORITE FOR MY FAMILY. IT BEGINS WITH A SPECIAL EUCHARIST IN THE LATE AFTERNOON AND ENDS WITH THE ANTICIPATION OF SURPRISES FROM SANTA. IN BETWEEN, WE ALL TAKE PART IN PREPARING A MEMORABLE MEAL FIT FOR THE OCCASION.

ON A HOLIDAY LIKE CHRISTMAS, GO ALL OUT WITH A SPECIAL BIRD OR CUT OF BEEF, GOOD WINES, AND A SELECTION OF 'FAVORITE' DELECTABLE DESSERTS. SET THE TABLE WITH GLEE USING REDS, GREENS, SILVER AND GOLD. EVERY PLATE, EVERY GLASS AND EVERY PIECE OF SILVER OR FLATWARE SHOULD SPARKLE AS YOU

THE NIGHT BEFORE...

Christmas Eve Dinner

FOR 10

Holiday Champagne Cocktails
Sherried Mushroom Strudel

Prime Rib in Rock Salt
Roasted Garlic Mashed Potatoes
Carrot Pudding
Salade Composée avec Coeur

Classic Apple Pie with Saint Cecilia Sauce
Espresso Crinkles

Crème Fraîche & Cinnamon Coffee Cake

Serve a Cabernet Sauvignon *with a medium/soft body with the prime rib. Serve* Calvados *with dessert.*

TIME LINE

I saw mommy kissing Santa Claus!

This dinner for ten can be served with dishes set on a buffet so guests can fill their plates and then return to the table for the meal. *For entertaining secrets see* Successful Co-Hosting, *p. 17.*

ONE WEEK BEFORE

Order prime rib from the butcher. Call aunts and in-laws with menu ideas and discuss what they might bring to help with the meal. *People like to help with the holiday meal. It makes them feel a real part of the celebration and provides an opportunity to bake and prepare time-honored dishes.*

DECEMBER 22ND

Enlist kids and house guests to decorate and begin preparing for the occasion!

Take a walk together and gather pine cones, tree branches and other found objects to use for decorations. Spray paint as desired. Then set a Christmas-ey table that twinkles with color and sparkles.

Coordinate the serving pieces and plan to serve dinner from a pretty buffet that incorporates china or pottery matching that on the dinner table. Set a buffet area for the desserts near the tree with plates, forks, napkins, a small pitcher for the sauce and coffee service.

Prepare cranberry mixture for champagne cocktails; refrigerate. Chill champagne. Roast 2 heads of garlic; seal and refrigerate.

Bake crinkles and freeze.

DECEMBER 23RD

Prepare strudel to refrigerate overnight. Prepare carrot pudding and bake for just 1 hour; cool, seal and refrigerate. Make pie dough; refrigerate.

THE MORNING OF DECEMBER 24TH

Get up early to get the baking done while the house is quiet: Make coffee cake for Christmas morning; seal and set aside. Assemble and bake apple pie. Make St. Cecelia Sauce.

LATE AFTERNOON, 3:30 TO 4:00 PM

Prepare salad, either on individual plates or a large serving platter. Cover and refrigerate.

Make vinaigrette dressing; place in serving carafe or small pitcher; cover and refrigerate. Assemble prime rib and roast, *time this to begin roasting just 2 hours from established serving time.*

FORTY-FIVE MINUTES BEFORE THE PARTY, 5:45 PM.

Now is a good time to line up helpers for the last minute tasks! Finish strudel and bake. Start potatoes, hold (after cooking and draining) in the hot pan. Bring carrot pudding to room temperature and bake for another 30 minutes. Set out crinkles to thaw; place on a serving platter; cover. Remove roast from the oven and allow to rest for 20 minutes.

WHEN THE PARTY STARTS, 6:30 PM

Make and serve champagne cocktails in the living or family room. Serve strudel, hot out of the oven on small plates with cocktail napkins.

FOR DINNER, 7:00 PM

Carve beef; serve with other dishes on a buffet when all are hot and ready. Add garlic, butter, salt and pepper to potatoes and mash; serve. Serve carrot pudding hot and bubbly. Dress salad(s) and serve. Pour wines and fill water glasses. After guests have gone through the buffet, invite them to the dining table. Clear plates and refill water glasses after the meal is finished. Offer coffee. Encourage guests to linger at the table a few minutes over coffee, while you heat the pie for 15 minutes at 375 degrees to crisp the crust.

WHILE EXCHANGING "JUST ONE GIFT" AND REMINISCING

Set a dessert buffet in the room where the Christmas tree presides, with hot apple pie, Saint Cecilia sauce and espresso crinkles. Ask guests to serve themselves and enjoy sweets around the tree. Serve Calvados and coffee, as desired.

ONCE GUESTS HAVE GONE HOME
Clear dinner dishes, put food away and tidy kitchen.

THE NEXT MORNING
Enjoy coffee cake and surprises from Santa!

Holiday Champagne Cocktails

What could be better than a little bubbly with cranberries on the eve of a special day?

YIELD: TEN TO TWELVE COCKTAILS

2 750-milligram bottles champagne, chilled
1½ cups water
1½ cups granulated sugar
12-ounce bag fresh or frozen cranberries
1 bunch fresh mint, rinsed

In a medium saucepan, make simple syrup by combining water and sugar over medium heat until sugar dissolves.

Add cranberries and bring just to boiling stage. Then reduce heat and simmer for 5 minutes, stirring frequently.

Remove cranberry syrup from heat and gently fold in the mint. Cover and let the mint steep in the sugar mixture for 15 minutes.

Press cranberry and mint mixture through a fine-mesh strainer; discard the solids.

Let the strained mixture cool completely and then chill in the refrigerator for **3 to 4 hours.** Chill Champagne and flutes at same time.

Cocktails can be made ahead to this point and held until the party begins.

To serve cocktails, combine the cold cranberry syrup with cold champagne in a large pitcher, stirring gently to combine. Pour into chilled flutes.

Skewer several cranberries and drop into each cocktail.

Happy Holidays!

Sherried Mushroom Strudel

This strudel of mushrooms, butter and curry is wrapped in crispy phyllo dough.

SERVES: TWELVE

¾ cup unsalted butter

6 cups mushrooms

1 teaspoon kosher salt

¼ teaspoon curry powder

6 Tablespoons sherry

2 shallots, minced

1 cup sour cream

1 cup plus 3 Tablespoons panko bread crumbs

8 sheets phyllo dough

Fresh chives

Additional sour cream

Clean and chop mushrooms very fine. *Any variety of fresh mushrooms will work for this strudel.*

In a large skillet, melt ¼ cup butter over medium low heat. Add mushrooms, salt, curry powder, sherry and shallots. Sauté until mushrooms are wilted and the liquid is evaporated, approximately 20 minutes. Cool.

Stir in 1 cup sour cream and 3 Tablespoons bread crumbs. Remove mixture to a plastic bowl and seal with a lid.

Refrigerate mixture overnight.

Preheat oven to 375 degrees.

Make the first strudel by using four sheets of phyllo dough and half of the mushroom mixture.

Start by melting the remaining ½ cup of butter. Then brush a sheet of phyllo with melted butter and sprinkle lightly with bread crumbs. Repeat until there are four layers of phyllo.

Spread half the mushroom mixture evenly onto the phyllo, leaving a 1-inch border on all four sides.

Roll lengthwise, jellyroll fashion and place on a cookie sheet lined with parchment paper.

Brush completed roll with butter and sprinkle lightly with bread crumbs. Then mark 8 equal slices in the dough with a sharp knife by piercing just the first 2 to 3 layers of the phyllo. *This will keep phyllo from crumbling apart when you slice the baked strudel.*

For the second strudel, repeat the above process using the remaining mushroom filling and phyllo.

Bake strudels until lightly browned, approximately 40 minutes.

Slice into bite-sized pieces using a pizza cutter at splice marks and serve with a small dollop of sour cream and sprinkle of chopped fresh chives on each piece.

Prime Rib in Rock Salt

This ancient method of cooking meat under a blanket of rock salt keeps the roast tender, with an end result that isn't too salty.

SERVES: EIGHT TO TWELVE

1 6-pound prime rib of beef
2 to 3 Tablespoons worcestershire sauce
2 teaspoons garlic powder
2 Tablespoons freshly ground black pepper
3 4-pound packages rock salt
½ cup water
Disposable aluminum foil roasting pan

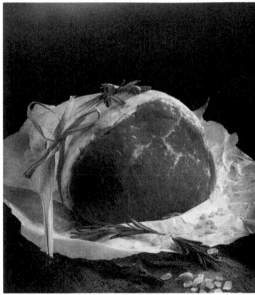

Preheat oven to 500 degrees.

Brush prime rib with Worcestershire sauce then sprinkle with garlic powder and pepper and rub into all sides of the roast.

Pour rock salt to depth of ½-inch in a disposable aluminum foil roasting pan; place roast in center of pan.

Rock salt will cling fiercely to the pan, so be sure to use a disposable one!

Add remaining rock salt, covering roast and patting with your hands to seal the roast on all sides. Use water as necessary to make a slurry with the salt to help seal meat entirely.

Roast for 12 minutes per pound (1 hour and 12 minutes), or until meat thermometer registers 150 degrees (medium rare) or to desired degree of doneness.

Allow roast to rest for 15 to 20 minutes before removing from the salt.

Crack salt with a hammer; remove roast and brush away rock salt. Slice into servings.

Prime Rib is the king of roasts and prized for its superior flavor and texture. It is made even more delicious cooked in rock salt.

This method is also delicious when cooking a whole fish.

Roasted Garlic

Roasted garlic is subtle, sweet, buttery soft and delicious in mashed potatoes, sauces or tossed with hot pasta. Garlic can also be served warm by squeezing cloves from their skins onto crisp crackers or bread. Roasted heads of garlic keep well in the refrigerator, and when roasted whole in the husk, you can easily squeeze out just what you need.

You can also open the foil for the last ten minutes of baking and allow the garlic to caramelize.

1 (or more) garlic head(s)
Olive oil, good quality
Kosher salt &
Freshly ground black pepper

Preheat oven to 350 degrees.

Slice off the top ¼-inch of garlic head to reveal the cloves.

Drizzle tops with a little (approximately ½ to 1 teaspoon) olive oil and season lightly with salt and pepper.

Loosely wrap each individual head in aluminum foil and twist foil together at the top to seal – *like a Hershey's kiss wrapper!*

Roast for 25 to 30 minutes, or until the garlic is very soft when squeezed.

Roasted Garlic Mashed Potatoes

To Cook: Peel and cube one Idaho potato for each guest.

Cut into uniform pieces before cooking. *This will allow all potato cubes to cook evenly and avoid lumps when mashed.*

In a large saucepan, boil potatoes in salted water until fork-tender.

To Mash: Drain water from the potatoes and then set the pan back over the heat for just a few minutes to dry the potatoes. While potatoes are drying, generously season with kosher salt and freshly ground black pepper, and add ½ to 1 clove of the roasted garlic for each potato.

Using an electric mixer, mash and lightly mix the dry potatoes and seasonings.

Once the potatoes are the consistency of a course meal, gradually add warm 2% milk and then butter. Now, whip potatoes, adding just enough additional milk to achieve a creamy consistency.

To Serve: Remove mashed potatoes to a serving bowl and top with a dollop of soft butter. Mashed potatoes should be served hot, so prepare these last and keep warm in a covered saucepan until ready to plate and serve.

Idahos make the best mashed potatoes.

Carrot Pudding

This sweet carrot pudding is a great choice to accompany any roast. Pudding can be assembled and partially baked then held, and cooked the final fifteen to twenty minutes just before time to serve.

SERVES: TWELVE

4 cups carrots
1 cup maple syrup
1 cup brown sugar, packed
½ cup unsalted butter
6 large eggs, slightly beaten
2 cups milk
5 Tablespoons all-purpose flour
1 teaspoon cinnamon
2 teaspoon baking powder
1 teaspoon kosher salt

Preheat oven to 350 degrees. Cook carrots; measure 4 cups.

In a large bowl, combine syrup and sugar with butter, eggs and milk.

Sift together remaining ingredients and mix with sugar and egg mixture until well incorporated.

Butter a 9 x 9-inch casserole dish, and add mixture. Dust top lightly with additional cinnamon.

Bake until set, approximately 1½ hours.

Salade Composée Avec Coeur

This composed salad is made with heart — hearts of palm and hearts of artichoke! It makes a beautiful presentation and the texture combination is really unusual. Salad can be made on a large platter and served Family Style, or composed on individual plates in the same manner.

PRONOUNCED: SAEL-AD COM-PO-SEE A-VEC COO-R

SERVES: TEN TO TWELVE

1 bunch kale and/or leaf lettuce

1 15-ounce can hearts of palm

1 15-ounce can artichoke hearts

1 cup walnuts

8 ounces roquefort cheese

½ bunch scallions

1 pound mushrooms, sliced

Vinaigrette dressing

A composed salad is a staple in the south of France and often performs as a complete meal. For a truly Provincial version of this salad, add a row of crumbled bacon or thinly sliced ham with a row of hard-boiled eggs.

Outline a large serving tray or individual salad plate with whole kale or lettuce leaves. Then remove the stems and tear remaining leaves into bite-sized pieces; add to center of the tray/plate.

Slice hearts of palm and quarter artichokes. Toast and chop walnuts. Crumble cheese and chop scallions (including the green parts).

Arrange in five **horizontal** strips onto the bed of greens: ½ artichokes, ½ mushrooms, hearts of palm, remaining mushrooms, and remaining artichokes.

Top with five **vertical** strips of: ½ walnuts, ½ Roquefort, green onions, remaining Roquefort, and remaining walnuts.

Sprinkle sparingly with a fresh vinaigrette dressing just before serving

To garnish, cut red pepper into the shape of holly leaves and set into inverted yellow rose petals.

Classic Apple Pie

Chop apples into cubes, rather than slicing, to ensure each bite is well coated with cinnamon and sugar.

When I bake apple pie, I like to mix apples for different textures and sweetness. Granny Smiths are drier and will stay firm on the bottom of the pie; Galas are sweet and good in the middle; and creamy sweet Jonathans are great on top.
To help ensure your success, see Baking Secrets, Rolling & Baking Pies, *p. 358.*

SERVES: EIGHT TO TEN

PIE CRUST

½ recipe Gladdie's Pie Dough

(See p. 245.)

FILLING

The flour and sugar added to fruit pies makes the scrumptious thick syrup that helps flavor the pie and bind the fruit and crust. For a perfect fruit pie, assess the sweetness and juiciness of your fruit and adjust the sugar and flour accordingly. For fruit that is very juicy, you will need a bit more flour. For fruit that is very sweet, use less sugar.

3 granny smith apples
2 gala apples
3 to 4 jonathan apples
1 to 1½ cups granulated sugar, 3 to 4 Tablespoons all-purpose flour
⅛ teaspoon salt
1 teaspoon cinnamon
½ teaspoon freshly ground nutmeg
Juice of ½ fresh lemon
3 pats unsalted butter

Preheat oven to 500 degrees.

Peel, core and cube apples, leaving skin on the Jonathans for a bit of red color. Keep different apple varieties in separate bowls. Squeeze fresh lemon juice on all apples and toss to distribute the juice.

Mix sugar, flour, salt, cinnamon and nutmeg; add to each bowl of apples and fold to coat apples cubes well.

Mound apples into a *chilled* (un-baked) pie shell with Granny Smith apples going in first to line the bottom, Galas in the middle, and Jonathans on top. Dot apple cubes with 3 pats of butter.

Place top crust over mound of apples and cut vents in the dough in a pretty design. Then crimp the edges of the pie to seal the two crusts together. Sprinkle the top of the pie liberally with granulated sugar.

Bake 500 degrees for 8 minutes. Reduce heat to 350 degrees and bake for 1 hour, or until crust is browned and filling is bubbly.

Saint Cecilia Sauce

This classic sauce is delicious over hot pastry or fresh fruit.

YIELD: APPROXIMATELY ONE CUP

3 large egg yolks, **organically grown**
⅔ cup powdered sugar
1 cup Half and Half cream
1 teaspoon calvados brandy

Consuming raw or undercooked eggs is not advisable for young children, pregnant women or those with certain medical conditions. Use flash pasteurized raw eggs to avoid salmonella concerns.

In a large bowl, whisk egg **yolks** with powdered sugar; set aside.

In a second large bowl with an electric mixer, whip cream with brandy until soft peaks form.

Fold the egg-sugar mixture into the whipped cream mixture. Keep refrigerated until ready to use.

Serve a dollop over pieces of hot apple pie.

Espresso Crinkles

This festive black and white cookie is perfect for the holidays! The chocolate dough rolled in powdered sugar makes an irresistible treat for young and old alike. Cookies can be kept in airtight container for a few days or frozen. To help ensure your success, see Baking Secrets, Cookies, p. 356.

YIELD: FORTY-FOUR CRINKLES

1 cup unsweetened cocoa powder

1½ cups granulated sugar

½ cup vegetable oil

4 large eggs

2 teaspoons pure vanilla extract

2 cups all-purpose flour

2 teaspoons baking powder

1 teaspoon instant espresso coffee powder

½ teaspoon salt

1 to 1½ cups powdered sugar

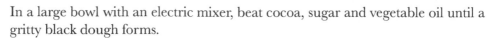

In a large bowl with an electric mixer, beat cocoa, sugar and vegetable oil until a gritty black dough forms.

Add eggs, one at a time, mixing just until combined. Add vanilla and beat thoroughly.

Sift flour with baking powder, espresso powder and salt onto a sheet of waxed paper; set aside.

Gradually add flour mixture to chocolate mixture and mix on low speed until just combined, being careful to not over mix.

Divide dough into four equal parts, wrap in plastic and chill for 2 hours.

Preheat oven to 350 degrees. Line two baking sheets with parchment paper.

Place powdered sugar into a large bowl.

Pinch off small sections of dough and roll into 1-inch diameter balls between the palms of your hands.

Place balls, four at a time, into powdered sugar. Lift bowl to swirl sugar around chocolate balls to coat heavily. The dough should be slightly sticky at this point and the sugar will adhere well.

Bake 10 to 12 minutes, or until cookies are lightly browned at edges.

Remove to wire rack and cool completely.

Crème Fraîche & Cinnamon Coffee Cake

While in the kitchen cooking for Christmas Eve, make this cake for Christmas morning. The sugary crunch from the nut topping makes this cake a favorite morning treat.

SERVES: TWELVE

CRÈME FRAÎCHE CAKE

½ cup unsalted butter, softened
1 cup granulated sugar
2 large eggs
2 cups all-purpose flour
1 teaspoon baking powder
1 teaspoon baking soda
¼ teaspoon salt
12 ounces crème fraîche
1½ teaspoons pure vanilla extract

NUT TOPPING

½ cup granulated sugar
1½ teaspoons cinnamon
½ cup hazelnuts

Preheat oven to 350 degrees. Lightly toast and chop nuts for approximately 5 minutes. In a small bowl, combine topping ingredients and set aside.

In a large bowl with an electric mixer, cream butter and sugar thoroughly. Beat eggs well and add.

Sift flour, baking powder, baking soda and salt onto a sheet of waxed paper; set aside. Mix crème fraîche and vanilla; set aside.

Add dry ingredients to egg mixture alternately with sour cream, working quickly to avoid over-mixing.

Turn half of the batter into a buttered and floured Bundt pan. Sprinkle on half of the topping mixture. Then add the remaining batter to the pan with the remaining topping sprinkled on top.

Bake 35 to 45 minutes, or until a toothpick inserted in center comes out clean. Allow cake to cool in Bundt pan for at least 30 minutes to shape before turning out onto a rack.

Crème Fraîche (a thicker, richer version of sour cream with a less tangy taste) makes this cake sweet and dense.

Hazelnuts are very rich and buttery and add a lovely complex flavor to desserts.
See p. 374-75.

New Year's Eve seems the ideal time to go over-the-top with silver and gold!

Create a winter wonderland on the table with metallic wrapping paper and ribbon. Then add spray painted and dried botanicals like poppy pods and pine cones or pomegranates and artichokes. Incorporate this glimmering array into a bed of sparkling candles to complete the mood.

Champagne at midnight will further compel merry guests to ring in the newest year in high style.

NEW YEAR'S EVE

New Year's Eve Buffet

FOR 20

Italian Fragolinis
Cheese Puffs – Voilà!
Ricotta & Olive Stuffed Endive

Tenderloin with Mushrooms & Wine Sauce
Broiled Shrimp with Basil
Parmesan & Leek Quiche
Stone Ground Grits with Gouda & Roasted Corn
Okra & Lucky Black Eyed Peas

Petit Gateaux Moelleux au Chocolat
Queen Cake
Jammin' Shortbread

RECIPES

ITALIAN FRAGOLINIS

CHEESE PUFFS – *VOILÀ!*

RICOTTA & OLIVE STUFFED ENDIVE

TENDERLOIN WITH MUSHROOMS & WINE SAUCE

BROILED SHRIMP WITH BASIL

PARMESAN & LEEK QUICHE

STONE GROUND GRITS WITH GOUDA & ROASTED CORN

OKRA & LUCKY BLACK EYED PEAS

PETIT GATEAUX MOELLEUX AU CHOCOLAT

QUEEN CAKE

JAMMIN' SHORTBREAD

Serve a Cabernet Sauvignon *with the tenderloin, a* Pouilly Fumé *with the shrimp, and* Champagne *at midnight.*

GRATING LEMON RIND – *ZESTING!*

295

TIME LINE

Good Friends & Midnight Champagne

This elegant celebration for twenty guests is designed to be served buffet style with help or co-hosts. *For entertaining secrets see* Entertaining Groups of Ten or More, *p. 15.*

IN EARLY FALL

Determine the layout for the dinner and party and consider re-arranging spaces to accommodate a large buffet and seating for 20 guests. *Experiment with various options, try to visualize the party and meal, and put yourself in the shoes of guests and consider both comfort and convenience.*

Rent tables, chairs, linens and serving pieces as necessary. Draft the guest list. *(See* The Guest list*:* Crafting the Right Mix, *p. 2.)*

IN EARLY NOVEMBER

Hire a minimum of three experienced wait and kitchen staffers to help with the event set-up, some cooking, service and break down/clean-up. Or, coordinate these tasks with co-hosts.

Make *a double recipe of cheese puffs* and freeze as directed.

AFTER THANKSGIVING

Finalize guest list, issue invitations.

Gather botanicals and experiment with spray painting; shop for metallic papers, etc.

Make Queen Cake and seal un-sliced layers in plastic and foil; freeze. Wait to make the curd and frosting.

Make *a double recipe of shortbread cookies;* freeze. Make *a double recipe of the miniature chocolate cakes;* bake just 7 minutes; cool, seal and freeze, wrapped in plastic in an air-tight container.

Make *two quiches* and bake just 40 minutes, or until set; cool, wrap and freeze.

ONE WEEK BEFORE

Buy all remaining ingredients needed for the meal. Buy the wine and champagne for 20 guests with all cocktail ingredients.

Finalize the plan for table decorations. Order flowers; arrange delivery (if you plan to incorporate fresh flowers).

Make lemon curd for cake; refrigerate.

TWO DAYS BEFORE

Assemble wait staff and kitchen help (if going this route) to assist and train. Lay the buffet table and review layout for balance, include serving pieces, bowls and platters, as well as serving utensils.

(See page 10-12, The Buffet Service.*)*

Assemble plates, silver and napkins for dessert table. Include coffee cups, saucers, and spoons. Assemble glasses & napkins for bar set up. Designate one area for making and serving Fragolinis, one area for the wines to be served from for the meal, and one area for champagne at midnight. *Having these areas pre-set saves an inordinate amount of time!*

Decorate all public spaces with silver and gold. Chill Fumé wine and champagne. Prepare cocktail glasses and chill.

Sterilize coins and prepare *a double recipe of okra and black-eyed peas*; refrigerate in its serving bowl.

Make *a double recipe of Fragolinis,* less champagne, and refrigerate. Prepare everything needed for the tenderloin and wine sauce; refrigerate until ready to cook.

THE MORNING OF THE 31ST

Thaw cakes, make frosting, and assemble and frost Queen cake with curd and sprinkles. Thaw cookies and seal with plastic wrap on their serving platter.

Remove quiches from the freezer to the refrigerator to thaw.

Make *a double recipe of ricotta and endive*; plate, so the tray can go straight from the refrigerator to the table; seal and refrigerate. Prepare *a double recipe of shrimp*; refrigerate until ready to cook.

ONE HOUR BEFORE GUESTS ARRIVAL

Wait staff and kitchen help or co-hosts to arrive and begin work. *When hiring help, provide clear and detailed instruction for completing the meal.*

Whip the cream and shave chocolate for petit moelleux.
Remove cheese puffs from freezer and bake as directed 30 minutes before guests arrive..

UPON ARRIVAL

Finish Fragolinis with champagne and serve to guests as they arrive. Serve hot cheese puffs, right out of the oven. Serve cold ricotta and olive stuffed endive.

30 minutes before serving buffet: Cook the tenderloin and wine sauce. Broil or grill shrimp and plate; cover to keep warm. Finish baking quiches for 10 to 15 minutes at 325 degrees; slice for guests to serve themselves.

Make *a double recipe of grits.*

FOR THE LATE NIGHT BUFFET

Designate one person to help serve and stock the buffet; one to serve the wines; and one to be on hand to assist guests as needed.

Lay buffet table with hot sliced tenderloin, warm shrimp, warm quiche, hot grits and cold black-eyed peas *with coins.* Set out chilled white wine and red wine.

Bake petit moelleux for 4 to 5 minutes at 400 degrees in a water bath just before midnight; ready the whipped cream and shaved chocolate to serve with cakes.

AT MIDNIGHT

Designate one person to slice and serve Queen cake; one to help garnish the mini cakes and serve the cookies; and one to serve champagne.

Set dessert buffet with Queen Cake, cookies and Mini Chocolate Cakes.

Serve champagne. Have plenty of cold water and hot coffee available.

Italian Fragolinis

The name for this cocktail comes from the Italian word for strawberries, fragola. It is inspired by the Italian peach Bellini, but is made with strawberries rather than peaches. Fragolinis are made sweet with fresh fruit and Grand Marnier liqueur. Prepare these drinks two to three hours before serve time to ensure ingredients and flutes are well chilled, and designate one helper during the party to mix drinks for guests.

YIELD: TWELVE COCKTAILS

4 cups ripe strawberries, hulled
6 Tablespoons simple syrup
4 teaspoons grand marnier liqueur
12 strips of orange zest
2 750-ml bottles champagne, chilled

See p. 386, Simple Syrup.

In a food processor, purée the strawberries until smooth; press through a fine sieve to remove the seeds.

Add simple syrup and Grand Marnier to the seedless purée; **refrigerate 2 to 3 hours,** or until well chilled. Chill champagne.

Rub the rim of champagne flutes with orange zest and dip in sugar to lightly coat the rims, then chill flutes in freezer for at least 30 minutes before serving.

Cocktails can be made ahead to this point and then held until ready to serve.

To serve, pour champagne into flutes to ¾ full; stir in 2 Tablespoons of the purée.

Drop orange zest curls into the top of glasses to garnish, and serve immediately.

Cheese Puffs – *Voilà!*

Store these easy appetizers in the freezer for unexpected guests and voilà, *instant treats for impromptu get-togethers and great easy appetizers for large parties!*

SERVES: SIXTEEN

2 cups unsalted butter

16 ounces cream cheese, cubed

16 ounces sharp cheddar cheese, grated

2 ounces parmesan cheese, shaved

1½ teaspoons cayenne pepper

4 cloves garlic, crushed and minced

4 large egg whites

1 French baguette loaf

Cube bread into bite-sized pieces, leaving the crusts on; set aside.

In a large saucepan with a double boiler, melt butter, cream cheese and cheddar. Stir in parmesan, cayenne pepper and garlic until well incorporated; Remove from heat.

In a large bowl with an electric mixer, beat egg **whites** until stiff; gently fold into the cheese mixture; cover to keep warm.

Spear bread cubes with a fork and dip into the warm cheese mixture. Allow excess cheese to dribble off, and then place cubes on a cookie sheet lined with parchment paper.

Once cookie sheet is filled, place in the freezer until cheese puffs are frozen. Then remove frozen puffs to a freezer storage bag or plastic container until ready to use. Return to the freezer to store.

When ready to serve, remove only the number of puffs you need to a cookie sheet lined with parchment paper, and bake frozen at 400 degrees for 10 minutes. Best served hot.

Ricotta & Olive Stuffed Endive

A creamy and light appetizer, with a bite!

SERVES: TWENTY

WRAP

2 bunches endive leaves

FILLING

2 15-ounce tubs ricotta cheese
1 ⅓ cups green olives, pitted
1 cup pine nuts, toasted
1 teaspoon kosher salt
½ teaspoon freshly ground black pepper
2 Tablespoons olive oil
1 cup Italian parsley leaves

Wash and separate endive leaves; set aside to dry.

In a food processor, add ricotta, olives, pine nuts, salt and olive oil.

Process until smooth.

Add parsley leaves and pulse 5 to 6 times to combine.

Stuff endive leaves with 1 to 2 teaspoons of the ricotta mixture.

Cover and chill until ready to serve. Garnish serving platter with additional parsley.

Tenderloin with Mushrooms & Wine Sauce

Simple and delicious, this elegant tenderloin of beef is a gift to your guests.

SERVES: TWENTY

20 4-ounce beef tenderloin steaks

½ cup fresh thyme leaves

½ cup kosher salt

5 teaspoons freshly ground black pepper

1 cup canola oil

2 quarts plus 2 cups beef broth

1 cup all-purpose flour

2½ cups cabernet sauvignon wine

10 cups wild mushrooms, sliced

5 yellow onions, diced

20 sprigs fresh thyme

½ cup plus 2 Tablespoons unsalted butter

2½ teaspoons granulated sugar

Tenderloin can be quite expensive when serving to a large party. A good substitute is sirloin fillet. This cut is less pricey, looks similar and can be a bit more flavorful. While sirloin fillet is less tender, when cooked in this recipe it can be a good alternative.

Pat beef dry and rub with salt and pepper. Tie thyme sprigs into a bundle with kitchen string.

In two extra-large skillets, heat oil over medium-high heat; swirl to coat the pans.

Add tenderloin in two batches of five steaks each; cook 3 to 4 minutes on each side, or to desired degree of doneness. Remove steaks from skillets and keep warm under foil. Cook the second batch.

Whisk broth and flour in a small bowl.

Add wine, mushrooms and diced onion to the skillets; cook approximately 30 seconds, scraping up any flavor-packed brown bits from the bottom of the pan.

Stir in broth mixture and thyme and bring to a boil. Cook 2 to 3 minutes, or until reduced to ½ cup. Remove thyme and discard. Whisk in butter and sugar.

Pour sauce over steaks to serve. Garnish serving platter with more fresh thyme.

Broiled Shrimp with Basil

This is an easy and delicious shrimp that can be prepared inside under the broiler when the weather is cold. In warmer months, prepare these shrimp on the grill for additional smoky flavor.

SERVES: SIXTEEN

2 pounds shrimp, peeled and deveined
½ cup fresh basil leaves, minced
Juice of 2 limes
½ cup olive oil

Skewer shrimp with 3 to 5 shrimp on each skewer and lay in an oblong casserole dish.

In a large bowl, combine basil, lime and olive oil.

Pour marinade over shrimp skewers and allow to marinate in the refrigerator for **30 to 45 minutes.**

Preheat broiler (or grill) to medium.

Remove shrimp from marinade and place on the broiler pan (or grill grate); then brush marinade over the shrimp.

Broil (or grill) shrimp 2 minutes per side. Serve warm or cold.

Parmesan & Leek Quiche

This recipe is inspired by the famed French onion tart, and showcases one of my favorite herbs, fresh thyme.

SERVES: TEN

¹⁄₃ recipe Gladdie's Pie Dough

(See p. 245.)

Bake 9-inch pie shell at 375 degrees for 12 to 15 minutes, or until golden brown.

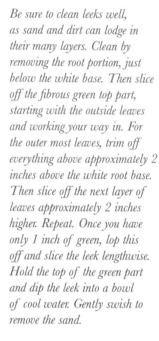

FILLING

2 Tablespoons unsalted butter

2½ cups leeks

1 teaspoon kosher salt

½ teaspoon freshly ground black pepper

1½ cups Half and Half cream

4 large eggs

2 teaspoons fresh thyme leaves

½ teaspoon freshly ground nutmeg

2 cups parmesan cheese, grated

Preheat oven to 325 degrees. Clean leeks and chop fine.

In a large saucepan, melt butter over medium heat. Add leeks, salt and pepper. Cook approximately 15 minutes. Set aside.

In a large bowl, whisk together the cream, eggs, thyme.

Stir in the parmesan cheese and taste for seasoning. Adjust as necessary.

Spread softened leeks into the partially-baked pie shell, taking care to not puncture the crust.

Pour egg mixture over the leeks. Dust the top of quiche with fresh nutmeg.

Bake for 45 to 55 minutes or until the filling is set but still moist, and the crust is golden brown. Serve warm.

Be sure to clean leeks well, as sand and dirt can lodge in their many layers. Clean by removing the root portion, just below the white base. Then slice off the fibrous green top part, starting with the outside leaves and working your way in. For the outer most leaves, trim off everything above approximately 2 inches above the white root base. Then slice off the next layer of leaves approximately 2 inches higher. Repeat. Once you have only 1 inch of green, lop this off and slice the leek lengthwise. Hold the top of the green part and dip the leek into a bowl of cool water. Gently swish to remove the sand.

Stone Ground Grits with Gouda & Roasted Corn

These grits are especially delicious with grilled shrimp. The savory Gouda cheese makes them extra creamy and the corn provides a flavor-packed sweet crunch to each bite.

SERVES: TWENTY

5 cups stone ground yellow corn grits

10 cups chicken broth

5 large cloves garlic, minced

10 ears fresh corn, roasted

2½ cups heavy cream

5 cups milk

5 teaspoons fresh (lemon) thyme leaves

3 Tablespoons kosher salt

Freshly ground black pepper

10 Tablespoons unsalted butter

2½ cups gouda cheese, grated

5 Tablespoons fresh chives, minced

Lemon Thyme is especially good with these grits.

Lightly roast corn kernels in 375 degree oven for 8 to 10 minutes, rotating periodically to roast all sides. Cool and remove the kernels from cob.

Bring broth and garlic to a boil; whisk in grits. Simmer on low heat for 20 to 25 minutes, stirring constantly.

Add cream, milk, corn, thyme, salt, pepper; stir to combine. Add butter and stir to melt.

Add Gouda and gently fold to incorporate. Fold in chives at the last minute and serve immediately.

Okra & Lucky Black Eyed Peas

Eating black eyed peas on New Year's is claimed to bring good luck all year long. When mixed in this fresh salad, what have you got to lose?

SERVES: TWENTY

3 cups fresh (or frozen) okra, cubed

2 15-ounce cans black eyed peas, rinsed & drained

2 Tablespoons olive oil

8 scallions, chopped (including green parts)

4 cloves garlic, minced

2 red bell peppers, chopped

2 jalapeño peppers, seeded & minced

4 large ears fresh corn kernels

⅔ cup fresh cilantro, minced

Kosher salt &

Freshly ground black pepper

Wash and prepare okra, scallions, garlic, red peppers and jalapeño peppers as directed. Remove corn kernels from the cob. Mince cilantro.

Heat oil in a large skillet over medium-high heat. Add scallions and garlic; sauté approximately one minute. Add okra; sauté approximately 3 minutes, or until it begins to soften.

Reduce heat to medium. Add bell and jalapeño peppers; cook 5 minutes. Add corn; cook 5 minutes. Stir in the black eyed peas; cook a final 2 minutes. Remove from heat.

Stir in cilantro; season to taste with salt and pepper.

Remove to serving bowl and refrigerate until ready to serve.

A NEW YEAR'S EVE TRADITION

A novel way to celebrate the New Year with friends is to
mix different coins into your black eyed peas.

Guests will delight in scooping up a coin with every spoonful of "good luck" peas as they ring in the New Year!

Collect an assortment of dimes, quarters and silver dollars and boil in water to sterilize. Then stir them into the black eyed peas and serve with a sly smile!

Petit Gateaux Moelleux
au Chocolat

These little cakes with a chocolate molten espresso heart are delicious topped with whipped cream and chocolate curls. Cakes can be prepared ahead and held, then baked the last few minutes just before ready to serve to ensure a delicious and gooey chocolate center.

YIELD: TEN FOUR-OUNCE CAKES

CHOCOLATE MOLTEN ESPRESSO HEARTS

1 4-ounce bar bittersweet chocolate

2 Tablespoons heavy cream

1 Tablespoon light corn syrup

1 teaspoon instant espresso coffee powder

In double boiler, combine chocolate, cream, corn syrup and espresso powder. Cook over medium heat, stirring frequently, until chocolate is melted and smooth. *Watch carefully to ensure chocolate does not get too hot, or it will separate.*

Spread melted chocolate into a 9 x 9-inch glass baking dish and freeze for 30 minutes.

Once chocolate is frozen, use a small scoop to create 1-inch balls, or chocolate hearts. Place hearts on parchment paper; set aside.

SMALL CAKES

2 4-ounce bars semisweet chocolate

1 cup unsalted butter

4 large eggs, *plus*

4 large egg yolks

½ cup granulated sugar

2 teaspoons pure vanilla extract

½ cup cake flour

2 Tablespoons cocoa powder

Whipped cream

White and dark chocolate curls

Preheat oven to 400 degrees. Place a water bath in the oven.

(See p. 255, The Water Bath.)

Spray ten 4-ounce cake ramekins or custard cups with baking spray and dust with cocoa powder.

In a double boiler, combine chocolate with butter; melt until smooth. Set aside to cool.

In a large bowl with an electric mixer, combine eggs, egg **yolks, s**ugar and vanilla. Beat until thick and pale yellow, approximately 4 to 5 minutes.

Fold the cooled chocolate mixture into the egg mixture, starting with just ¼ of the chocolate to temper the eggs first. Once incorporated, add the remaining chocolate.

Then add the flour and cocoa; fold to combine.

Spoon batter into prepared ramekins to ¾ full. Press one chocolate heart into the center of each ramekin. As necessary, smooth the batter over the top of the heart to cover it completely.

Place ramekins in the water bath already in place in the oven. Bake 10 minutes, or until the cakes are spongy and spring back when touched.

Remove ramekins from the water bath to cool on a wire rack for 2 to 3 minutes, then invert onto serving plates and serve immediately while center is still liquid.

Top inverted cakes with a dollop of whipped cream and curls of shaved chocolate. *This is especially pretty with a mix of dark, milk and white chocolate curls.*

See p. 79, Making Chocolate Curls.

Queen Cake

This triple lemon cake, layered with tangy curd and coated with a tart butter frosting, is fit for a queen! Be sure to use fresh lemons and make your own curd, as nothing compares to the bright taste of fresh citrus. You will need seven lemons for this recipe. See p. 377, Measuring Lemons, *and to help ensure your success, see* Baking Secrets, Light & Airy Cakes, *p. 361.*

SERVES: TWENTY

SIX-LAYER CAKE
2 ⅓ cups cake flour
2¾ teaspoons baking powder
¼ teaspoon salt
1¾ cups granulated sugar
2 Tablespoons zest of fresh lemon
12 Tablespoons unsalted butter, softened
1 cup whole milk
5 large egg whites
¼ teaspoon cream of tartar
1 six-inch wooden skewer

Set butter (for cake and frosting), milk and eggs on counter and bring to room temperature before beginning. Reserve extra flour and butter to prepare pans.

Preheat oven to 350 degrees and position rack in the middle of oven. Generously butter and flour three 6-inch cake rounds.

Grate lemon zest, then measure all other ingredients and have ready.

Sift cake flour with baking powder and salt; set aside. Whisk ¼ cup of the sugar with lemon zest until well-combined.

In a separate large bowl, beat egg whites with an electric mixer on medium speed just until foamy. Add the cream of tartar, increase speed to medium high, and beat until soft peaks form when the beaters are lifted out.

In a large bowl with an electric mixer, beat butter and lemon sugar until light and fluffy, approximately 3 minutes. Add remaining 1½ cups sugar and beat until smooth, another 1 to 2 minutes.

Beat in ¼ cup of the milk until just blended.

You may have a bit of the curd leftover. Just save it. Lemon curd is delicious with scones and other sweet breads and will keep for up to two weeks refrigerated.

On low speed, add the flour mixture alternately with the remaining ¾ cup of milk in three batches, scraping the bowl with each addition. Beat just until blended.

Add ¼ of the whites to the batter and gently fold in by hand using a spatula; continue to gently fold in whites by hand, a quarter at a time, being careful to not deflate the mixture.

Divide the batter evenly between the prepared pans. Gently swish cake pans to and fro on the to deflate any large air bubbles and to smooth the tops of the cakes. Bake for 20 to 25 minutes, or until toothpick inserted into center comes out clean.

Let cakes cool in pans for 5 minutes. Then run a knife around the inside of the pans and carefully invert onto a cooling rack flipped right side up. Cool completely.

LEMON CURD

Curd can be made one day to one week in advance and refrigerated.

½ cup unsalted butter
¾ cup granulated sugar
½ cup juice of fresh lemon, including pulp
3 Tablespoons zest of fresh lemon
⅛ teaspoon kosher salt
6 large egg yolks

While cake is baking, make the curd.

Melt butter in medium saucepan over medium-high heat. Remove the pan from the heat and whisk in sugar, lemon juice, zest and salt.

Whisk in the **yolks** *one at a time* until well combined and smooth.

Return pan to medium heat and cook curd, whisking constantly, until the mixture thickens, approximately 5 to 6 minutes. Be sure to not allow the mixture to boil. Cool and refrigerate covered, until ready to use.

FROSTING

Frosting can be made a couple hours ahead, and kept covered and cool (but not cold), until ready to use. Allow cake to come to room temperature before serving.

1 cup unsalted butter, softened

2 Tablespoons zest of fresh lemon
3½ to 4 cups powdered sugar, sifted
3 Tablespoons juice of fresh lemon

While cake and curd are cooling, make the frosting.

In a large bowl with an electric mixer, beat the butter and lemon zest on medium speed until light and fluffy, approximately 2 to 3 minutes. Add the powdered sugar in 3 batches and beat until light and fluffy. Add the lemon juice and beat for another minute. Check consistency and add a bit more powdered sugar if necessary.

ASSEMBLY

To ensure six uniform cake halves, start by trimming any peaks from the tops of the three cakes, using a long serrated knife. Then, with the palm of one hand gently pressed on top of cake layers, cut each of the three cakes in half horizontally, again using a serrated knife.

Put one of the six cake layers on a pretty cake plate, cut side up.

With a spatula, spread about $1/5$ of the chilled curd on top of the cake layer, allowing the curd to soak into the cake as much as possible. Lay another layer on top, spread it with another $1/5$ of curd, and repeat with the third through fifth layers and last $1/5$ cup of curd. Top stack with the sixth cake layer, top side up.

At this point, you will see the cake is very tall and a bit precarious! Steady the cake by inserting a wooden skewer down the center of the six layers and use extra care when transferring cake to and from the refrigerator.

TO FROST

Spread a thin layer of frosting on the sides and top of the cake, filling in any gaps as you go. Chill cake until the frosting firms, approximately $1/2$ hour (*an essential step for setting this very tall cake in place*).

Divide remaining frosting into four equal parts. Color $1/4$ of the frosting dark yellow, $1/4$ light yellow; and $1/2$ leave white. Spread the dark yellow on the bottom third of cake, the light yellow in the center third, and white on the top third and across the top of the cake.

Frosting Options	Bottom of Cake	Middle	Top of Cake
Amount of Frosting	$1/4$ recipe	$1/4$ recipe	$1/2$ recipe
Colors	Light Purple	Light Aqua	Light Pink
	Dark Pink	Pink	Light Pink
	Dark Yellow	Light Yellow	White (no color)

Use a long offset spatula, designed for frosting cakes for this task.

Then sprinkle top of cake with crystals and sprinkles, or candied fruits and flowers. Use a damp paper towel to clean any excess frosting and cake crumbs from the cake plate, and refrigerate until ready to serve your queen!

Allow cake to come to room temperature before slicing. Store leftover cake in refrigerator.

GRATING LEMON RIND – ZESTING!

To zest lemon and orange rind, gently run the whole fruit up and down a micro plane grater.
For curls or long strips of rind, use a vegetable peeler.

Rather than composting lemon and orange rinds, grind them in the garbage disposal and your kitchen will smell citrus fresh!

Jammin' Shortbread

These jam filled shortbread sandwiches are derived from the traditional Christmas cookie of Austria, the Linzer. You won't believe how good they are!

YIELD: TWENTY-SIX COOKIES

¾ pound unsalted butter, softened
1 cup granulated sugar
1¼ teaspoon pure vanilla extract
3½ cups all-purpose flour
¼ teaspoon salt
¼ teaspoon cinnamon
Zest of 1 lemon
8 to 10 ounces good apricot jam
Powdered sugar, for dusting

In a large bowl with an electric mixer, mix butter with sugar until just combined. Add vanilla and zest and mix in.

Sift the flour with salt and cinnamon onto a sheet of waxed paper, then gradually add to the butter mixture and mix on low until the dough begins to come together, approximately 2 to 3 minutes.

Onto a lightly floured surface, pour out the dough and shape into 2 rounds. Wrap rounds in waxed paper and chill for **30 minutes.**

Preheat oven to 350 degrees.

On a lightly floured surface, roll the first round into a ¼-inch thick round. Cut the dough into 26 2-inch rounds.

Cut the second half of the dough into 2-inch rounds, and then cut a triangle or circle shape from the center of each round. Roll cut out/dough scrapes until you have 26 rounds with the centers cut out.

Place cookies on cookie sheet lined with parchment paper and chill for 15 minutes.

Bake for 15 to 20 minutes, or until the edges are just beginning to brown and cookies look crisp yet soft. Remove to a wire rack and cool completely.

Spread apricot jam generously onto the bottom side of each of the 24 cookies *without* the cut outs.

Then top jam with 24 cookies *with* the cut outs to make a sandwich, placing the bottom side down onto the jam.

Using a fine mesh sieve, dust the tops of each cookie sandwich with powdered sugar.

AFTER THE RICH FOODS AND SWEETS OF THE HOLIDAYS, NOTHING SOUNDS BETTER IN JANUARY THAN A DE-LIGHT-FUL MEAL.

THIS MENU STARTS WITH A LEAN AHI TUNA RUBBED WITH LAVENDER FLOWERS AND ENDS WITH LEMON SORBET SERVED IN TINY PORTIONS WITHIN ACTUAL LEMON CUPS!

WINE IS OPTIONAL.

AT THE START OF A NEW YEAR

de-Light-ful Dinner

FOR 4

Lavender Seared Ahi Tuna
Roasted Vegetables in Lemon Thyme Tart
with
Cornmeal Crust
Apple Slaw with Raisins & Pomegranate

Lemon Sorbet in Lemon Cups
and/or
Mixed Fruit & Ricotta Tartlets

RECIPES

LAVENDER SEARED
AHI TUNA

ROASTED VEGETABLES
IN LEMON THYME
TART WITH CORNMEAL
CRUST

APPLE SLAW
WITH RAISINS &
POMEGRANATE

LEMON SORBET IN
LEMON CUPS

MIXED FRUIT &
RICOTTA TARTLETS

*Serve Sparkling Water for a
light touch.
Or a Malbec,
with its deep aroma and soft
tannins, would be especially
good with the tuna steaks.*

TIME LINE
Resolutions

This meal should be served Family Style. *For entertaining secrets, see* Setting a Formal Table – Napkins & Linens, *p. 28-36.*

THE DE-LIGHT-FUL MORNING

Make sorbet and freeze.
-or-
Make ricotta tartlets, but wait to assemble. Chill water.

Make cornmeal crust, roast vegetables, assemble tart filling; cover each separately and refrigerate.
Assemble slaw and refrigerate.
Set a simple table including serving pieces for Family Style service.

TWO HOURS BEFORE DINNER

Trim, rub and sear tuna, then refrigerate for at least one hour. Bring ingredients for tart to room temperature, assemble and bake.

JUST BEFORE SERVING

Slice tuna and plate.
Serve tart and slaw.
Serve sparkling water or Malbec wine.

TO END

Scoop sorbet into lemon cups and place on dessert plates with a spoon.
-or-
Assemble tartlets and serve on plates to each guest.

Lavender Seared Ahi Tuna

This elegant preparation creates a tuna steak that is rare inside with an aromatic and crispy crust.

SERVES: FOUR

1 pound center-cut ahi tuna
1½ teaspoons dried lavender flowers
1 teaspoon kosher salt
3 teaspoons *peppercorn mix
3 to 4 Tablespoons good olive oil

Trim and cut tuna into four 4-ounce steaks approximately 2-inches across.

Using a mortar and pestle, crush the salt with the peppercorn mix and lavender.

Oil the tuna steaks by rubbing with half of the olive oil, then coating with salt and lavender mixture on all sides.

In a large skillet, heat the remaining oil until hot and sear tuna quickly on each side, being careful to not overcook. *Tuna should be rare inside.*

Immediately place tuna on a plate, cover and refrigerate to chill and rest for **1 to 3 hours** before serving.

To serve, slice tuna very thin.

The aromatic oils of lavender add a delicious herbal smoked flavor to grilled meats and are also delicious used in salads and baked goods.
For recipes that call for rosemary, try substituting lavender for something different. See p. 376.

Ask your fishmonger for help in finding fresh ahi.

*PEPPERCORN MIX

Toasted & ground black & pink peppercorns, coriander & ground star anise.

Roasted Vegetables in Lemon Thyme Tart with Cornmeal Crust

This cornmeal crusted tart finds its roots in the cooking conventions of rural France. The rustic cornmeal crust combined with a ricotta filling is seasoned with the dry aroma and slightly mint flavor of fresh thyme, then filled with naturally sweet roasted vegetables.

Make this tart any time of year using fresh vegetables in season.

SERVES: EIGHT

ROASTED VEGETABLES

½ **cup cherry tomatoes, halved**
½ **cup winter squash, sliced**
½ **bell pepper, sliced into strips**
Kosher salt

Preheat oven to 325 degrees.

Prepare vegetables, then sprinkle lightly with salt and place on a jelly roll pan lined with foil. Slowly roast for 30 minutes, or until tender yet crisp; set aside.

CORNMEAL CRUST

½ **cup unsalted butter, softened**
2 Tablespoons honey
1 cup yellow cornmeal
2 large eggs
1 teaspoon kosher salt
1½ **cups all-purpose flour**

In a food processor, combine butter with honey and process until smooth. Add cornmeal, eggs and salt and continue processing until well combined.

Add flour and pulse just until dough forms into a ball.

Wrap mixture in plastic wrap and chill for **1 hour.**

Preheat oven to 350 degrees.

Butter a 9-inch tart pan with a removable bottom.

On a lightly floured surface, roll dough to ¼-inch thick and fit snuggly into tart pan. Press the dough to fit into pan. Crimp the top edges of the crust. Then prick dough with a fork on all surfaces to prevent air bubbles.

Bake for 8 to 10 minutes, or until lightly browned.

When the shell has cooled, line the bottom with roasted vegetables.

LEMON THYME FILLING

1 Tablespoon unsalted butter
2 large shallots, minced
⅔ cup Half and Half cream
½ cup sauvignon blanc wine
1 teaspoon kosher salt
Freshly ground black pepper
¾ pound fresh ricotta cheese
3 large eggs
½ Tablespoon each: thyme, chives & parsley

In a medium saucepan, melt butter and sauté shallots until soft.

Add the cream, wine, salt and pepper. Bring to a simmer and then reduce by half. Remove to a mixing bowl and cool.

Add ricotta, eggs and herbs to mixture and beat until smooth.

Pour ricotta mixture into prepared tart shell that has been lined with roasted vegetables. Sprinkle freshly ground black pepper over the top.

Bake 35 minutes, or until filling is just set and lightly browned.

Serve warm, or room temperature.

Apple Slaw with Raisins
& Pomegranate

Pomegranates are very flavorful without a lot of sugar, and unlike most fruits, the seeds are the edible portion of a pomegranate. See p. 383.

This crisp slaw is both sweet and tart with a light cream dressing.

SERVES: FOUR

½ **cup golden raisins, plumped**
½ **cup brandy**
2 **jonathan apples, chopped**
Seeds of ½ **pomegranate**
¼ **cup sour cream (light)**
1½ **Tablespoons mayonnaise (reduced-fat)**
1 **Tablespoon (reserved) brandy**
½ **teaspoon sourwood honey**
¼ **teaspoon kosher salt**
⅛ **teaspoon freshly ground black pepper**
8 **ounces coleslaw mix**

Plump raisins in ½ cup brandy for 20 to 30 minutes, or until soft and supple. Separate raisins and set aside; reserve brandy.

Core and cube apples, leaving skin on; Seed ½ of a pomegranate.

In a small bowl, whisk together sour cream, mayonnaise, half of the reserved brandy, honey, salt and pepper.

In a large bowl, toss raisins, apples and pomegranate seeds and coleslaw mix; add mayonnaise mixture gradually to desired amount; toss to coat fruit and combine. Serve cold.

Lemon Sorbet in Lemon Cups

This fruit-flavored ice is the perfect way to end a satisfying meal. Sorbet is the essence of pure flavor and an intense experience of the fruit(s) used. The citrus and sugar in this sorbet balance one another to create a de-light-ful dessert.

PRONOUNCED: SORE-BAY

SERVES: FOUR

½ cup juice of fresh lemon
¼ cup juice of fresh orange
⅔ Tablespoon zest of lemon
⅓ Tablespoon zest of orange
¾ cups granulated sugar
⅛ teaspoon kosher salt
2 cups Half and Half cream
Fresh mint leaves

Cut two lemons in half horizontally to make serving "cups." Gently hollow out the pulp and juice, using a citrus juicing tool, and reserve to a small bowl.

Then slice just a bit of the rind off the bottom of each lemon half so that the cups will sit up straight on your service plate. Cover the four hollow lemon halves tightly with plastic wrap and refrigerate until ready to serve.

In a large bowl, combine all ingredients and mix well.

Pour into ice cream freezer; freeze per instructions.

After mixing with citrus juice the cream may look clotted when poured it into the freezer. This is fine, it will smooth out when frozen.

Allow sorbet to soften just slightly before serving.

Then, using a medium-sized ice cream scoop, spoon sorbets into lemon cups and dust with a pinch of sugar. Top each serving with mint before placing on service plates.

Mixed Fruit & Ricotta Tartlets

What could be better than ricotta piled onto crisp spicy cookies and topped with fresh seasonal fruits? Pair these with Madeira wine for a light after-dinner sweet.

YIELD: EIGHT TARTLETS

TARTLETS

¾ **cup all-purpose flour**

½ **teaspoon cinnamon**

¼ **teaspoon kosher salt**

¼ **teaspoon ground cloves**

¼ **cup unsalted butter, softened**

1 **Tablespoon brown sugar, packed**

1 **Tablespoon granulated sugar**

1¼ **Tablespoons lavender honey**

½ **teaspoon molasses**

Sift the flour with cinnamon, salt and cloves onto a sheet of waxed paper; set aside.

In a large bowl with an electric mixer, beat butter with sugars until fluffy, approximately 3 minutes. Mix in honey and molasses. Scrape down the sides of the bowl and then fold in the flour mixture until just incorporated.

Pat dough into a disc and wrap in waxed paper. Refrigerate for 1 hour.

Preheat oven to 350 degrees. Line a baking sheet with parchment paper.

On a lightly floured surface, roll dough to ¼-inch thick. Cut into 3-inch rounds; place on baking sheet. Re-roll dough scraps as necessary until you have 8 rounds.

Bake 12 to 15 minutes, rotating pan after five minutes. Cookies should be golden brown at edges.

Transfer to cooling racks to cool completely.

MIXED FRUITS

1 **fresh pear, cored and sliced thin**

1 **apple, cored and sliced thin**

Juice of ½ **lime**

1½ **Tablespoons honey**

1 **teaspoon pure vanilla extract**

¼ **cup walnuts, toasted and chopped**

Toast and chop walnuts; set aside. Mix vanilla with honey.

Wash, core and slice pears and apples.

Coat fruit with lime juice, then sprinkle with honey and vanilla mix to get the juices running. Refrigerate until ready to assemble.

FILLING

5 ounces ricotta cheese
1½ Tablespoon honey
½ teaspoon zest of lime

In a medium bowl, mix the ricotta with honey and lime zest.

Assemble by spreading approximately 1 to 1 ½ Tablespoons of the filling onto each cookie, then spooning approximately 1 to 1 ½ Tablespoons of sugary fruits over the top. Drizzle with more syrup from the bowl and top with toasted walnuts.

WAKING UP TO A BLANKET OF SNOW NEVER FAILS TO THRILL. WHEN THE FORECAST CALLS FOR FLURRIES, I LIKE TO MAKE MUFFINS THE NIGHT BEFORE TO SERVE WITH HOT CHOCOLATE ON SNOWY MORNINGS. WITH A QUICK AND SATISFYING BREAKFAST OUT OF THE WAY, WE ARE FREE TO RACE OUTSIDE AND SPEND THE DAY SLEDDING AND SKIING.

BY LATE AFTERNOON, I'M READY TO COME IN AND PREPARE SOMETHING HEARTY FOR THE GANG, AND THIS MENU OF HOLY MOLE FITS THE BILL.

A SNOWY DAY IN JANUARY

Powder Day

FOR 4 TO 6

Hot Chocolate with Whipped Cream & Cocoa Powder
Pumpkin Chocolate Chip Muffins

Holy Mole!
English Muffin Bread
Apple Butter

Baba au Rhum with Whipped Cream

Serve a full-bodied Petite Sirah *with the Mole.*

MAKING LEMON CURLS

WHIPPING CREAM

TIME LINE

On the Slopes or Home from School

Make powder day easy! Serve the meal from a simple buffet set up on a kitchen island and invite friends and family to help themselves, and then gather in the dining room to enjoy the meal and share stories of escapades in the snow! *For entertaining secrets see* Stocking the Pantry & Freezer, *p. 39.*

THE NIGHT BEFORE

Make pumpkin muffins.

Assemble mole and refrigerate in a slow cooker bowl.

SNOWY MORNING

Make hot chocolate and serve muffins with a selection of dried fruits.

Place mole into slow cooker to be ready in 8 hours.

Bundle up and head outside!

LATE AFTERNOON

Make English Muffin Bread and bake.

Thaw apple butter – *made last fall and frozen!*

Bake rum cake; add syrup. Whip cream.

WHEN TIME FOR DINNER

Slice and toast bread; serve with butter and apple butter. Serve hot mole.

FOLLOWING THE MOLE

Serve rum cake with whipped cream and sugar crystals.

Hot Chocolate with Whipped Cream & Cocoa Powder

When the snow is falling, serve this yummy chocolate drink and you'll stay warm and toasty!

SERVES: FOUR TO SIX

3 cups two-percent milk

3 cups Half and Half cream

2 cups ghirardelli milk chocolate chips

Whipped cream

Cocoa powder

Simmer milk and cream just to boiling stage.

Add chips and stir while they melt and cook through.

Pour into mugs and top with a dollop of whipped cream and curls of semi-sweet chocolate that have been shaved into the mugs with a micro plane zester/grater.

Serve hot chocolate with a selection of dried fruits.
Figs, pear and pineapple are especially tasty with chocolate.

Pumpkin Chocolate Chip Muffins

These muffins are a combination of moist pumpkin bread and sweet milk chocolate. When the forecast calls for snow, bake these the night before so that breakfast will be ready when the gang wakes up and you can be the first ones on the slopes!

YIELD: TWENTY-FOUR MUFFINS

3 ⅓ cups all-purpose flour

2 cups granulated sugar

2 teaspoons pumpkin pie spice

2 teaspoons cinnamon

2 teaspoons baking soda

½ teaspoon baking powder

½ teaspoon salt

4 large eggs

1 15-ounce can pure pumpkin

1 cup unsalted butter, melted and cooled

2 cups ghirardelli milk chocolate chips

Always break eggs into a separate bowl to ensure no shell slips in, and that the eggs are good, before adding to batter.
Never use eggs that have red or brown color inside.

Preheat oven to 350 degrees.

Whisk the dry ingredients onto a sheet of waxed paper to combine; set aside.

In a large bowl with electric mixer, beat eggs, pumpkin and butter until well combined and fluffy, approximately 2 minutes.

Add dry ingredients to the egg mixture gradually and mix until just moistened.

Fold in chocolate chips by hand.

Spoon batter evenly into muffin tins filled with parchment paper liners.

Bake for 18 to 20 minutes, or until a toothpick inserted into the center of each muffin comes out clean.

Use canned pure pumpkin, not pumpkin pie filling for this recipe.

Holy Mole!

This traditional Mexican chicken mole is a "heavenly" delight! The turbo-charged chicken is spicy and succulent, and the sauce a blend of sweet chocolate, cinnamon and raisins - with hot chilies!

PRONOUNCED: MOE-LAY

SERVES: SIX

2 pounds organic chicken, (breasts and thighs with skin removed)
Kosher salt
¼ cup almonds, toasted
⅛ cup sesame seeds, toasted
1 15-ounce can whole tomatoes
½ yellow onion, chopped
1 dried chili, re-hydrated in very hot water
1 small can chipotle peppers in adobo sauce
⅛ cup raisins
1½ ounces bittersweet chocolate, chopped
2 cloves garlic, peeled
1½ Tablespoons olive oil
½ teaspoon ground cumin
¼ teaspoon ground cinnamon
Lightly toasted sesame seeds

Season chicken with salt and place into a slow cooker set on low heat.

Toast nuts and seeds; chop onion.

In a food processor, combine all ingredients (except chicken) and pulse to mince ingredients and incorporate.

Add tomato-chili mixture to chicken in slow cooker; cover and cook for

8 hours.

Remove bones from chicken. Serve hot, garnished with fresh cilantro.

Mole is a very spicy dish. If you need to bring down the heat, add a bit of honey.

English Muffin Bread

This sticky dough transforms into the most wonderful toast, and is terrific with Holy Mole and Apple Butter. Made by hand, it requires a strong arm for kneading.

YIELD: ONE TEN-SLICE LOAF

1¾ cups lukewarm water
1 Tablespoon active dry yeast (2 envelopes)
2 Tablespoons all-purpose flour
1½ teaspoons kosher salt
2¾ to 3½ cups *additional* flour
Cornmeal

When baking bread, spritz your oven with water to create a more humid environment. This will give the bread a nice crisp crust. Use a spray bottle filled with tap water to do the job.

Yeast should be dissolved in lukewarm water (105 to 115 degrees) not hot.

In a liquid measuring cup, add **¼ cup** of lukewarm water with 1 Tablespoon yeast and 2 Tablespoons flour. Cover with plastic wrap and make a "sponge" by letting the mixture stand until doubled in volume with tiny bubbles across the surface (10 to 15 minutes).

In a small bowl, mix the salt with additional flour; set aside.

Transfer the sponge into a large bowl; add remaining **1½ cups** of lukewarm water and stir to combine well.

With a wooden spoon, begin adding the additional flour to the water, little by little, mixing well with each incorporation.

At approximately 3 cups, check to ensure the dough is sticky and clings to your spoon. If it is still very very wet, add up to ½ cup of additional flour.

Transfer dough to a clean dry surface to knead by hand.

This dough is very sticky, and is kneaded much like making taffy – pulling the dough up as it "walks" across the counter.

Grab the center of your dough and pull it straight up, stretching the mass to 8 to 10 inches above the counter top. Let your hand follow the dough down.

Repeat until the ball of dough cleans itself from the countertop for just an instant. *It takes approximately ten minutes to get to this stage.*

Preheat oven to 350 degrees.

Butter a 10-cup loaf pan then dust the bottom and sides of the pan with cornmeal. Transfer dough to pan and cover with a kitchen towel and set in a warm place. Allow to rise to ¾ of pan depth. (30 minutes to 2 hours, depending on humidity.)

Bake on the middle rack of oven for 45 minutes.

This bread will not brown, but only become slightly darker in color than the shade of the dough.

To unmold bread, place the pan on a damp cloth for several minutes, then run a knife around the edges and invert to a wire cooling rack.

Cool completely, then wrap in foil until ready to serve. Serve by cutting bread into thin slices and toasting.

Apple Butter

Apple butter is delicious on English Muffin Bread, and is also great with pork. This Apple Butter has no preservatives, but will keep in the refrigerator for up to two weeks. It also freezes well.

YIELD: TWO PINTS

3 pounds apples
½ cup granulated sugar
½ cup brown sugar, packed
½ Tablespoon maple syrup
½ Tablespoon ground cinnamon
¼ teaspoon freshly ground nutmeg
¼ teaspoon ground cloves
1 teaspoon kosher salt
½ Tablespoon pure vanilla extract

Peel, core and cube apples; place in a slow cooker.

Mix all remaining ingredients *except vanilla extract* and pour over the apples; Stir to combine.

Cook on low setting for **10 hours,** stirring occasionally, until mixture is thick and dark brown.

Stir in vanilla and continue cooking for **2 more hours**.

Cool and remove to a food processor; purée apples until smooth and buttery; Spoon into sterile jars. Refrigerate or freeze.

I like to make a couple batches of this easy spread in the fall when apples are at their peak of freshness. I store the butter in small (seven to fourteen ounce) jars and freeze. This allows fresh apple butter all winter long as well as enough to give as gifts during the holidays.

Baba au Rhum with Whipped Cream

This rum cake recipe is from the tiny island of Bermuda where they make delicious rum. The moist pound cake is infused with buttery rum syrup then sprinkled with Demerara Sugar Crystals.

PRONOUNCED: BAE-BAE O RUM

SERVES: TWELVE

CAKE

½ cup, plus 6 Tablespoons unsalted butter, softened
½ cup granulated sugar
5 large egg yolks
2 cups cake flour
1 Tablespoon baking powder
2 Tablespoons rum extract
2 Tablespoons sour cream
6 large egg whites
¼ cup additional granulated sugar

Preheat oven to 350 degrees.

In a large bowl with an electric mixer, cream butter and sugar until pale yellow, approximately 3 minutes. Add egg **yolks** *one at a time*, mixing after each addition.

Sift the flour with baking powder onto a sheet of waxed paper, then gently fold into the butter mixture in three batches. Add sour cream and rum extract; combine.

In a separate, clean bowl, beat egg whites and remaining sugar until small peaks form. Gently fold **whites** into cake batter by hand.

Turn batter into a buttered and lightly floured Bundt pan. Bake 20 to 30 minutes, or until toothpick comes out clean.

If rum extract cannot be found, pure vanilla extract also works well.

BERMUDA RUM SYRUP

½ cup unsalted butter
¼ cup water
1 cup granulated sugar
½ cup Bermuda rum

In a small saucepan, place sugar, water and butter; heat just to boiling stage when sugar mixture begins to thicken slightly. Remove from heat and add rum. Cool.

Using a skewer, puncture several small holes into the top of cooled rum cake. Drizzle rum syrup over cake slowly and evenly, allowing the cake to absorb the syrup between drizzles.

TOPPING

1 cup heavy cream
3 Tablespoons powdered sugar
Optional: Lemon rind curls & Demerara sugar crystals

Beat **cold** cream and sugar at high speed with an electric mixer until soft peaks form.

To serve, top cake slices with a dollop of whipped cream and dusting of powdered sugar, a sprinkle of Demerara sugar crystals.

Opposite of egg whites that should be beaten at room temperature, cream should be chilled before whipping for best results.
If you over-whip your cream and it begins to look curdled, just add a bit more cream and continue whipping until soft peaks form once again.

LEMON RIND CURLS

Make lemon rind curls with a channel knife zester.

Simply hold clean lemon over a bowl, and using a zester, pull gently across the lemon with one edge of the zester. Twist the thin strips of lemon rind to curl.

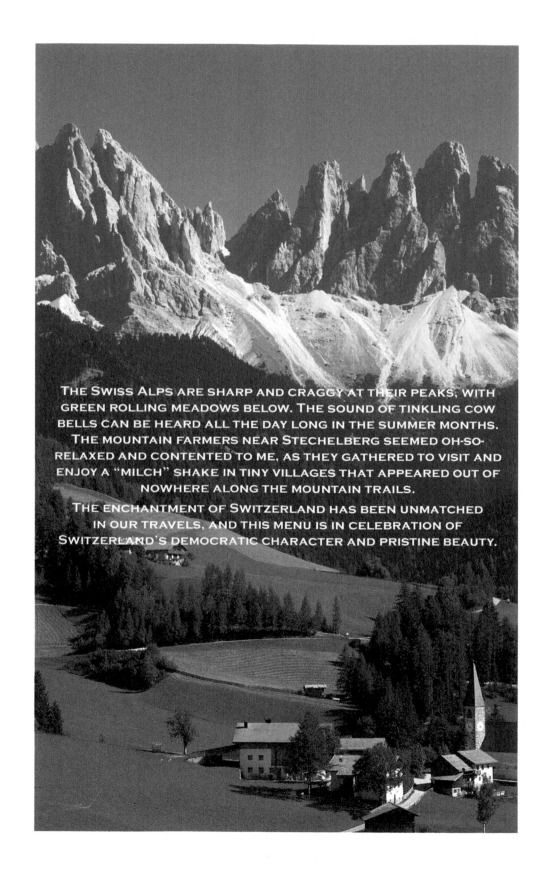

THE SWISS ALPS ARE SHARP AND CRAGGY AT THEIR PEAKS, WITH GREEN ROLLING MEADOWS BELOW. THE SOUND OF TINKLING COW BELLS CAN BE HEARD ALL THE DAY LONG IN THE SUMMER MONTHS. THE MOUNTAIN FARMERS NEAR STECHELBERG SEEMED OH-SO-RELAXED AND CONTENTED TO ME, AS THEY GATHERED TO VISIT AND ENJOY A "MILCH" SHAKE IN TINY VILLAGES THAT APPEARED OUT OF NOWHERE ALONG THE MOUNTAIN TRAILS.

THE ENCHANTMENT OF SWITZERLAND HAS BEEN UNMATCHED IN OUR TRAVELS, AND THIS MENU IS IN CELEBRATION OF SWITZERLAND'S DEMOCRATIC CHARACTER AND PRISTINE BEAUTY.

A COLD WEEKEND IN FEBRUARY

Alpine Feast
FOR 8

Cassoulet of Fowl & Hot Sausage
Watercress, Orange & Sweet Potato Salad

Lemon Soufflé – *Mais Oui!*

RECIPES

CASSOULET OF FOWL & HOT SAUSAGE

WATERCRESS, ORANGE & SWEET POTATO SALAD

LEMON SOUFFLÉ – *MAIS QUI!*

Serve a Merlot with a berry and/or vanilla influence with the cassoulet. Serve Marc with the Soufflé.

SECRETS TO SUCCESSFUL SOUFFLÉS

TIME LINE

Willkemmen Friends!

This dinner for eight can be served two ways. Either Family Style with the dishes on the table and passed, or with dishes set on a buffet (or kitchen island) so guests can fill their plates and then return to the table to dine.

For entertaining secrets see Good Cooking Habits *and* Kitchen Essentials*, p. 38.*

TWO DAYS BEFORE

Begin the cassoulet and prepare as directed through simmering the beans; refrigerate overnight.

Purchase yummy Swiss chocolates to send home with guests.

THE DAY BEFORE

Set a mountain lodge-themed table, and lay a fire.

Prepare second steps for cassoulet through assembling ingredients in casserole.

TWO HOURS BEFORE FEAST

Prepare the gratin for the cassoulet and finish the dish.

30 MINUTES BEFORE FRIENDS ARRIVE

Prepare and plate salads; cover and refrigerate.

Assemble all ingredients for soufflé.

FOR THE ENTREE

Serve cassoulet, salad and wine.

AFTER THE ENTREE

Invite guests to adjourn to the living room for a glass of marc while you prepare and bake the soufflé.

45 MINUTES LATER

Treat guests to a delicious lemon soufflé right out of the oven.

Send Swiss chocolates home with friends.

Cassoulet of Fowl & Hot Sausage

This hearty casserole is moist but not soupy and laced with a "boquet" of flavors. This is true Alpine cooking and worth the time to prepare. The chicken can be substituted with duck or pheasant, and the beans should rest at least one day before final assembly.

PRONOUNCED: KAES-EAU 'LEI
SERVES: EIGHT TO TWELVE

CASSOULTET

1   4-pound whole chicken
3 quarts chicken broth
2 pounds great northern beans, dry
4 cups sauvignon blanc wine
1 pound lean bacon
2 cloves garlic
3 large onions, finely chopped
2 pounds fresh tomatoes
1 pound hot Italian sausage
Kosher salt
Olive oil
Additional chicken broth

In a large stock pot, bring chicken broth to a rolling boil. Wash (and inspect) beans in cold water; drain. Add beans to broth and boil for 10 minutes, stirring occasionally.

Remove pot from the heat, skim off any foam, and set aside to cool.

Preheat oven to 450 degrees.

Remove giblets; wash and quarter the chicken; pat dry. Rub the cavity with salt and the skin with olive oil.

Place bird on a rack set over a roasting pan; roast for 25 to 30 minutes, uncovered. Remove partially cooked bird from the oven and cool.

Debone and skin the chicken and refrigerate until final assembly. Place the bones and skin back into the roasting pan and roast for 30 minutes. Add 1 cup water and roast another 15 minutes.

Cool; remove bones and skins, retaining the fat and drippings. Add 2 cups of wine to the drippings and cook 5 minutes more. Return beans to heat and cook until soft.

Cut bacon into ½-inch cubes. In a separate pan, sauté the bacon until browned with all the fat is rendered. Remove bacon from frying pan and add to the cooking beans.

Peel, seed and chop tomatoes, reserving juice. Chop onions and garlic. Add garlic and onion to bacon fat and sauté until transparent, scraping up any flavor packed brown bits from the bottom of the pan. Add tomatoes and cook another 10 minutes.

Pour the vegetable mixture into the pot of beans. Add the Boquet Garni and the clove-studded onion. Bring beans to a simmer over medium heat and cook approximately **1½ to 2 hours,** or until the beans are tender.

At this point you can refrigerate the bean mixture overnight and finish the cassoulet the next day.

BOQUET GARNI

2 sprigs fresh parsley
1 sprig fresh thyme
3 carrot tops
2 bay leaves, dried
2 large leek whites, cleaned
1 large carrot, peeled and sliced lengthwise
1 yellow onion, peeled and studded with 12 cloves

Bundle all ingredients except studded onion, into a piece of cotton cheese cloth and tie with kitchen string.

FINAL ASSEMBLY

Preheat oven to 350 degrees.

Brown sausage; crumble; set aside.

Place bean mixture over medium heat and add remaining wine. Cook to heat through.

Cut chicken meat into bite-sized pieces.

Press the boquet garni packet in the bean mixture to release all the liquid; remove and discard.

In a 9 x 11-inch casserole layer beans, chicken and sausage alternately until all has been added, ending with the beans as the top and final layer.

Prepare gratin per following directions.

Bake casserole for 2 hours, or until a golden brown crust forms on the top.

Check periodically. If cassoulet appears dry, add additional chicken broth. If cassoulet begins to brown too quickly, cover with foil.

GRATIN

2 cups dried bread crumbs
¾ cup parsley, chopped
3 cloves garlic, minced

Toss bread crumbs, parsley and garlic.

Sprinkle over casserole. Serve with additional parsley sprigs to garnish plates.

This casserole is involved. To alleviate spending all day in the kitchen, note the following: The bean mixture can be prepared as much as 3 to 4 days ahead; the chicken 2 days ahead. Leaving only the final assembly on the day you plan to serve. Cassoulet also freezes well. Always remember to add more broth when re-heating.

Watercress, Orange & Sweet Potato Salad

Peppery watercress flavors this fresh-tasting salad that is topped with a fruity vinaigrette dressing. The sweet potatoes can be roasted ahead and refrigerated to save time in the preparation.

SERVES: SIX TO EIGHT

SALAD

1 medium sweet potato
2 cloves garlic, minced
3 oranges, divided into sections
⅛ red onion, sliced thin
½ Tablespoon fresh rosemary, minced
1 teaspoon olive oil
2 Tablespoons pine nuts, toasted

3 to 4 ounces fresh watercress, washed

Preheat oven to 400 degrees.

Peel and cut sweet potato into ½-inch cubes; roast in a jelly roll pan for 45 minutes.

Mince rosemary and garlic; peel and divide oranges; slice onion; toast pine nuts in dry skillet; clean and stem watercress.

In a large bowl, whisk to combine rosemary, oil, garlic and onion.

Combine roasted potatoes with orange sections, then toss with rosemary mixture. Add nuts and watercress. Toss lightly again to incorporate all ingredients.

FRUITY VINAIGRETTE DRESSING

¼ cup olive oil
1½ Tablespoons juice of fresh orange
½ Tablespoon dijon-style mustard
½ Tablespoon rice wine vinegar
½ Tablespoon honey

1 clove garlic, minced
½ teaspoon kosher salt
¼ teaspoon freshly ground black pepper

In a small bowl, whisk olive oil with all remaining ingredients.

Drizzle lightly over salad and toss well.

Lemon Soufflé – *Mais Oui!*

Say **Yes!** *to this light airy dessert, because it is worth mastering.*

PRONOUNCED: SU 'FLEI

PRONOUNCED: MAY -WE

Just hearing the word "soufflé" can make even the most accomplished cook run for cover. But great care has been taken to document what I've learned from practice. If you will follow these directions precisely, you'll be delighted with a magical puffed-up creation and the accolade of accomplishing a soufflé.

SERVES: SIX TO EIGHT

6 large eggs

3 Tablespoons unsalted butter, softened

3 Tablespoons all-purpose flour

¾ cup whole milk

¼ cup juice of fresh lemon

½ cup granulated sugar

1 teaspoon pure vanilla extract

1 Tablespoon zest of lemon

¼ teaspoon kosher salt

Powdered sugar

Lemon curls

SECRETS TO SUCCESSFUL SOUFFLÉS

Preheat oven to 400 degrees.

Prepare a water bath by setting a jelly roll pan filled to ½-inch with water on the *lower rack* of the oven as it preheats.

Then start your soufflé by carefully separating the eggs and preparing the mold.

When separating eggs, ensure no yolk gets into the whites; place egg whites in a perfectly clean, dry mixing bowl. *You will need 6 whites & only 4 yolks for this recipe.*

Butter a 7-inch in diameter soufflé mold *very well.* Toss in approximately ¼ cup of sugar to dust the mold, and shake and tap to coat the mold well. Shake out any excess sugar; set dish aside. *Dusting the mold with sugar will help the soufflé to rise by giving it something to cling to on the sides of the pan.*

The trick to serving true soufflé is to know that it absolutely cannot be held.
This is a dish you want to serve to folks who will understand the need for last minute preparation. Just either excuse yourself from the table and make this as soon as the entrée has been served, or ask guests to adjourn from the table after the entrée for coffee and conversation while you prepare the soufflé and then serve informally.

Is it worth it?
Mais Oui!

Second, prepare all other ingredients and have measured and ready.

Measure/prepare/assemble all ingredients except egg whites near your stove.

Leave the egg whites in the clean mixing bowl to warm up to room temperature so that you can beat them later.

Now, prepare the soufflé base sauce.

(The base is a thick béchamel sauce.)

Bring milk to a boil; set aside. Melt butter in a large, heavy-bottomed saucepan. Add flour to melted butter and whisk over medium heat for 2 minutes, or until the mixture bubbles. Remove from heat and whisk in the hot milk all at once.

Cook, stirring constantly but gently, until the mixture has almost reached the boiling point and is thick and smooth.

Add lemon juice and sugar and cook an additional 2 minutes.

Remove from heat; add vanilla and cool slightly.

Whisk 4 egg **yolks,** one at a time, into the base. *Whisk* to incorporate each yolk before adding the next. Then stir in lemon zest.

Return the pan to the stove and cook over medium heat, stirring constantly, for another minute. Remove sauce from the heat and let cool until just warm.

Now it is time for the most important step – beating the egg whites.

Add salt to room temperature egg whites and beat with spotlessly clean and dry beaters until soft peaks form.

Stir ¼ of the beaten whites into the sauce. This will make it lighter and facilitate the folding of remaining whites.

Carefully, fold in the remaining whites.

With a rubber spatula, cut through the mass in the center of your bowl. Bring the mixture at the bottom of the bowl to the top, turning the bowl clockwise each time you repeat the motion of cutting into the mixture. Repeat this figure-8 pattern just until the whites and the soufflé base are mixed. (Having a few white streaks remaining is fine.)

Gently ladle finished soufflé batter into prepared mold. Run your finger around the top edge of mold to clean the rim.

Place mold on the *lower* rack of your oven in the water bath, then immediately drop the oven temperature to 375 degrees.

Bake for 25 to 30 minutes, or until the top is browned and the soufflé has risen to approximately 2 inches over the top of your dish.

Do not open the oven door while your soufflé cooks.

Serve immediately .Using a fine-mesh sieve, dust soufflé with powdered sugar and top with lemon curls.

Remember that the trick to serving soufflé is to serve straight from the oven
before it is tempted to fall!

WHEN I FIRST PREPARED THIS MENU, IT WAS
FOR MY HUSBAND TODD'S BIRTHDAY, AND THE
CELEBRATION INCLUDED SOME OF OUR CLOS-
EST FRIENDS. THAT MADE IT EASY FOR ME TO
SLIP IN AND OUT OF THE KITCHEN WHILE OUR
GUESTS HAD TIME WITH THE BIRTHDAY BOY.
DURING THE MEAL, I CLEARED AND SERVED.
AFTER OUR GUESTS HAD GONE HOME, TODD
AND I WASHED DISHES AND TALKED ABOUT
WHAT FUN WE'D HAD. BEFORE WE KNEW IT
THE KITCHEN WAS TIDY AND THE NIGHT
CONSIDERED GREAT FUN!

FEBRUARY 25TH
Formal Birthday Dinner Party
FOR 8

Sidecars
Chili Cheese Wafers with Jam

Citrus Salad with Lavender Honey
Vinaigrette

Roasted Fillet of Beef
Basil Rémoulade
Mousseline Potatoes
Green Peas in Butter

Italian Cream Torte

RECIPES
SIDECARS
CHILI CHEESE
WAFERS
CITRUS SALAD
WITH LAVENDER
HONEY
VINAIGRETTE
ROASTED FILLET
OF BEEF
BASIL
RÉMOULADE
MOUSSELINE
POTATOES
ITALIAN CREAM
TORTE

Serve Bordeaux
with the fillet of beef.

TRIMMING A
FILLET

FOLDING EGG
WHITES

TIME LINE

May you have many more!

This four-course formal meal requires a good deal of planning. It can be done alone, but is not recommended for the inexperienced host/hostess without help. A timeline will make a complicated meal doable by determining what can be done in advance. Help can come from a co-host or hired assistant.

For entertaining secrets see Cocktail Glasses, *p. 43.*

ONE MONTH BEFORE THE PARTY

Issue invitations/save-the-date. Determine menu.

THURSDAY BEFORE THE SATURDAY PARTY

Set Table and make place cards. Shop for groceries, wine and flowers – *and don't forget the pepper jam!* Place flowers in treated water and refrigerate.

FRIDAY AFTERNOON BEFORE THE PARTY

Make wafer dough and refrigerate. Make rémoulade sauce and refrigerate. Steam cherries for sidecars and refrigerate resulting infused cognac. Bake torte and frost as directed, seal tightly and refrigerate.

SATURDAY MORNING

Ready coffee for quick and easy brewing after dinner. Arrange centerpiece. Prepare a tray with dessert plates, forks, coffee service and champagne flutes for easy access after the entrée. Toast nuts and coconut for salad, cool, seal and set aside. Prepare vinaigrette and refrigerate.

3:00 PM

Prepare potatoes and cover. Prepare beef for roasting and cover. Assemble salads (less nuts, coconut and dressing) cover and refrigerate on individual salad plates. Set up the bar, cube lemons and limes/refrigerate. Prepare glasses for sidecars and set aside to dry. Assure there is plenty of ice for both the cocktails and dinner.

5:00

Slice wafers, place on cookie sheet, brush with egg mixture and salt. Pre-mix side cars (less ice). Put beef in to roast – *removing when 136 degrees and covering with foil to rest*. Put peas into saucepan with butter, set aside.

6:00

Check beef temperature to ensure cooking properly. Dress for dinner. Check lighting in each room, and put on music at a volume that will also allow for conversation. Bake potatoes – cover and set aside. Fill ice bucket. Fill water pitcher with ice and water; refrigerate. Uncork wine.

7:00

Bake wafers and serve when just slightly cooled and still nice and warm. Assemble sidecars and enjoy cocktails with guests.

7:30

Broil potatoes for final 2 to 4 minutes. Steam peas in butter. Slice beef. Fill water and wine glasses. Finish salads and place on table for first course, setting the salad plates on top of the dinner plates.

Invite guests to the table and enjoy the first course. Clear plates. Set out the beef, sauce, potatoes and peas in a buffet. Allow guests to take their dinner plates form the table and serve themselves from buffet line, then return to the table Clear dinner plates.

Serve torte, champagne and coffee.
Box up pieces of torte for guests to take home.

Sidecars

This cocktail, made famous at the Ritz Hotel in Paris, can often be very sour or very sweet. This version is a nice balance of flavors and subtly sweetened with dried cherries.

YIELD: TWO COCKTAILS

4 ounces cognac
6 to 8 dried cherries
2 ounces grand marnier liqueur
Juice of 1 fresh lemon, divided
4 teaspoons granulated sugar

Prepare two old fashion glasses by dipping the rims into lemon juice, then into a small amount of granulated sugar. Set aside to dry completely.

In a microwave-safe bowl, heat the cherries and cognac for 1 minute. Remove cherries and reserve cognac.

In a cocktail shaker filled with ice, add the cherry-infused cognac, Grand Marnier and remaining fresh lemon juice.

Shake for a full **30 seconds t**o mix and chill well.

Pour into an old fashion glasses filled with ice.

These cocktails should only be made two at a time, but by preparing the mix ahead (infused cognac, grand marnier and lemon juice) all you have to do is shake and pour when guests arrive – it goes pretty quickly and your friends will enjoy watching the process!

Chili Cheese Wafers

These peppery cheese biscuits are crisp and salty — brilliant with cocktails! Logs will keep for three to four months frozen; defrost in the refrigerator before baking.

YIELD: SIXTEEN OR THIRTY-TWO WAFERS

For a party of eight, one log of these wafers is plenty. After making up your dough and wrapping in plastic, place one log in the freezer for another time and just bake the one.

7 ounces cheddar cheese, grated

2 cups all-purpose flour

1 teaspoon kosher salt

⅛ teaspoon baking powder

½ cup plus 5 Tablespoons unsalted butter, cold

1½ jalapeño peppers, seeded and minced

¼ teaspoon chili powder

3 Tablespoons ice water

1 large egg

1 Tablespoon milk

Himalayan pink salt

Scotch bonnet pepper jelly or Jalapeño pepper jam

In a food processor, combine flour, salt and baking powder. Add cold butter and pulse until a coarse meal forms. Add cheese, pepper, and powder and pulse to combine.

While processor is running, pour in ice water. Pulse until mixture forms into a ball.

Place dough onto a lightly floured surface. With your hands, roll into two 7-inch logs. Wrap logs in plastic wrap and refrigerate for 1 hour. (Dough will keep in refrigerator for a week.)

If you are making these well ahead, place logs in the freezer after wrapping in plastic and sealing in a plastic baggie.

When ready to bake, preheat oven to 400 degrees. Line a baking sheet with parchment paper.

Cut logs into 16 uniform slices each, and place on prepared baking sheets.

Whisk egg with 1 Tablespoon milk. Brush each wafer with egg wash; sprinkle with 2 to 3 grinds of pink salt. *You will only need a fraction of the egg wash; just a couple of brush strokes on each wafer are plenty.*

Bake wafers for 13 to 15 minutes, or until golden brown and slightly crisp. Serve warm with Scotch Bonnet Pepper Jelly or Jalapeño Pepper Jam.

Citrus Salad with
Lavender Honey Vinaigrette

Sweet and tart, this salad will brighten a rich wintry meal. Use a packaged prewashed salad mix of baby greens to make this salad in no time at all.

SERVES: EIGHT

SALAD

1 prepared salad mix
2 navel oranges, peeled and sliced
2 ruby grapefruits, peeled and sliced
½ cup pistachios, toasted and chopped
1 cup coconut, toasted
8 mint leaves, sliced thin

Rinse salad mix and spin dry. Peel, and without separating the sections, slice oranges and grapefruit horizontally into ¼-inch thick slices. Toast nuts and coconut.

Prepare vinaigrette dressing as instructed below.

Mound salad mix on individual serving plates. Arrange 2 to 4 (mixed) citrus slices over greens. Drizzle vinaigrette over fruit and greens.

Spoon nuts and toasted coconut over each salad just before serving, and top with a leaf of fresh mint.

Use honey as a flavor rather than a sweetener like sugar.
See p. 375 for more on honey.

LAVENDER HONEY VINAIGRETTE

⅛ cup olive oil
1 clove garlic, crushed and minced
1 Tablespoon balsamic vinegar
1 Tablespoon lavender honey
¼ teaspoon kosher salt
Zest of 1 orange

Whisk oil with garlic, vinegar, honey, salt and zest until frothy. Spoon over composed salads.

Roasted Fillet of Beef

When using tarragon, be sure to only chop it two to three times or use whole. Dicing this herb will cause it to oxidize, giving it a ghastly taste. Tarragon should also be used in moderation and on its own, as it is a fairly strong herb.

There is a luxurious buttery tenderness to fillet mignon, but it is a less flavorful cut. The sharp tarragon with its light anise licorice flavor is an incomparable accompaniment.

SERVES: EIGHT

1 3½ to 4 pound fillet of beef
tenderloin
1 Tablespoon cognac
3 Tablespoons olive oil
4 teaspoons kosher salt
2 teaspoons freshly ground black pepper
5 to 7 sprigs fresh tarragon

Preheat oven to 275 degrees. Cover a jelly roll pan with aluminum foil. Rinse tarragon and allow to dry.

Trim and tie fillet per instructions that follow. Pat dry and place on prepared baking sheet.

Mix cognac with olive oil and brush on beef, reserving 1 Tablespoon of the mixture. Then salt and pepper the fillet generously. This is a large piece of meat and will need a good deal of seasoning.

Tuck 5 to 7 tarragon branches under the cooking twine uniformly around the fillet. Brush tarragon with reserved oil and cognac to keep it moist while roasting.

Roast for 1 hour and 15 minutes, and then check the internal temperature of the fillet. *The center of the fillet should register 135 degrees for medium rare; 125 degrees for rare.*

Remove fillet from oven when cooked to desired degree; tent with foil to rest for 20 minutes.

Slice into 1 to 1½-inch slices. Serve warm topped with Basil Rémoulade.

TRIMMING A FILLET

Place fillet in front of you with the head (large extremity) to your left. Tear as much of the silver skin off with a boning knife as possible.

Remove the gristle of fat that runs along the side.

Trim the fat from the head flap and main body of the fillet.

Turn the fillet underside up and trim off all fat with a sharp boning knife.

Turn back to right side up and continue trimming fat and sinews (tendons).

Be sure to remove sinew or it will cook into a tough outside crust.

When fillet is totally clean, use cooking string to wrap it from one end to the other, tying at every inch.

When choosing a fillet at the Butcher's, look for good marbling and beef that is a slightly darker color.

For hints on cooking beef, see Steak, p. 387.

Basil Rémoulade

Bring egg and oils to room temperature before beginning. This is essential for a properly emulsified mayonnaise.

Rémoulade is a mayonnaise sauce made with herbs and other ingredients to create a briny taste, and it is a "must" with roasted fillet. The salty bite of pecorino balanced with sweet basil makes this delectable with roast beef - or on sandwiches.

PRONOUNCED: REIM-U 'LA D

SERVES: EIGHT

¼ cup pecorino cheese
1 large egg yolk
½ cup vegetable oil
¼ cup olive oil
2 teaspoons dijon-style mustard
2 Tablespoons juice of fresh lemon
1 large clove garlic
½ teaspoon kosher salt
⅛ teaspoon freshly ground black pepper
¼ cup fresh basil leaves
½ teaspoon lemon zest

Put egg **yolk** in a bowl and whisk for **10 seconds**; set aside.

Then combine the two oils in a liquid measuring cup; set aside.

In a food processor, place pecorino cheese and grind into small pieces; remove from processor and set aside.

In the food processor bowl, process whisked **yolk,** mustard, lemon juice, garlic clove, salt and pepper until smooth.

While processor is running, slowly drizzle oil mixture into the egg mixture until it is thick and creamy.

Add basil, pecorino and zest and continue processing to make a thick emulsion. Taste for seasoning to ensure enough salt.

Mousseline Potatoes

These double whipped potatoes are perfect for a formal dinner, because they are not only a buttery delight but can also be made ahead and held to finish just before serving. The potatoes can be completed through baking and held for two to three hours, covered. Just before ready to serve, broil as directed or until hot and bubbly.

PRONOUNCED: MU-S'LI N

SERVES: EIGHT

8 Idaho potatoes
½ cup unsalted butter, melted
¼ to ½ cup milk
1 cup heavy cream, whipped
1 Tablespoon kosher salt
1 teaspoon freshly ground black pepper

Wash and cut potatoes into uniform cubes leaving skins on.

In a large pot, place potatoes and cover with cold salted water to 1-inch above potatoes. Bring to a boil, then reduce heat and gently cook for 10 to 15 minutes or until fork tender.

Meanwhile, preheat oven to 250 degrees. Butter a 9 x 11-inch casserole dish; set aside. Whip cream; set aside.

When potatoes have finished cooking, drain and return to heat to dry for 1 to 2 minutes.

Using an electric mixer, mash potatoes while still in the saucepan.

Stir in ¼ cup of melted butter and ¼ cup of milk. Add additional milk as needed for a mashed but not too creamy consistency.

Fold in the whipped cream and season with salt and pepper.

Spoon whipped potatoes into prepared casserole dish and top with remaining ¼ cup melted butter.

Bake for 30 minutes.

Just before serving, turn on oven broiler and broil potatoes for 2 to 4 minutes, or until toasted and brown on top and heated through.

Mousseline Potatoes *Occasions* 351

Italian Cream Torte

This rustic Italian Cream Torte is iced like a torte, with the rich cream cheese frosting placed only between the sweet and dense coconut cake layers. To help ensure your success, see Baking Secrets, Light & Airy Cakes, p. 361.

SERVES: EIGHTEEN

CAKE

It is important to carefully fold egg whites into batter. Use a figure eight motion with a rubber spatula to turn whites up and over very gently, so as to not over-mix and deflate the meringue.

2 cups granulated sugar
½ cup unsalted butter, softened
½ cup crisco shortening
5 large eggs, separated
2 cups all-purpose flour
1 cup buttermilk
1 teaspoon baking soda
1 3½-ounce can angel flake coconut

Separate eggs into two bowls and allow to come to room temperature. Soften butter.

Preheat oven to 350 degrees.

In a large bowl with an electric hand mixer, beat egg **whites** until stiff; set aside.

In a large bowl with an electric stand mixer, cream sugar, butter and shortening until light and fluffy, approximately 3 minutes.

Add egg **yolks,** one at a time. Add soda to buttermilk and add alternately with sifted flour. Add coconut. Mix to incorporate.

By hand, fold in 5 beaten egg whites.

Divide batter evenly into three buttered and floured 8-inch cake pans. Bake for 25 minutes. Cool and frost.

FROSTING

Powdered sugar, also called Confectioner's Sugar, typically comes in a one-pound box which is the equivalent of four cups.

1 8-ounce package cream cheese
½ cup unsalted butter, softened
1½ teaspoons pure vanilla extract
1 cup toasted and chopped nuts (pecans, pistachio and/or hazelnuts)
1 1-pound box powdered sugar

Mix cream cheese, butter and vanilla; sift sugar and add, blending well. Add nuts; blend well. Frost only the top layer of each cake, leaving sides bare like a torte.

Keep torte refrigerated until party time, then allow to come to room temperature before slicing. Store leftover torte in refrigerator.

Baking Technique

Baking Technique

When baking, you cannot rely on instinct or good taste, but need accuracy and skill. There are techniques to master, such as folding, creaming and whipping, and rules of chemistry to adhere to carefully. When baking it is important to follow the recipe exactly, measure accurately, and use the correct size of pan while being sure to prepare it well. But don't let this keep you from trying your hand, for baking techniques can be quickly mastered. When you can turn out a light and moist cake, perfect cookie or mouth watering pie your pride will swell and the pleasure of pleasing your guests will make the practice time well worth the effort.

Cookies

Cookie Baking Tips

When baking cookies and cakes, it is best to have all ingredients at room temperature before you begin. This will ensure your baked goods are light and flaky. Also, use all-purpose flour for cookies unless otherwise directed.

It is not necessary to sift flour when baking cookies unless specified in recipe instructions. However, I do recommend always whisking flour with salt, soda and/or powder to ensure all dry ingredients are thoroughly combined. Skipping this step can result in a bite of cookie that is overly salty or bitter.

Use sturdy cookie sheets that are the right size for your oven, with room for air to circulate around each sheet. Avoid using pans with a high side for baking cookies (sides deflect heat and cookies will be misshapen).

When cookie dough contains a good deal of butter (like shortbread), it is not necessary to butter the sheets. To use butter to prepare sheets, use the unwrapped paper from a stick of butter, or use cooking spray. Lining sheets with parchment paper also works well, especially for cookies with a great deal of butter.

There is no need to wash sheets between batches of cookies, just scrape off any crumbs and continue using until all the batter has been baked.

How to Roll & Bake Perfect Cookies

Always Chill Dough for Rolled Cookies

Solidifying the batter will ensure your dough does not stick to your counter top when rolled out. When dough is sticky, more flour is required in the rolling process – and too much can alter the texture and taste of cookies. If your dough still seems sticky after chilling, sprinkle the counter and rolling pin with *a bit* more flour. But if this does not work, return the dough to the refrigerator to chill longer.

Roll Dough to ¼-Inch Thick Before Cutting Into Shapes

Using either cookie cutters or the rim of a glass. After the shaped cookies have been cut out, gather up the scraps, put them together (handling dough as little as possible) and roll or pat them out again to make more cookies.

Bake Cookies in a Preheated Oven

Only bake one sheet at a time (unless using a convection oven). Watch cookies carefully while baking. Some thinner cookies especially, can take as little as five minutes to brown. Baking time also varies with ovens, *so be sure to set your timer for less time than the recipe calls for,* check cookies half way through and rotate pan(s), then cook for more time if necessary. Chewy cookies should be baked slightly less time and crisp cookies more, depending on personal preference.

Let Cookie Sheets Cool Before Adding Another Batch

On a hot sheet the second batch may not hold its shape. Remove cookies to cooling rack as soon as they are cool enough to handle. If cookies remain on sheets too long and begin to stick to pans, just pop them in the oven for a few minutes to soften them, and then try removing again.

Do Not Stack Cookies or Store Until Cooled Completely

When freezing cookies, place sheets of waxed paper between the rows to prevent sticking. *When freezing cookies that have been iced, drizzled with chocolate or glazed, freeze cookies on a flat surface first and allow the icing to freeze and set in place.* Otherwise, the icing will stick to your paper and come off the cookies when unpacked.

Rolling & Shaping Pie Dough

For best results, roll pie dough on a cool hard surface and use heavy-gauge steel or aluminum pans for baking. Glass or ceramic pans also work well, but should be baked at 25 degrees less heat than the recipe calls for.

Bottom Crust

Divide pie dough and pat each piece into a flattened round. Place it on a lightly floured and clean counter top and sprinkle both sides with flour. Using a rolling pin dusted with flour, start in the center and roll lightly in all directions until round is large enough to cover bottom and sides of pie plate (approximately ⅛–inch thick and two inches greater than the diameter of pie plate.

Lift and turn the dough frequently to ensure it does not stick to the counter, and do not roll quite to the edge of the dough until the last few turns. If the dough seems to be sticking, dust the counter with more flour.

Then, carefully roll the dough loosely over the rolling pin, then lift and place over the pie plate. Unroll from one edge of the plate to the other. Use your hands to carefully adjust and center the dough. *Avoid stretching dough or it will fall in the oven.* Pat dough into all edges of pie plate, and then trim extra dough that is not uniform around the outside rim.

At this point, chill the bottom crust, in the pie plate, to keep your finished bottom crust from being soggy.

Open-Faced Pies

If you are making a single crust pie, crimp the edge of the crust by using your thumb and forefinger. Press and pinch the dough together evenly at intervals around the rim. Build the rim up to approximately ¾-inch, then using your two fingers, press and pleat at intervals to make the dough stand up and create a scalloped edge.

Before baking an unfilled shell, be sure to prick the dough all across the bottom and along the sides. Shells should be baked at 375 degrees for 12 to 15 minutes, or until lightly browned. During the first 8 to 10 minutes of specified baking time, place a second, slightly smaller pie plate into the shell to help the crust hold its shape while baking.

Top Crust

While your bottom shell is chilling, prepare the pie filling. Add filling to pie shell and dot with butter. Prepare second/top crust just like the first and roll onto the filled pie. Crimp the edges as instructed above, and then slice a clever design into the top crust (or use a pie bird) to create vents for steam to escape while baking.

Baking

Sprinkle the unbaked pie with granulated sugar before baking. Use a pie crust shield for the first half of baking time. When baking fruit pies, it is advisable to place a pie shield sheet or aluminum foil beneath the pie plate to catch run-off juices.

For a crisp bottom crust, be sure to bake pies on the lowest rack of a thoroughly preheated oven.

PHOTOS L TO R: PAT DOUGH INTO A BALL AND PLACE ON A COOL, HARD AND LIGHTLY FLOURED SURFACE FOR ROLLING; ONCE ROLLED AND SHAPED, FILL PIE PLATE BY USING ROLLING PIN TO HOLD DOUGH WHILE TRANSFERRING; FIT DOUGH INTO PIE PLATE AND TRIM EDGES FOR UNIFORMITY; CRIMP, SCORE AND SPRINKLE - READY TO BAKE.

Baking Pie Shells

Many pies with a pudding or gelatin filling call for baking the pie crust empty first. The trick to doing so is to add some weight.

Begin by pricking the pie crust all over with a fork; this helps prevent it from puffing up while it bakes.

Then cover the bottom of your shell with a piece of parchment paper, and place a slightly smaller aluminum pie tin inside the shell, atop the paper.

Turn upside down and bake for the first 8 to 10 minutes, upside down, to prevent the middle and sides from slipping down into the plate.

Bake the crust in a preheated 375°F oven for a total of 12 to 15 minutes.

After the first 8 to 10 minutes, you can remove the smaller tin and parchment and finish cooking your shell right side up, allowing the crust to brown.

Using Pie Shields

Remember to place fruit pies on a pie shield sheet, to avoid juice over flow onto oven.

If you do not have a pie shield (a thin, round cooking sheet with the center removed), place strips of foil on your oven rack to form a circle just larger than your pie plate. Leave the center of the circle open to encourage bottom crust to cook completely. *Remember to also use a pie crust shield when baking any pie. Shield pie crusts during the first half of baking to prevent your crust from cooking faster than the pie.*

If you do not have a pie crust shield, you can easily make a shield with aluminum foil. Simply tear off approximately a 12-inch piece of foil, fold the piece in half, and tear in two. Fold these two strips in half lengthwise.

With side of your hand, indent the strips to form half circles, and then carefully fit over crust, being careful to not crush the dough.

Crimp two pieces of foil together to hold in place.

Should your pies overflow onto your oven floor and the juices begin to burn, throw salt onto the spill to stop the smoke.

If you do not have a pie crust shield, make a shield with aluminum foil. Indent the strips to form half circles and shape around crust. Crimp pieces together to hold them in place as a shield to prevent burning.

Baking Fruit Pies

The flour and sugar added to fruit pies makes the scrumptious thick syrup that helps flavor the pie and binds the fruit and crust.

For a perfect fruit pie, assess the sweetness and juiciness of your fruit and adjust the sugar and flour accordingly. For fruit that is very juicy, you will need a bit more flour. For fruit that is very sweet, use less sugar.

If your fruit is drier, as Granny Smith apples can often be, add a bit of apple juice or Calvados.

Cakes

Secrets for Light & Airy Cakes

Butter Temperature

Most baking recipes call for the butter to be softened, or at room temperature. This is because the purpose of creaming butter is to beat tiny air bubbles into it for a light and airy cake. Butter holds air bubbles best at approximately 68 degrees. So for best results on baking morning, let your butter sit on the counter overnight, or a minimum of 30 minutes before beginning to bake. You will know when your butter is ready when your finger can easily make an indent in the stick. *To speed the softening process, place butter in a sealed plastic bag and gently pound with a rolling pin, or microwave for 15 seconds.*

Be Organized

Not only should you have all of your ingredients at room temperature before you begin, but make it a habit to measure everything before getting started and have things close at hand as well. Get in the practice of preheating the oven as you assemble your ingredients and prepare to begin. Then add ingredients exactly as the recipe specifies and in the order listed – not all at once. Remember that baking is a science and ingredients are to be incorporated in specific ways to ensure the correct chemical reaction(s).

Adding Eggs Separately

Another way to ensure a light and airy cake is to add eggs separately. When a recipe calls for adding eggs one at a time, it is because this helps keep the batter blended and creamy, which is important to the final texture. If you add the eggs all at once, the batter can break and look curdled because air pockets have collapsed. When this happens, your cake will taste okay, but will not be fluffy.

I also recommend always breaking eggs into a separate bowl, as opposed to directly into the batter. This way you can ensure all of your eggs are good and that no shell is added accidently. If your eggs are red or any color other than yellow and clear, throw them out.

Creaming Butter & Sugar

Creaming the butter and sugar is important for a light cake. With an electric mixer, you can cut the sugar into the butter and create tiny air bubbles via the power of the machine. A common mistake is to cream too little. A good rule of thumb is to cream for at least three minutes, and sometimes as long as five. You should continue creaming the butter and sugar until the mixture both grows in volume and lightens to a pale yellow color. Scrape the sides of your bowl once or twice during the creaming process to make sure all of the ingredients are being incorporated, and watch the batter, stopping if it begins to look curdled.

Over Mixing

Once you begin adding dry ingredients, over mixing your cake batter becomes a real danger. Over mixing will destroy the air bubbles you've worked to incorporate and will result in a cake that is tough and heavy. To avoid this, start with the mixer on low speed and stop it when most of the flour has been incorporated. At this point, remove the bowl from the mixer and finish mixing and folding by hand with a spatula. This way you can both scrape the bottom of the bowl to get any pockets of flour, and avoid unnecessary strokes. In fact, I typically only use a mixer to cream the butter and wet ingredients, then fold/mix in the dry ingredients by hand.

The Wet-Dry Method of Baking

When recipes call for mixing all the dry ingredients in one bowl and wet (liquid) ingredients in another, it is to avoid the formation of gluten, which can make cakes heavy. The wet-dry method results in cakes that are very tender and moist. By adding the liquids to the dry ingredients in batches, you are essentially allowing the fat in your recipe to coat all the flour proteins and are preventing the formation of heavy gluten. Be sure to always follow the method specified in the recipe to guarantee the correct results.

The Sifting Quandary

Most flour sack labels claim the contents to be pre-sifted. However, you have no way of knowing how long ago it was milled. Flour compacts as it stands, so to be safe be sure to always freshen your flour by sifting before measuring. Likewise, always **use a dry measuring cup** and a knife to level your measurement as opposed to shaking your measuring cup to level the flour or using a cup designed for liquids. If you are also adding an agent like baking powder or soda to your recipe, sift your flour a second time with these ingredients added to thoroughly blend all dry ingredients. And just like flour, be cognizant of soda and powder to ensure you are always using fresh. *To ensure your baking ingredients stay as fresh as possible, store flour and leavening agents in the freezer until ready to use.*

To Beat or Not to Beat

Be sure to start with room temperature eggs and pay close attention when beating egg whites. As whites whip, their color changes from very pale yellow to white. Properly beaten whites will look smooth, wet, and shiny, and will form soft peaks when the beaters are raised out of the bowl. If in doubt, it is preferable to under beat egg whites, because whites that have been over beaten will appear lumpy and form large white clumps when you fold then into the batter. When air bubbles have been overworked, cakes are more likely to collapse in the oven. This will result in a cake that is chewy rather than tender.

A neat trick for cleaning beaters when finished is to very slowly raise them from the batter or meringue while the mixer is still running. The egg white, batter or icing will whisk itself off as the beaters are raised up and out.

Preparing Cake Pans

Buttering the bottom of cake pans, or using cooking spray, does not always guarantee that your cakes will come out in one piece. Even though it adds a step, using parchment paper along with buttering your pan, will guarantee your cakes do not stick to the pan and break apart when you are trying to remove them. Coating cake pans with butter before topping with paper will also help prevent the paper from sliding and curling up when the batter is added. And be sure to only butter the bottom of your layer cake pans. Cakes will naturally release from the sides of pans during baking, and buttering the sides will cause your batter to slide down, preventing your cake from rising to its fullest.

To ensure your paper is exactly the same size as the bottom of your pan, trace the bottom of pan onto paper with a pencil then carefully cut out the rounds.

Filling Cake Pans

Be sure to fill pans only two-thirds full to allow room for the cake to rise. Gently spread the batter in a circular motion with a spatula to fill the entire pan, then gently swish pans to and fro on the counter top a few times to remove any large air bubbles and assure a smooth texture for your cake.

Testing to See if Your Cake is Done

Always bake cakes in a preheated oven. Glass or dark colored pans will retain more heat. Bake cakes in glass pans the same amount of time, **but at 25 degrees lower heat.** Bake cakes in the center rack of the oven, and near the center to keep them from baking unevenly. If using two racks, stagger the pans to allow the heat to circulate.

My preferred method for testing cakes is to insert a toothpick into the center of the cake. If the pick comes out clean, the cake is done. If you see nothing, or just a few crumbs, remove cake from the oven and place on a cooling rack. If still-wet batter clings to the pick, return to the oven and set your timer for just a few minutes more and check again. Always stay near the kitchen when baking cakes to monitor the last ten minutes of baking time, especially.

When you begin to smell the cake, it is nearly done.

Another tip is to only allow cakes to cool in the pan for the first *five to ten minutes.* Once the pans have cooled enough to handle, remove cakes to a cooling rack to cool completely.

To remove cakes from pans, run a knife around the edge of the pan, loosening any pieces of cake that are clinging. Gently use your knife or spatula to partially lift and loosen cake from bottom of pans as well. Then place an inverted cake plate or cooling rack on top of cake pan and quickly flip while holding the two pieces together. Once the cake is right side up, gently lift the cake pan off.

Using a Kitchen Timer

Always set your kitchen timer to check cakes approximately three-quarters of the way through established cooking time. Rotate your pans at this juncture to ensure even baking, and double check that the cakes are not overcooking. If one side of your cake is browning unevenly, it is because it is too close to the side of your oven, so rotate the pan and adjust accordingly. There is often as much as a ten minute time difference in recipes and given the way your oven cooks. It's always better to be safe than sorry, for nothing is more disappointing than a cake that has baked too long and become dry.

If your oven is convection (preferred when baking) the cooking temperature is lower than what is recommended for a conventional oven. Newer ovens calculate the difference automatically.

You can also check older ovens for accuracy with a simple and inexpensive thermometer designed for the task.

Make-Ahead Cakes

When serving large complicated meals that include cakes, consider partially baking ahead of time to leave more time the day of your event. If un-frosted and unfilled butter or pound cakes are stored in airtight containers, they can keep at room temperature for one to two days.

You can also make cakes even further ahead by freezing.

FREEZING CAKES

Wrap baked and cooled cakes in layers of plastic wrap and then aluminum foil; freeze for up to four months. A lighter or foamy cake will keep for up to two months frozen. Wrap layers separately before freezing.

FREEZING FROSTING

A buttery frosting can be frozen for up to two months in an airtight container.

FINAL ASSEMBLY

When freezing cakes, be sure to let all ingredients thaw before assembling. Thaw frosting in the refrigerator and cake layers at room temperature.

How to Frost a Cake

Creating beautiful cakes can be accomplished in five easy steps.

Position & Level Your Cake

Set your cake plate on a Lazy Susan or use a cake plate with a pedestal so it can be rotated easily and avoid possible jarring. Place the first cake layer upside down. Because the top of a cake is sticky, this will help prevent the layers from slipping off of each other, and your plate!

Fill the Layers

Dust your cake for any excess crumbs using a long, offset spatula knife designed for icing cakes (this purchase is worth the investment if you like to bake). Spread the filling evenly on top of the first layer; don't worry about getting the frosting smooth. Place the second layer on the frosting and align the layers. Add additional layers if you have them, ending with the top layer (un-frosted).

Seal in the Crumbs

Spread a very thin layer of frosting over the sides of your cake to seal in the crumbs. Then place the cake in the refrigerator to set-up for approximately 20 to 30 minutes. Once your thin layer of frosting is set, finish frosting the cake with the remaining icing.

Finish with Flair

Spread the remaining frosting evenly over the sides and top of cake. Use your knife lengthwise to spread the icing on the sides of your cake to create even and smooth sides. Top your masterpiece with a "baker's signature," or that extra whorl or pattern that will be remembered as your stamp. Swirl the frosting by dipping your knife up to create peaks and texture.

Clean Your Plate

Finally, take a slightly damp paper towel and wipe any remaining crumbs, smudges and excess frosting from the plate. Top cakes with candied flowers, lemon zest or chocolate curls as desired.

Volume Equivalencies

VOLUME	EQUIVALENT	VOLUME	EQUIVALENT
3 teaspoons	1 Tablespoon	Brown sugar	1 pound = 2 ½ cups
2 Tablespoons	1 fluid ounce	Powdered sugar	1 pound = 4 cups
8 Tablespoons	½ cup or 4 fluid ounces	Nuts, chopped	4 ounces = ¾ cup
16 Tablespoons	1 cup or 8 fluid ounces	Root Vegetables, sliced	1 pound = 3 cups
2 cups	1 pint or 16 fluid ounces	Butter	4 Tablespoons = ½ stick 8 Tablespoons = 1 stick
4 cups	1 quart or 32 fluid ounces	Cream cheese	3 ounces = 6 Tablespoons
1 quart	0.95 liters	Heavy cream	½ pint = 2 cups whipped
4 quarts	1 gallon	Flour, all-purpose	1 pound = 4 cups sifted
Pinch	¼ teaspoon		
Dash	½ to 1 teaspoon		
Jigger	1 ½ ounces or 3 Tablespoons		

Glossary of Ingredients, Techniques & Terms

A-B

Aïoli – French; A garlic-infused sauce or condiment. Delicious served with fresh vegetables, grilled seafood or poultry.

Alfresco – Served out of doors/open air.

Al Dente – Italian; To briefly cook (pasta) just long enough to be firm to the bite and almost tender; slightly under cooked. *Translation, "To the tooth."*

Au Jus – French; A term applied to meat, usually roast beef, served in its own juices. *Translation, "With the juice." Pronounced*: Oh Zhu.

Avocado – A fruit with a leathery dark green skin and large stony seed that has a mild, nutty flavor and buttery texture.

Easy to prepare using this method:

Start with a large knife. Insert it into the top of the fruit where the stem was, and gently press down until you reach the pit. Holding the knife steady, rotate the fruit so that the knife traverses the pit, cutting the entire avocado in two. Remove the knife, and then gently twist the two sides away from one another with your hands to separate. Now, hold the fruit in the palm of your hand, nestled in a kitchen towel, pit side up. Carefully strike the pit with your knife, and pierce it with the blade. Twist and remove the knife; the pit will come out with it. Then, use the knife's tip to slice the flesh in both horizontal and vertical rows, being careful not to cut through the skin. Remove the meat from fruit by gently scooping it out with a spoon. Your avocado will spill out already diced and ready to use! Be sure to quickly squeeze fresh lemon juice on the diced fruit to prevent browning.

Haas Avocado - Available fresh year-round from California; dark-green colored with a bumpy skin that becomes dark purple to black, and yields to gentle pressure when ripe.

Baba au Rhum – French; A rum infused sponge cake.

Baguette – A long, thin loaf of French bread.

Bake – To cook by dry heat in an oven. *Do not crowd foods in the oven as air circulation is important. Always preheat the oven for 10 to 15 minutes, and check older ovens periodically for accuracy in temperature.*

Balsamic Vinegar – Vinegar made from the juice of white grapes matured in wood for 10 to 50 years, giving it a rich sweet-sour taste and characteristic dark color.

Barbecue – To cook on a grill over intense heat.

Basmati Rice – A long-grained aromatic rice.

Baste – To moisten, especially meats, with pan drippings or melted butter, during the cooking time to add flavor and keep things from drying out. *Use a bulb baster, spoon or brush to baste.*

Batter – A mixture of flour and liquid that is thin enough to pour.

Bay Leaf – An aromatic leaf of the Mediterranean bay tree associated with hearty dishes like pot roast and broths with big flavors. *Bay is a strong herb and it only takes one or two leaves to alter the flavor of a dish. Fresh leaves are especially pungent, much more so than dried.*

When using dried bay leaves, remove them after they have simmered in recipes because they cannot be digested and should not be consumed. The dried leaves are too coarse for the human stomach to process.

Beat – To mix ingredients by vigorously stirring with an electric mixer in order to make smooth and light and incorporate as much air as possible.

Béchamel – A medium-thick white sauce and important base to soufflés. Made from a *roux* (butter and flour) with heated milk then whisked in gradually. Béchamel is one of the five "Mother Sauces" of classic French cuisine.

> **Five Mother Sauces** – The grand sauces from which hundreds of "petites" can be composed. They include:
>
> > **Béchamel** – A milk-based sauce thickened with a white roux.
> >
> > **Espagnole** – A fortified brown sauce made from veal stock and thickened with a brown roux.
> >
> > **Hollandaise** – An emulsion of egg yolk, butter and an acid of either lemon or vinegar (shown at left).
> >
> > **Tomate** – A tomato-based sauce.
> >
> > **Velouté** – A light stock-based sauce, thickened with a roux, or a mixture of egg yolks and cream (a liaison).

Blanch – Typically used with vegetables and fruit. To immerse briefly into boiling water to inactivate enzymes when canning or freezing, loosen skin or soak away excess salt. Blanching can also set the color, seal in juices and remove strong flavors.

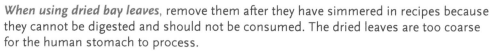

Blend – To combine two or more ingredients thoroughly, one being liquid or soft, to quickly produce a mixture of uniform consistency.

Boil – To heat liquid until bubbles break continuously on the surface (approximately 212 degrees for boiling water).

Braise – A method of slowly cooking meats, usually covered, in a small amount of liquid or fat and often in a bed of aromatic herbs and/or spices.

Brine – A process of seasoning and moistening poultry before roasting by soaking in salt and sugar water for ten to twelve hours. In this process, salt draws out the blood, cleanses the bird and is absorbed in the meat, and the meat becomes juicy and seasoned to the bone. The sugar in turn rounds out the salty taste and helps the poultry brown. *This process is especially beneficial when roasting a frozen bird.*

Broil – To cook by direct exposure to intense heat, such as a flame or heating unit at the top of an oven.

Brown – To sear in order to seal in the juices and give good color. Typically done under a broiler, in fat in a skillet, or in the oven. ***When browning meat for a stew,*** *be sure it is completely dry before beginning, and sear all sides. Do not overcrowd the pan or your meat will steam rather than brown.*

Brown Butter – Butter with a dense, caramel flavor that adds a delicious dimension to recipes both sweet and savory.

> *To brown butter simply melt very slowly, stirring occasionally, until it smells like caramel and is almost ready to burn (approximately 10 minutes). When the butter suddenly turns*

amber, either stop the cooking by plunging your pan in a bowl of ice water (when baking), or whisk vigorously and remove from heat (when making a syrup or sauce).

Buttermilk – The liquid left behind after cream has been churned into butter.

If you do not have buttermilk on hand, you can make it:

Add 1 Tablespoon of white vinegar or lemon juice to 1 cup sweet milk. Allow this mixture to stand at room temperature for 10 to 15 minutes then add to recipe.

Avoid wasting buttermilk by freezing: Pour unused buttermilk into ice cube trays. Freeze and then remove to a plastic baggie and store in the freezer until you need it. (Most ice cube tray compartments fill with 2 Tablespoons of liquid.)

C

Cake Flour - Cake flour is soft wheat flour blended with a little cornstarch, and makes a lighter, more crumbly cake.

If a recipe calls for cake flour and you do not have it on hand, use 2 Tablespoons less all-purpose flour for each cup of cake flour specified. Then replace the 2 Tablespoons of flour removed with 2 Tablespoons of cornstarch and sift with the remaining flour.

Calvados – French cider brandy.

Candied – Fruits or flowers drenched in syrup or egg white then saturated with sugar.

Caramelize – The process of melting sugar until golden brown to give it a special taste. This can be done in a heavy sauce pan over a low heat (stirring constantly) or atop a cookie or cake while it is baking.

Cassoulet – French; A slow-cooked casserole.

Char – To sear or singe meats over an open flame.

Chèvre – French; A cheese made from goat's milk. AKA: Goat Cheese.

Chiffonade – To shred stacked herbs with a fast, quick pass of the knife, ensuring the flavor is not left on the cutting board from excessive chopping.

Chill – To cool in the refrigerator or in ice.

Chili Peppers – A spicy vegetable with an intense hot taste.

Hot chilies set your taste buds on fire, and can also burn your hands if not prepared properly. Serrano, jalapeño and other hot peppers add wonderful depth to recipes via a chemical called capsaicin. Control the capsaicin "kick" by removing the seeds and veins with the tip of your knife, wearing surgical or rubber gloves until you are comfortable working with hot peppers. Seed peppers by using a paring knife to cut off the stem, and then slice lengthwise. Cut each half lengthwise to create four separate pieces. Lay the skin side down on a cutting board and slide your knife against the pepper to cut away the vein and seeds. Wash your hands while still in the gloves with warm soapy water – then remove the gloves, thus ensuring that none of the capsaicin touches your skin. If your hands tingle, rub some aloe gel or lotion on them.

If you eat something too spicy, don't reach for water or an alcoholic beverage! This will intensify the heat and the liquid will spread the capsaicin throughout your mouth. Eat a bite of cheese or sour cream or drink some milk instead to cool the burn.

Roasting chilies helps remove the bitter taste of their skin and brings out the earthy flavor. The easiest way to roast is over a gas burner. You can also roast on the grill or under an oven broiler. The objective is to blister and blacken the skin without damaging the flesh. Once this has been accomplished, place the chili in a plastic or paper bag. The steam in the enclosed bag will loosen the skin so it can be easily removed. *Do not run roasted chilies under water* because this will remove the essential oils and smoky taste. After skinning, cut the chili open and remove the ribs, seeds and core. Roasted chilies can be stored in the refrigerator for up to 2 days, or frozen for 6 months.

When buying chilies, choose those that are flexible and without blemishes. If you do not plan to use them immediately, prevent drying out by storing them in the freezer. Soak dried peppers in hot water for about 30 minutes to reconstitute.

CHILIES

The Chili-Culinary Heat Scale - Starts at 1 & peaks at 10	1	2	3	4	5	6	7	8	9	10
Ancho - Sweet and slightly fruity.	■	■								
Chipotle - Smoky-sweet and well-rounded.					■	■				
Hatch - Lightly pungent, similar to an onion. Subtly sweet, spicy and smoky taste.			■	■	■	■	■			
Jalapeño - Flavor is similar to a green bell pepper.						■	■			
Paprika - Piquant and fruity.			■	■						
Poblano - Fruity and herbaceous with a hint of licorice.	■	■					■	■		
Serrano - Citrusy.									■	■

Chop – To cut solids into pieces. *It is worth learning good knife skills and chopping techniques to save time in preparation.*

Coat - To sprinkle with flour or sugar until covered or to roll in flour sugar, etc. until coated.

Cool - To let stand at room temperature until no longer warm to the touch.

Corn – The grain of a tall annual cereal plant that produces densely packed ears attached to a central core. Used as a vegetable, ground into flour and to produce oil.

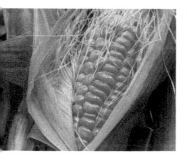

When purchasing, check for natural moisture. The husks should not appear dry or show signs of wilting, and when pulled back, the kernels should be plump, tight, and vivid yellow (or bright white) in color. Squeeze the ears to check for freshness and ensure the kernels are full and juicy. Avoid corn that has been pre-shucked and packaged in plastic, as this indicates corn that is far from its point of harvest and the least fresh.

To shuck fresh corn, hold the tip facing down and pull the husks and silk toward your body. Use a damp paper towel to remove any remaining silks by twisting back and forth on the ear. Trim about a half-inch from the top of each ear before cooking.

To trim the kernels from the cob, stand ears upright in a pie plate. Use a sharp knife from top to bottom in a slow, sawing motion. Remove kernels in rows, capturing all of the kernels and none of the cob.

Coulis – A (often thin) purée of fruits and/or vegetables used as a garnish or complementary sauce to another dish.

Cream – To blend one or more foods together (butter or shortening with a granulated sugar or crushed ingredient) until soft and creamy or light and fluffy.

Crème Frâiche – French; A cultured cream that is less sour than US-style sour cream with a richer consistency and higher fat content.

Crimp – A method of sealing the edges of double-crusted pies for a scalloped edge that is done by pinching at intervals. See Flute.

Crimp by using the index finger of one hand to push the inner edge out, while pinching the outer edge in with the thumb and index finger of other hand.

Crostini – Small, toasted slices of bread with a topping.

Crudité – French: Appetizers consisting of sliced or whole raw vegetables which are sometimes dipped in vinaigrette or other dipping sauce. Crudité often includes celery sticks, carrot sticks, bell pepper strips, broccoli, green beans and asparagus spears; sometimes olives.

Cube – To chop into small squares of approximately ½-inch.

Curd – A solid substance formed when milk coagulates. Used for making cheese.

Curdle – To congeal milk or milk fat until soft lumps or curds are formed. Certain foods curdle, or separate, when too much heat is applied too quickly. Sometimes you can correct this, but other times (when using eggs) you will need to start over.

Cut in – To disperse solid shortening into dry ingredients with a pastry blender or knife. The finished texture resembles coarse meal and looks crumbly. *It is essential that the shortening is chilled.*

D

Deglaze – To make a small amount of natural sauce to pour over meats or use as enrichment for a more elaborate sauce. A liquid such as stock or wine is added to the natural glaze that accumulates in the pan in which meat has been cooked. When liquids are mixed with the pan drippings, the liquid forms a flavorful gravy or sauce base that can be boiled down to a concentrated form or swirled with butter.

Demerara Sugar - Originates from India and retains much of the Sugar Cane flavor.

Use the large light brown crystals to dress up desserts while adding flavor dimension. Demerara sugar is also great on yogurt, in cereals and for glazing ham.

Dice – To cut into small squares, approximately 1/8-inch.

Dissolve – To thoroughly mix a granular substance with a liquid.

Dollop – To lump or blob a small quantity.

Dot – To scatter small bits (like butter) over the surface of foods.

Dough – A mixture of flour, liquid and other ingredients stiff enough to shape and knead.

Dough Scraper – A stainless steel blade with a handle used for cutting dough, sectioning pie crusts, and scraping sticky dough from counter tops while baking or making pasta.

Dredge – To cover a solid food with sugar, flour or bread crumbs. Done by dragging the solid food through the powdery substance, shaking together in a bag, or by using a sifter.

Drippings – Valuable for sauces and gravies, drippings are the juices, fats and brown bits that collect in the pan when meat or poultry are roasted.

Drizzle – To lightly sprinkle drops of liquid over foods in a casual yet controlled stream.

Dry Ingredients – Flour, baking powder and soda, salt, spices, etc.

Dust – To sprinkle foods with a dry ingredient such as sugar or nutmeg.

Dutch Oven – An iron or earthenware container with a lid, used for cooking stews and/or casseroles.

E-F

Egg – A bird's egg; used in both cooking and baking.

Very fresh eggs will cling together, hold their shape and have a tighter yolk. You can tell if your eggs are old if they float or tip/stand upward on their own in a bowl of water.

For hard boiled chicken eggs that are tender and delicious, follow this simple formula:

Place eggs in a heavy saucepan and cover with cold water, being careful to not overcrowd the pan with too many eggs touching one another. Fill water to 1-inch above tops of eggs, just to cover. Bring the water to a boil, then remove the pan from the heat and allow eggs to steep, with the lid on tight, for 17 minutes. Remove eggs to an ice bath to stop the cooking. Chill eggs in the refrigerator before peeling. Peel eggs under cool running water for best results.

Egg White - The clear liquid surrounding the yellow egg yolk.

Use room temperature eggs when making meringues (beaten egg whites), and add the sugar very slowly, so as not to defeat the meringue.

Fava Bean - A large flat green seed from the pea family grown inside long pods that produce broad beans. Eaten as a vegetable, fava beans have a delicate yet bitter flavor and are in season in the spring and summer months. Favas are delicious both raw or lightly sautéed.

These bright green beans need to be shucked twice.
After popping them out of their larger pod, be sure to remove the individual skins. In the spring when beans are tender, the individual skins can be eaten.

Figs – An intensely sweet fruit with a grainy texture that is in season summer to autumn. Fresh figs can sometimes be hard to find. *If you are unable to find fresh, use black Mission dried figs and re-hydrate in very hot water with a squeeze of fresh lemon.*

Fillet – To remove the bone(s) from meat or fish. A fillet is also the piece of lean flesh that remains after meat has been boned.

Flash Pasteurized – A method of heat pasteurization of perishable beverages and dairy products such as eggs and milk that maintains color and flavor better and kills spoilage in order to make products safer.

Fleur de Sel – French; Hand-harvested sea salt collected by workers who scrape only the top layer of salt before it sinks to the bottom of large salt pans. *Best used to add flavor to a finished dish, not to season.*

Flour – A powder made by grinding the edible parts of cereal grains.

Cake flour - A soft wheat flour blended with a little cornstarch, which makes a lighter, more crumbly cake.

All-Purpose – This white flour delivers consistent results for a wide range of baking needs. It is a blend of soft and hard wheat grains with the bran and germ removed.

Almond - Made from ground almond nuts.

Bread – Ideal for baking bread, this flour is unbleached and made from gluten-rich hard wheat, making for highly resilient dough.

Gluten – High in protein and treated to reduce its starch content, gluten flour is good for people with wheat allergies.

Self-Rising – A blended all-purpose flour with baking powder and salt added, making this great for quick breads.

Whole Wheat – Yields dense, heavier bread. This flour is milled from wheat grains, bran and germ. It is high in nutrients as well as particles that interfere with gluten formation. Often used in combination with other flours.

Flute – To make a decorative scalloped edge with pie crust. See Crimp.

Foie Gras – French; A luxury pâté or spreadable paste made from the liver of a duck or goose that has been specially fattened.

Fold In – To blend and aerate a delicate frothy mixture into a heavier one so that none of the lightness, volume and air is lost. *This is best done by using a rubber spatula, turning under and bringing it up and over, rotating the bowl one-quarter turn after each motion.*

Fork-Tender – To soften by cooking until fork pierces easily.

French Dragées - Small, spiced balls of hardened sugar or honey, and can be coated in silver or pastel colors.

Frothy – To beat until slightly foamy.

Fruit Spreads - All fruit spreads are made with fruits, sugar and pectin.

Preserves are made with chunks of fruit stored in its own juice or syrup.

Jellies are made from fruit pulp and crushed fruit.

Jams are a transparent gel in which the fruit comes from fruit juice.

Fry – To cook in a pan or skillet with hot oil in which the oil does or does not totally cover the food.

Fry in batches as necessary to ensure foods do not touch, and avoid frying foods that are very cold. Use oil or fat with a high burning temperature and do not let the fat or oil smoke or the interior will likely be under cooked. For best results, use flavorless oil with a high smoke point (corn oil or Crisco shortening). Drain, as soon as food has finished cooking, on paper toweling that has been lightly salted. Season immediately; salt will stick to and dissolve quicker on a hot surface.

Reuse oil. Once oil has cooled, it can be strained, stored and used again – up to six or eight times. ***See Oils & Fats.***

G

Garlic – A bulb or clove with a pungent odor and flavor commonly used in cooking. Choose plump, firm heads that are free of sprouts and dark spots. Garlic will stay fresh for months when stored in a cool, dark place – but not in the refrigerator.

To peel and mince garlic, *place the flat side of a large knife on an unpeeled clove. Then gently break open the clove by popping the knife down with the heel of your hand. Peel off the skin and trim the rough end with your knife. Mince the clove by cutting lengthwise, then cutting crosswise.*

When cooking minced garlic be sure to sauté over low heat and watch carefully. Garlic typically only needs 30 to 60 seconds to cook, and burns very quickly, which will result in a bitter taste. If you burn your garlic, discard it and start again.

Roasted Garlic & Infused Oil - Garlic in bulk can be peeled, broken into cloves and submerged in olive oil, then baked slowly in a 200 degree oven for 2 to 3 hours. This method yields a large supply of garlic that will keep in the refrigerator, preserved in the oil, for up to 3 months. To enjoy this roasted garlic on bread, in hamburgers or any other recipe, just warm it in the oven a few minutes until it is buttery soft again. *Use the garlic infused olive oil for cooking.* Roasting brings up the garlic flavor in the oil without any bitterness and makes delicious oil for sautéing meats and vegetables.

Garnish – To decorate food with herbs, flowers or candies to enhance appearance. Garnishes are often fresh herbs, citrus fruits and/or florals.

Ginger "In a Snap" – A hot-tasting edible underground stem rhizome of an Asian plant that is eaten fresh, dried or candied, sometimes pickled. The distinct flavor of ginger is refreshing, sweet and spicy-hot at once.

Fresh Ginger - The knobby, tan, root-like stem of fresh ginger can be found in the produce section. To use: peel, slice and then mince or grate.

Ground Ginger - This dried spice is delicious used in cakes, cookies and breads.

Crystallized Ginger - These candy-like nubs are made from pieces of young ginger that have been cooked in sugar syrup. They are terrific on baked goods as well as in hot tea.

Glacé – The process of coating (fruits) with a sugar solution that results in a glazed finish.

Glacée, Crème – French; Cold or iced cream.

Glaze – To cover or coat with a sauce, syrup or egg white after application – adding a final sheen that is both colorful and flavorful.

Grate – To rub food against a rough perforated utensil to break up a solid into small particles and produce slivers, curls or chunks.

Gratin – The browning process of toppings of bread crumbs and/or cheese. Gratin also refers to the baking dish used to bake or broil foods in this manner.

Grease – To rub lightly with butter. Also known as, to "butter."

Griddle – A heavy flat metal plate used for cooking.

Grill – To broil over charcoal or hot coals/intense heat.

Grilling Fruits & Vegetables - From asparagus to peaches, seasonal fruits & vegetables roasted on the grill have a delicious smoky flavor with an exterior that is crisp and just slightly charred. But the intense heat of the grill can also burn tender veggies.

To protect grilled produce, mix ¼ cup mayonnaise with 1 to 2 teaspoons of olive oil and brush over fruits and vegetables before grilling. The mayonnaise burns off over the flames and does a great job protecting vegetables and fruits alike while cooking. Grill produce for 4 to 5 minutes until crisp yet tender. Turn veggies and brush again with the mayo mix as you go. Grill fruits & vegetables directly on the grate to get the grill marks.

If you do not have an outdoor grill, vegetables can be roasted in a hot oven. Wash, trim and dress as directed above, then place in a jelly roll pan in 425 degree oven for 5 to 15 minutes (depending on vegetable), turning 1 to 2 times.

Grind – To produce small bits by cutting, crushing or forcing through a chopper.

Hazelnut – An edible nut from the Hazel tree.

*Hazelnuts have a bitter hull that must be removed before adding to recipes. **After toasting, when nuts are cool enough to handle, remove hulls by vigorously rubbing a handful at a time in a clean dish towel. (Some skin may remain on hazelnuts, but they should be mostly free of the bitter hull.)***

Heaping – Term used to mean mounding just a bit more of an ingredient than measurement.

Herbs – A low-growing aromatic plant used fresh or dried for seasoning. Herbs are more than mere garnishes, but essential ingredients that add fresh dimension and flavor to cooking and baking.

***When cooking and baking with fresh herbs**, be cognizant of pairing delicate varieties with delicate flavors. For example, a gentle chive will pair well with a gentle white fish because this herb has the same intensity as the protein.*

It is also nice to pair herbs according to their affinity. Pair Mediterranean herbs with dishes from the Mediterranean region (rosemary with lamb), and Asian herbs with Asian foods (lemon basil or lemon grass with a Thai noodle dish). It is a natural pairing to marry summer herbs with summer vegetables and winter herbs with winter vegetables. Keep these tips in mind as you experiment with different flavors.

Soft-Leaved Herbs - Do not cook soft leaved herbs, but add them at the very end of the cooking time. Herbs best used fresh include: *Parsley, Basil, Mint, Cilantro, Chervil, Chives, Dill, Sorrel, and Tarragon.*

Tough Leaved Herbs - Should be cooked and will stand up to heat. Herbs that are best cooked: *Oregano, Rosemary, Marjoram, Bay leaf, Thyme, Sage, and Savory.*

***To store fresh rinsed herbs (and cut or peeled vegetables)**, place a damp paper towel in a plastic bag or plastic container. Add herbs or veggies, seal, and store in the refrigerator for up to one week.*

When using dried herbs remember that they are far more concentrated than fresh.

Use a fraction of the measurement for fresh herbs, or roughly one third of the amount. For example, if a recipe calls for 1 Tablespoon of a fresh herb, you will need only 1 teaspoon of dried. (3 teaspoons equal 1 Tablespoon.) Dried herbs should be stored in a cool dry place and checked for potency periodically.

***Use fresh herbs in table settings.** Try incorporating a sprig of fresh rosemary (or another herb) with the silverware and napkins, or in other places on your table scape such as in the centerpiece or on the place card. Woody herbs like rosemary and lavender are tough enough to stay fresh-looking for several hours without water and smell wonderful without competing with foods.*

Honey – A sweet sticky golden-brown fluid produced by bees from the nectar of flowers. *Use honey as a flavor rather than a sweetener like sugar.*

Hull – To remove husk, shell, stem or outer covering of a seed or fruit.

Immersion Blender – An electric stick used to purée foods (soups and sauces especially) by submersing into a liquid mixture. *If you do not have an immersion blender, use a food processor.*

Infuse – To steep herbs or other flavorings in a liquid until the liquid absorbs the flavors.

Julienne – To cut vegetables, fruit, etc. into long thin matchstick strips. To julienne, make a stack of 1/8-inch pieces and then slice downward at 1/8-inch intervals.

Kale & Swiss Chard – Edible, leafy vegetables.

The first step to enjoying kale and Swiss chard is to remove the stems, which can be tough and stringy even when cooked. Start by removing the stem from the center of the leaf by folding each leaf in half. With the back of the leaf on the outside, cut away the center vein from the bottom to top in a V-shape. Wash greens in cool water and pat dry. Unlike lettuce, which should be gently torn to avoid bruising, kale leaves can be cut/chopped with a knife.

Kelp Caviar - A seaweed-based delicacy that tastes of the ocean but contains no fish roe. This product is great for Vegetarians, is low in fat, salt and cholesterol, and is a fraction of the price of sturgeon roe caviar.

Knead – To press, fold and stretch dough until smooth and elastic, thus developing the gluten in the flour (Method usually indicates a time frame and result.)

Lavender - An aromatic herb with oils that add a delicious smoked flavor to grilled meats and are also delicious used in salads and baked goods. For recipes that call for rosemary, try substituting lavender for something different. Lavender is terrific in buttery desserts and pairs well with most all nuts – almonds, hazelnuts, pistachios and walnuts. Lavender does not pair well with chestnuts, however.

*Like fresh herbs, dried lavender is far more potent than fresh. **Reduce the amount by 2/3 if using fresh buds - ½ teaspoon dried is equal to 1½ teaspoons fresh.***

When grilling, add the stems and leaves of the lavender plant to the hot coals to further enhance the smoky herbal flavors. And try putting lavender into our outdoor fire pit. The aroma is just lovely on a summer night!

Lavender Honey - An intensely sweet honey with a floral aroma. Both light and tart, it originates from the south of France and Mediterranean coastal area of Spain. It is delicate in both color and consistency.

Leaven – Using a chemical leavening agent to cause batters and dough to rise. The process may occur before or during baking.

Leeks – An edible plant with dark green leaves rising from a close-set white base; related to the onion. Must be cleaned well before using because sand and dirt can lodge in its many layers.

Clean by removing the root portion, just below the white base. Then slice off the fibrous green top part, starting with the outside leaves and working your way in. For the outer most leaves, trim off everything above approximately two inches above the white root base. Then slice off the next layer of leaves about 2 inches higher. Repeat. Once you have only one inch of green, lop this off and slice the leek lengthwise. Hold the top of the green part and dip the leek into a bowl of cool water. Gently swish to remove the sand.

Lemons & Citrus – Yellow, green and orange fruits with a thick fragrant rind and sweet or sour juicy flesh. The natural acid from lemons, limes and oranges enhance flavors without adding salt.

Lemons are a Superfood because of their soluble fiber content, which stabilizes blood sugar by slowing its absorption into the bloodstream.

To zest lemon, orange or lime rind, gently run the whole fruit up and down a micro planer or grater. For curls or strips of rind, use a vegetable peeler.

Save Lemon Juice in Ice Cube Trays - When recipes call for lemon zest only, save the lemon juice by freezing rather than throwing it away.

Rather than composting citrus rind, grind in garbage disposal and your kitchen will smell citrus fresh!

MEASURING LEMONS	Number of Lemons	Teaspoons or Tablespoons	Cups
For Lemon Juice	½	3 teaspoons juice	
Lemon juice adds both acid and a tart yet mild citrus flavor. If a recipe calls for water, try using citrus instead.	1 2		1/8 cup juice ¼ cup juice
For Lemon Zest	½	1 to 2 teaspoons zest	
Lemon zest is grated lemon rind. Zest adds lemon flavor with the perfume of lemon in essential oils. Great for baking and cooking.	1 2	1 Tablespoon zest 2 Tablespoons zest	

Fresh lemons used in baking and cooking add a bright flavor that cannot be matched, and should be considered a staple in the kitchen.

Liaison – A mixture of egg yolks and cream. Used to thicken sauces.

Lukewarm – A temperature that is neither cold nor hot.

M-O

Macaroon – A French confection of buttercream in almond meringue.

Mâche – A lettuce-like vegetable with leaves that are mild and slightly nutty with a subtle tang. The oval leaves taste almost juicy. Mâche was named "corn salad" because it was found growing in cornfields, so be sure to wash it well before using to remove sand. *Mâche can be hard to find; butter lettuce is a good substitute.*

Marc – A French brandy made from the residue of wine grapes.

Marinate – To soak in a highly seasoned or wet solution to flavor and/or tenderize foods. Marinades always contain an acid like lemon, vinegar or wine to tenderize and infuse flavor.

Mascarpone - Italian; A cheese made from whole cream and citric acid with a milky and lightly sweet and tangy flavor. Similar to cream cheese; often used in desserts.

Measure – The use of cups and spoons to ensure an accurate measure when filled. *Do not pack dry ingredients when measuring - except for brown sugar.* Always use liquid measuring cups to measure liquids and dry measuring cups for dry ingredients.

Melt – To liquefy a solid food, via the action of heat.

Meringue – A dessert made from whipped egg whites and sugar.

The Secret to a Good meringue is to use room temperature eggs, and add the sugar very slowly, so as not to defeat the meringue. Also, be sure to always use spotlessly clean and dry beaters. If egg whites are loose or wet, add a pinch of cream of tartar to help them stay stiff and weep-free. Eggs are easiest to separate while cold.

Mince – To cut or chop into very small, tiny pieces. *After chopping roughly, mince foods by rocking the blade back and forth, using one hand on the tip and one on the handle, and marching from one end of the pile to the other. Then repeat crosswise.*

Mint – An herb often used to garnish desserts with a pungent taste and lovely bright green color.

A sprig of mint can completely change the balance of your desert, so avoid garnishing indiscriminately with mint. If it doesn't make sense to the overall balance, leave it off.

Mix – To combine foods by distributing ingredients uniformly.

Mocktail – A cocktail-like drink containing no alcohol.

Mojito – Spanish; A cocktail traditionally made of rum, sugar, lime and mint.

Mold – To shape into a particular form or attractive shape by steaming, baking or chilling.

Mound – To spoon or heap ingredients, but not blend.

Mousseline – A sauce or mixture made by folding in whipped cream.

Mushrooms – An umbrella-shaped spore that is cultivated and available year round.

Seasons for naturally grown mushrooms are:

Spring – Morels are in season.

Summer – Porcinis, Oysters & Chanterelles are fresh.

Fall – Enjoy Matsutakes, Porcinis, Oysters, Portobello & American Truffles (less flavorful than European truffles but also far less expensive).

When purchasing, look for fresh-looking, firm, evenly-colored and dry mushrooms. If they look shriveled, soft or spongy, or smell of mildew they are likely old and not worth the purchase.

Roasting Mushrooms - All mushrooms are good roasted. Place on a large baking sheet and spread apart to ensure good evaporation of these watery morsels. Sprinkle with olive oil, salt, pepper and fresh thyme leaves. Roast for 30 to 45 minutes at 400 degrees, or until liquid has evaporated and the mushrooms are browned and about half of their original size.

Seasoning & Sautéing Mushrooms - Mushrooms should always be paired with a savory seasoning. Parsley and garlic are a good choice. Start by sautéing mushroom in olive oil and/or butter then toss in parsley and garlic (or shallots) with a pinch of salt. Mushrooms are also good prepared in a dry sauté. If roasting Oyster or Porcinis, try doing so on a bed of savory or thyme for added flavor.

Store mushrooms in a plastic bag with the top left open in the refrigerator. Mushrooms will keep in the refrigerator for up to 3 days.

All mushrooms need to be well cleaned to avoid a mouthful of grit. Mushrooms are very porous so it is important to use care when washing them in water. Always wash just before using, not in advance, and blot dry immediately. Mushrooms can be cleaned without water by gently rubbing them with a kitchen towel to remove the dirt and then simply trimming off the bottom of the stems.

Morel mushrooms – A delicacy in springtime but very pitted, so it is important to clean them well. Start by brushing off any dirt and/or bugs with a dry pastry brush. Then rinse them well in water, or soak briefly in salt water, and pat dry. Slice lengthwise to check a second time for bugs and worms. If you see white threads that look like mold on the surface of morels, that is likely a worm hole and needs further investigation and/or cleaning. Morels are delicious with a grilled steak and in pastas.

> *Fried Morels* - Coat morels in approximately ½ cup of all-purpose flour and fry in 2 to 3 Tablespoons butter until crisp.

> *Sautéed Morels* - Sauté morels in dry skillet until brown, then add approximately 2 Tablespoons butter (or olive oil) and minced garlic and/or shallots. Cook an additional 1 to 3 minutes.

> *Dried Morels* - Available year round, dried morels can be re-hydrated in very hot water for 20 to 30 minutes. Squeeze out moisture before cooking.

Portobello mushrooms *should have their underbellies scraped clean, or the gills/black fibers will discolor the other ingredients in your dish.*

Shitake mushrooms *need to have their entire stem removed as it is rubbery.*

Nut – The fruit of a plant or tree with a hard outer shell and edible seed.

> *Toasting brings out the essential oils in nuts and seeds, resulting in much more flavor. Nuts are a delicious addition to both sweet and savory dishes and add a crunch of texture to anything from salads to soups to entrées and desserts. Nuts absorb moisture readily and toasting will both dry them out and heighten their flavor. Go slowly and use care as nuts burn easily. To toast nuts, place them on a baking sheet in a 350 to 375 degree oven until they are fragrant and slightly brown, approximately 5 to 10 minutes depending on the size of nut. Toss once during toasting time.*

> *Smaller, less dense seeds and nuts are best toasted in a dry sauté pan over low heat so they can be closely watched to prevent burning. Pan toast cumin, pepitas or peppercorns, as well as pine nuts until aromatic and slightly brown, about 5 minutes.*

> *If nuts are to top a tart or other dessert, there is no need to toast them in advance as they will do so while the dessert bakes.*

> *Avoid buying chopped nuts, the flavor quality cannot compare to whole nuts. Chop by hand or in a hand-cranked grinder, but avoid the more powerful food processor or the natural moisture in nuts may turn to powder.*

> *Consider the geographic origin.* As with using herbs, when creating a dish with nuts, use nuts from the same region. For example, if you are making a southern dish, pecans are a good match. If you dessert is Italian, consider pistachios because that is the nut they would use in Sicily.

Oils & Other Fats, *see table on the following page.*

> *Re-Use & Store Oils* - Clarify first by adding a few slices of peeled potatoes to the hot oil to absorb flavors. Then remove the potato and let the oil cool. Strain oil through a fine mesh strainer or cheesecloth before storing.

> *Store oils* at room temperature in a cool dark location, or for best results in the refrigerator. Taste or smell oil before reusing to ensure it has not become rancid. Rancid oil has a noticeably off scent. Oils will darken with each use, and that is okay. Oils will keep for up to one year after opening and can be reused up to eight times.

> *Never pour oils* down the kitchen sink because it will congeal and clog pipes. Toss it

OILS & OTHER FATS

Oil Type	Flavor	Use	Pair with (a sampling)	Fat Content: Oils average 120 calories per Tablespoon	Burning Temperature/ Smoke Point
Hazelnut	Rich hazelnut taste.	Sautéing, pan/deep/stir frying, searing, grilling, broiling.	Apples, artichokes, cheese, figs, fish, pears, spinach.	80% unsaturated fat	400°F
Olive (Extra Virgin)	Slightly fruity, bitter & peppery.	Cooking, salad dressing, baking, sautéing, pan/deep/stir frying, searing, grilling, and broiling.	Anchovies, beans, fish, garlic, Italian cuisine, olives, Parmesan, salads, soups, vegetables.	78% unsaturated fat	325–375°F
Almond	Subtle toasted almond.	Sautéing, stir frying.	Asparagus, chicken, fish, pasta, salads, baked goods.	72% unsaturated fat	420°F
Canola	Neutral, pleasant flavor.	Frying, salad dressing, shortening. Avoid deep-frying.	Salads.	72% unsaturated fat	400°F
Sesame	Strong toasted flavor.	Cooking, salad dressing.	Asian cuisine, beef, cabbage, chicken, garlic, ginger, lemongrass, noodles.	40% unsaturated fat, 45% neutral fat	350–410°F
Walnut	Nutty flavor & aroma.	Sautéing, pan/deep/stir frying, searing, grilling, broiling.	Apples, beets, bread, figs, bitter greens, potatoes, steaks.	35% unsaturated fat, 55% neutral fat	400°F
Corn	Mild taste.	All purpose. Salad dressing, cooking.		30% unsaturated fat, 55% neutral fat	450°F
Vegetable Shortening	Mild.	All purpose.		70% unsaturated fat	360°F
Vegetable Oil	Mild.	All purpose.		70% unsaturated fat	400–450°F
Butter	Nutty flavor.	Baking & sautéing.		30% unsaturated fat, 50% saturated fat	250–300°F
Coconut	Slight coconut.	Replacement for butter in cooking & baking.		Less than 10% unsaturated fat, 85% saturated fat	350°F

What sets *coconut oil* apart as a healthy alternative is that more than half of its fat is rapidly metabolized and less likely to be stored as fat in the body.

Butter - Use unsalted butter to provide the pure, sweet cream taste of butter and allow control of the salt content in recipes. Store butter in an airtight container in the refrigerator.

out in the garbage instead, sealed in a plastic baggie or other sealed and throw-away container.

Onions – A rounded edible bulb with a hard pungent flesh in concentric layers beneath a flaky skin that can be eaten raw or cooked. Onions form the foundation for every cuisine. They increase the appetite and pair with virtually all savory foods.

Vidalia– Available in late spring to early summer, has a sweet, light taste and is good served raw.

Spanish – very mild with a delicate taste and best grilled or sautéed just a few minutes.

Yellow – Has a stronger onion flavor and a good balance between sweet and savory flavor. Yellow is the most common onion.

Bermuda or Red – Has a sweeter, milder taste and a bold purple color. They are best served raw, and rarely used for cooking.

White – Mild in taste and should be used in dishes where you do not want a strong onion flavor.

Shallots are tiny cousins of the onion. They have a sweet, pungent flavor that is good raw or cooked. Shallots provide the flavor of onion without overwhelming the dish.
To slice onions, start by halving the onion lengthwise with the grain and notching out the ends. Then hold one half of the onion, flat center side down with your fingertips. Start slicing through to center at bottom edge of one side. Place your knife at a low angle and follow the natural curve of the onion. Adjust the angle of your knife as you slice, keeping it at 90 degrees. Slice until you reach the center, then flip the onion and continue in same manner through opposite side. If you want to dice your onions, simply continue cutting through these slices in the opposite direction.

When slicing a red onion, take advantage of the large knob where roots are attached. Cut red onion in half with root knob at ends. Leave the knob in place and slice just up to it both horizontally and vertically. Then dice onion from outside in. The knob will hold all of the layers and slices together until diced, at which time you can just slice off the knob and have a neatly diced onion!

Store onions in a cool, dry, dark place – but never in a sealed container.

P-Q

Pancetta – Italian; A type of bacon sliced very thin, often consumed raw.

Pan Broil - To fry in a skillet that is often salted or rubbed with fat first.

Parboil – To partially cook in boiling water. Most parboiled foods require additional cooking. This is good way to bring up the bright colors of vegetables when serving crudité. See Blanch.

Pasta – A fresh or dried food of Italian origin made from a dough typically made of water, flour and eggs and produced in a variety of shapes and forms. To cook:

Dried Pasta - Use a large pasta pot filled to ¾ full with water and a handful of salt. Bring water to a rolling boil and add pasta, then turn down the heat slightly. Ensure all pasta is submerged and stir to divide each strand. Boil pasta for 15 minutes. Drain and rinse briefly in cool water to remove the sticky paste and stop the cooking.

Fresh Pasta - Fill pasta pot to ¾ full with water, a handful of salt and 1 teaspoon olive oil. Bring water to a rolling boil, add pasta, then turn down the heat slightly and stir to ensure pasta is not sticking. Boil fresh pasta just 3 to 5 minutes. Drain and serve.

Rehydrated Pasta - To "hold" cooked and drained pasta and ensure it is supple when ready to serve, simply dip it back into a pot of simmering water for a few seconds to rehydrate just before plating.

PASTA & SAUCE PAIRINGS

Bow Tie – Great with vegetables and tomato-based sauce.

Fettucine – Good with Bolognese sauce.

Fusilli – A corkscrew pasta, good in salads and with pesto.

Pappardelle – This rustic pasta is good with game and fish.

Spaghetti – Great with everything from tomato sauce to pesto, most all sauces will stick to spaghetti.

Angel Hair – This very thin pasta is served to the elderly in Italy, or people who are sick or have trouble chewing! It is too thin for cooking al dente and not as robust as other choices.

BASIC PASTA SAUCES

Bolognese – A red meat-based sauce, also known as ragù, good with fettuccine pasta.

Tomato – Works well with all pastas.

Pesto – Works well with fusilli because it can cling to the corkscrew shape.

Garlic & Olive Oil – Good with spaghetti pasta.

Cream – Because cream is rich, it should be paired with strongly flavored pasta. Use fettuccine, pappardelle or gnocchi with a cream sauce.

Carbonara – Use pasta this sauce will cling to, like spaghetti.

Pastis – A popular drink in the south of France with a licorice or anise flavor, served diluted with cool water.

Pâté – A well-seasoned and baked loaf of various ground meats and fats, served cold.

Peel – To remove the peel from vegetables or fruit.

Pepita – Spanish; Sunflower seed.

Pepper – A hot condiment or seasoning made from ground dried berries of a tropical climbing plant.

PEPPER

PEPPER TYPE	FLAVOR	CONSISTENCY	USE
Black: Made from berries that have been dried before ripened. *My recipes always call for freshly ground.*	Complex, spicy flavor. Pungent, hot.	Suggests heat, stimulates the appetite. *Best added at the end of cooking process.*	Good with tuna and red meat. Good with fresh fruit, especially lemons, limes, cherries & apricots.
Red	Hot, strong; can burn.	Best added at the end of cooking process.	Also known as Cayenne. Good with Indian, Italian & Mexican cuisine.
White: Made from berries that have ripened before being dried.	Hot, but milder than black.	Best added at the end of cooking process.	Good with white fish because it does not overwhelm.
Mix: Toasted & ground black & pink peppercorns with coriander & star anise.	Pink pepper is hot.		Great with tuna, beef, bison & pork, Good with dressing & sauces.

Petit Four – French; A small confectionery or mini cake that is iced or glazed.

Pesto – Italian; A sauce made from crushed garlic, pine nuts, basil and (Parmesan) cheese. *Save pesto over the winter months by freezing in an ice cube tray, and then in a sealed baggie.*

Pinch – A trifle amount, typically about 1/8 teaspoon.

Pipe – To squeeze a soft smooth food, such as frosting, through a pastry tube to make a border or decorative shape.

Pit – To remove the hard inedible seed from olives, peaches, plums, etc.

Plump – To soak dried fruits, such as raisins or currants, in a liquid or liqueur until soft and swollen. See Reconstitute.

Poach – To cook in a small amount of gently simmering liquid.

Pomegranate - Pomegranates are a very tart and flavorful fruit without a lot of sugar. Unlike most fruits, the seeds are the edible portion of a pomegranate.

There are a number of ways to seed this fruit, here are two methods: Cut pomegranate in half and hold the open end over a bowl. Using a wooden spoon, pop the back of fruit to release the seeds, which will spill out into the bowl with each rap of the spoon. Or, with a large knife, cut fruit into four quarters. Hold each quarter over a bowl and use your fingers to gently fleck out the beautiful red ruby seeds. With either method, be sure to use care when separating the seeds from the inner white membrane and to not burst the individual juice sacs. Once the seeds are removed, pick any bitter membrane from the seeds. Seeds will keep for up to one week refrigerated. Pomegranate juice stains, so protect your clothing!

Pomegranate Juice - To make juice, slice open 2¼ pounds of pomegranate fruit and remove seeds from membrane. In a medium-sized saucepan, cover seeds with water and simmer to release the juice from the seeds sacs, about 5 minutes. Run mixture through a fine mesh sieve; discard seed pods. Measure amount of strained juice, then use that same amount for sugar measurement.

Pot de Crème – French; An egg and milk based dessert custard.

Preheat – To turn on oven to desired temperature, and allow to come to said temperature, before putting foods into oven.

Puff Pastry – A flaky, light pastry of laminated buttery dough. *When using puff pastry, shop for the kind made with butter, and thaw pastry overnight in the refrigerator to avoid dough that is sticky on one side.*

Purée – To reduce the pulp of cooked fruit and vegetables to a smooth and thick liquid by straining or blending.

Quesco Fresco – Spanish; Fresh cheese.

R

Ravioli – A type of dumpling with a filling sealed between two layers of pasta dough.

Reconstitute – To soak dried fruits or vegetables in a liquid or liqueur until soft and swollen. See Plump.

Red Bud Blossoms - Blossoms from the Red Bud tree that have a slight nutty flavor and pink magenta color, add a striking beauty to any dish. The Redbud blooms in early spring.

Toss redbud blossoms into salads, pancakes, or other baked goods. **They also make lovely** *garnishes and are great pickled. When green, the redbud seed pods are also edible. Steam and serve with butter just like peas.*

Reduce – To boil stock, gravy or other liquid until volume is reduced, liquid has thickened, and flavor intensified.

Refresh – To place blanched and drained vegetables in cold water to halt the cooking process.

Remoulade – French: A condiment that is mayonnaise-based with strong seasoning.

Render – To cook meat or meat trimmings slowly at low temperature until fat melts and can be drained and strained.

Rest – The (essential) process of allowing meats to relax after roasting or grilling so that their internal juices can redistribute evenly. Resting 10 to 15 minutes will make any roast or large cut of meat tastier, and ensure the juices remain in the meat - and not on the cutting board!

Ricotta – Italian; A whey cheese. Similar to mascarpone or cream cheese.

Risotto – Italian; A rice dish cooked in broth to a creamy consistency.

Roast – To: 1) Cook by dry heat in an oven or over hot coals or, 2) Dry or parch by intense heat.

Root Vegetables – A vegetable grown for its fleshy edible underground parts that is sweet and full of sugar in the fall and especially good roasted in a slow oven.

Beets – Varieties in red, gold, pink and white, their flavor is intensified by baking.

Carrots – Orange and sweet. Carrots are great raw, steamed, sautéed and roasted.

Celery Root – These knobby relatives of celery are great shredded into salads or cooked and mashed with potatoes.

Parsnips – These subtly sweet and ivory-hued cousins of the carrot are terrific roasted with other vegetables. They are also good French-fried or boiled and mashed.

Radishes – These crisp and pungent roots are best eaten raw. The small round or long goodies come in varieties of red, lavender, black and white.

Rutabaga – Large and bulbous, this pale yellow relative of the turnip is slightly pungent in taste and delicious roasted or puréed.

Turnips – Turnips are excellent simmered, roasted or puréed. The white bulb is mild and sweet.

Rediscover the pleasure of these humble comfort foods. Try mixing in lemon slices, bay leaf, whole green beans and a few pomegranate seeds to bring up the sweetness of these vegetables and make the mixture a visual masterpiece.

Roux – A mixture of butter and flour. Used to thicken sauces.

S

Salmon – A large fish that spends most of its life in the ocean, but migrates up freshwater rivers to spawn. Salmon can be either farm raised or wild.

King Salmon – (AKA: Chinook) King salmon is the most popular species with large, thick fillets that are easy to cook. King salmon is not the most flavorful variety, and farm raised King salmon is a bit smaller than wild. *Wild King Salmon* is thought to be the granddaddy of salmons, however, and always a good choice.

Sockeye Reds – The best sockeye comes from the icy cold rivers of Alaska. Premium sockeye has a high oil content, deep red flesh, full flavor and firm texture.

Caution - these thin fillets can be easily overcooked.

Coho – This silver salmon can be found in market during the summer months. Coho is small and has a brighter more flavorful taste. It is especially good grilled.

Wild Arctic Salmon – *Many wild salmon populations are threatened. Be sure to ask your fishmonger if the salmon you are buying comes from a sustainable fishery. Wild salmon has a reddish-orange flesh and tends to be a bit more fatty*

SALT

SALT TYPE	FLAVOR	CONSISTENCY	USE
Kosher *My favored salt.*	Less intense, more pure salty taste.	Coarse, craggy crystals. Easy to pick up.	Good for all cooking; best with meats. Also good for pasta water and brining. Dissolves fast but does not break down too fast. Flavor disperses quickly.
Sea	Subtle brine, sweet & even bitter taste. Pungent boost of flavor to just cooked foods.	Fine to coarse.	Use with delicate foods like fish and vegetables. Holds natural impurities of sea.
Himalayan Pink	Rich flavor; 95% sodium.	Light, translucent pink color. Easy for the body to digest.	The purest salt on earth. Mined by hand in Himalayan mountains.
Fleur de Sel	Delicate flavor with just a hint of saltiness.	Fine crystal. Produced through evaporated ocean water.	Use on cold dishes & salads. Good with meats like beef, rib eye, bison or roast chicken added just before serving. A special occasion table salt.
Table *If my recipes do not specify a type of salt, use table salt.*	Heavily processed with added iodine.	Very fine. Best used for baking.	Mined from underground deposits.
Rock	Not edible.	Large chunky crystals.	Used to make ice cream & slow-cooked meats & fish.
Infused	Infused salts are not intended for cooking, but rather to bring up the flavors of a dish after it has been prepared.		

Saucing – Sweet or sour sauces served with steak that use acid or sweetness to cut through the fat and richness of the meat. *A simple wine with caramelized shallots, or bourbon and peppercorns are good beef sauces.*

Saucisson – French; A cured sausage similar to salami.

Sauerbraten – German; A pot roast marinated for several days until sour or pickled.

Sauté – To cook, stirring frequently, in a skillet containing a small amount of hot cooking oil. (Food is not immersed in oil.) Often the food is browned first, tossing to seal all sides, then gently sautéed, covered or uncovered.

Scald – To bring milk nearly to boiling point. (Process makes yeasts breads lighter.) To scald a solid food means to drop it in boiling water for just a second.

Scallop – To bake with a sauce in a casserole. The food may either be mixed or layered with the sauce. Also means to make a decorative pie crust.

Score- To make shallow cuts in meat or fish to both tenderize and help keep its shape.

Scramble – To cook and stir simultaneously, especially with eggs.

Sear – To cook meats at a very high heat in order to seal in the juices and brown the surfaces.

Shred – To cut or shave food into slivers.

Shrimp – A small and edible, mainly ocean-dwelling crustacean.

Always shop for the freshest shrimp you can find and buy shrimp that has been peeled and deveined by machine.

To clean yourself: Tear off the heads and slit the shell; peel off shell and legs. Once shrimp are peeled, run a small paring knife along the top back of the shrimp. You will find a dark, slimy vein as you cut just below the surface. Use the tip of your knife to scrape this out, trying to get it all in one piece. Be sure to run your knife the full length of the shrimp. Once the vein has been completely removed, rinse shrimp in cool water before cooking.

Shuck – To remove the husk from corn, beans or the shell from oysters or clams.

Sift - To pass, usually dry ingredients, through a fine wire mesh to produce a uniform consistency.

Simmer – To cook in or with a liquid at or just below the boiling point (barely bubbling).

Simple Syrups - Simply sugar (sweetener) and water (liquid) that have been reduced to a syrup consistency.

Classic Simple Syrup - Make simple syrup by bringing to a boil equal parts sugar and water, and then simmering until the sugar dissolves (approximately 10 minutes). Let cool before using.

Citrus Simple Syrup - Add strips of orange and/or lemon rind to the mixture as it boils.

Not-So-Simple Syrup - Make not-so-simple syrup by boiling together equal parts brown sugar and orange juice until the sugar dissolves.

Herbed Simple Syrup - Add 4 sprigs of fresh thyme and zest from ½ lime per each cup of sugar and water mixture. This is great with lemony and citrus drinks.

Lavender Simple Syrup - Add 1 Tablespoon fresh lavender blossoms to sugar and water mixture as it boils.

Cranberry Simple Syrup - In a medium saucepan, make simple syrup by combining water and sugar over medium heat until sugar dissolves. Add cranberries and bring just to boiling stage. Then reduce heat and simmer for 5 minutes, stirring frequently. Remove from heat and gently fold in mint. Cover and let steep for 15 minutes. Press cranberry mixture through a fine-mesh strainer; discard solids. Let mixture cool completely and chill in refrigerator for 3 to 4 hours.

Skewer – To hold in place by means of a metal or wooden skewer.

Skim – To ladle or spoon off excess fat or scum from the surface of a liquid or pudding.

Slice – To bring a knife down firmly in order to make slices.

Slow Cooker – AKA: Crock Pot. A clay pot within an electrical bowl that slowly cooks foods.

Sorbet – A frozen dessert made from sweetened water and flavored with juices, liquors and/or honey.

Soufflé - A baked egg-based dish made from beaten whites and cooked yolks. Can be sweet or savory.

Sourwood Honey – Honey made from the blossoms of the Sourwood tree, also called the Lily of the Valley tree that grows up to 60 feet tall in the Appalachian Mountains of north Georgia and western North Carolina.

Showcasing clusters of white bell-shaped flowers in late June and early July, the Sourwood tree blooms after most other flowering trees in the mountains have come and gone. The honey from the Sourwood tree is extra-light and extremely aromatic with a distinctive, rich honey flavor. No other honey can match this Appalachian wonder. Available from farms in the Appalachians and by mail order.

Spices – An aromatic plant substance used as a flavoring. Unlike herbs which should only be combined one or two at a time, spices can be combined in a myriad of ways. Freshly grated spices, especially nutmeg, cinnamon, cloves and pepper are far superior to pre-ground. Use a micro plane grater or spice grinder for best results.

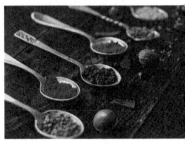

Spices have a shelf life and should be checked periodically. Unless you cook large quantities regularly, look for dried spices and herbs in smaller, ½-ounce quantities. This way if you need to discard you won't waste as much.

Sriracha – A type of hot sauce made from the paste of chili peppers with distilled vinegar, garlic, sugar and salt. Named after the coastal city of Si Racha in eastern Thailand.

Steaks & Beef – Preparing, cooking, serving:

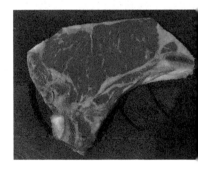

Aging - Aging tenderizes beef and concentrates its flavor. A dry-aged steak has a mineral sharp edge to it, as opposed to a fresh cut of beef that tastes sweeter. Aging takes a minimum of four weeks and will add to the cost.

Seasoning - Season beef with kosher salt and freshly ground black pepper on both sides just prior to cooking. This will draw out the flavor while it cooks.

Cooking - Steak should be cooked rare to medium rare over indirect heat. Cooking beyond this point will cause the meat to toughen and become dry because the fat is oozing out.

Searing - Once you are within 10 degrees of desired doneness, move meat to the hot side of the grill to sear. Leave the lid of the grill open and turn meat frequently to build up a charred crust.

Rare is a touch cool on the inside with a hot exterior, (Approximately 2 minutes per side, 120 degrees).

Medium Rare is cooked just a shade past rare with a warm center, (3 minutes per side, 130 degrees).

Medium = 140 degrees, ***Medium Well*** = 150 degrees, ***Well Done*** = 160 degrees.

Resting - Transfer steak to a cutting board and allow to rest for 10 minutes to ensure juices remain in the meat.

Saucing - Sweet and sour sauces are a good choice with steak because the acid and sweetness can cut through the fat and richness in the meat. A simple red wine with caramelized shallots, or bourbon and peppercorns are good beef sauces.

Steam – To cook with water vapor in a closed container, usually in a steamer or on a rack.

Steep – To pour boiling water over something and let it sit.

Sterilize – To purify and cleanse through exposure to intense heat.

Stew – To simmer meats or vegetables for a long period of time. Also used to tenderize meats.

Stir – To rotate ingredients in a bowl or pan to ensure even cooking and prevent sticking.

Strain – To pass through a strainer or cheesecloth to break down or remove solids and/or impurities.

Strudel – Austrian; A layered pastry with filling that is sweet or savory.

Stuff – To fill or pack cavities in meats, vegetables and poultry.

Superfine Sugar – A very fine form of sugar (not powdered) used for candied fruits and flowers.

If you do not have superfine sugar in your pantry, you can easily make it. Simply pulse granulated sugar in a blender until it becomes powder-like in texture. Do not try to substitute granulated sugar for superfine.

T

Tart – A baked dish with a pastry base that is filled and has an open top.

Temper – To prepare eggs to be added to a hot liquid by adding just a small amount and incorporating it well first.

Tent – To cover roast or bird loosely with foil after roasting.

Thicken – To stir flour or other ingredient into hot liquid to thicken its consistency.

Toast -   To brown and crisp by means of direct heat, or to bake until browned.

Toast Points – Toasted triangular slices of bread that have been cut diagonally from one corner to the opposite corner.

Torte – A multi-layered cake filled with cream and/or jam.

Toss – To mix lightly with two forks or other utensils.

Translucent – Cook until semitransparent; clear.

Truss – To bind poultry legs and wings close to body of bird before cooking in order to hold its shape and ease in slicing.

U-Z

Unmold – To turn out of a mold so that the interior contents keep their shape.

Vanilla - Vanilla and vanilla beans are derived from the orchid plant and have a cherry-like, woody flavor that should always be used as the star of the show. Vanilla is to baking as salt is to cooking, and is especially good in dairy desserts. Vanilla also pairs well with sweet herbs like bay leaf and tarragon.

Capture vanilla beans from the pod by slitting lengthwise and scraping out the copious tiny seeds with a knife.

Choose shiny, black bean pods that are supple. When purchasing vanilla beans, it is often hard to see the pods as they are packaged with labels that cover much of the ingredients. So shake the glass or jar containers to see it the bean pods rattle. If so, they have likely dried out and are not good.

After opening the container, store bean pods by wrapping tightly in plastic wrap inside a glass jar.

Vino Santo – AKA: Holy Wine. A late harvest Italian dessert wine. (**Vendage** is a late harvest French dessert wine)

Vichyssoise – A thick soup of leeks, onions, potatoes and cream that is served cold.

Vinaigrette – A mixture made from oil and acids enhanced with salts, herbs and spices. Commonly used as a salad dressing.

Water Bath - A method that ensures even, slow cooking and guards against curdled custards or cracked cheese cakes.

Start by placing a jelly roll pan in a cold oven and filling it with enough water to reach the half-way point. Now, preheat oven as per recipe and allow the water to heat while the oven heats. When custard or cakes are ready to bake, set the smaller cups or ramekins directly into the hot water for a constant heat source while baking. When finished baking, allow the water to cool in the jelly roll pan before removing from the oven.

Whip – To beat a mixture until air has been thoroughly incorporated and the mixture is light and fluffy, volume is greatly increased, and mixture holds its shape.

Whisk – A quick light brushing or whipping motion.

Wilt – To apply heat to cause dehydration and a droopy appearance.

Wine Spritzer – A cocktail made by mixing half wine with half soda water that can be made with any kind of wine. Served over ice and garnished with lime and/or fresh mint or other fruits and herbs as appropriate to the wine being used. *If using a white or rosé wine, be sure to also chill soda water.*

Zest – The process of grating very fine slivers of citrus rind. Zest is used to provide a concentrated flavor of fruit in both baking and cooking.

Index by Category

COOKIES

CUSTARD

DRESSINGS & SAUCES

EGGS

FISH & SEAFOOD

FROSTING

FRUITS

GARNISHES

GLAZES & SAUCES

ICE CREAM & SORBET

PASTA & SAUCES

PANCAKES & SYRUP

PIES

Thank You

CARL BRUNE
Art Direction & Consultation

D'ANN BARTLEY
DORIS FRAMPTON
Reading & Editing

ACE CUERVO
Ace Cuervo Photography
Cover Photography, Title Page & Photos on pages 1, 122, 194, 219, 267, 307, 321 & 355.

INSTRUCTION
Handmade Pasta
EMI CHIAPPA-STARNES
Dough, Asheville, North Carolina

Wines
TIZIANA INFANTINO
Poderi Arcangelo, San Gimignano, Italy

RESOURCES
Food Affinities
KAREN PAGE & ANDREW DORNEBURG
The Flavor Bible

Entertaining Etiquette
LETITIA BALDRIGE
The Amy Vanderbilt Complete Book of Etiquette

Thanks also to
DANNY SADLER
Photography Consultation

MADELINE CRAWFORD
Tulsa People Magazine
Photos on pages 95 & 180.

JENNIFER & MARSHALL WELLS
for MISS E.B & MASTER CAMERON (photo on page 175).

and
My deepest gratitude to my friends & family who have listened as I babbled, encouraged as I brainstormed, and assisted whenever I asked over the past two years as this project evolved into the publication it is today. Thank you -
BETTY, EMILY, LURLINE, MICHAEL, ROBBY, ROBIN, TODD & COOKING PARTNERS JULIE & MEREDITH. *I love you all!*

CPSIA information can be obtained
at www.ICGtesting.com
Printed in the USA
LVOW06*1559190417
531394LV00023B/465/P